THE THIRTIES AND AFTER

Stephen Spender was born in 1909, the second son of a Liberal journalist. He was educated at University College School, London, and University College, Oxford, where his friends included those writers with whom his name was to be linked as the Thirties Generation: Auden, Day Lewis, MacNeice, Isherwood and Upward. In 1928 he printed his and Auden's first books of poems on his own hand press. His book, *Poems*, was accepted by T. S. Eliot for Faber and Faber and it appeared in 1933.

He went to Spain during the Spanish Civil War and worked as a propagandist for the Republicans. With Cyril Connolly he founded *Horizon* in 1939 and co-edited it until 1942 when he joined the National Fire Service in London. At the end of the Second World War, under the auspices of the Foreign Office, he travelled in Germany and France. With Irving Kristol he founded *Encounter* in 1953 and was its co-editor until 1965.

Since the late 1940s he has spent much time in the United States where he has been Visiting Professor at many universities; and in 1965–6 he was Consultant in Poetry at the Library of Congress. In England, he was Professor of English at University College, London, from 1968 to 1973. He has also travelled widely in Europe.

Stephen Spender published his *Collected Poems* in 1955 and has since published a further collection, *The Generous Days* (1971). His autobiography, *World Within World*, appeared in 1951. He has also published one play, *Trial of a Judge* (1938), a novel, *The Backward Son* (1940), and several books of criticism including *The Destructive Element* (1935) and *The Struggle of the Modern* (1963). His other prose books include *The Year of the Young Rebels* (1969) and *Love-Hate Relations* (1974). Among those writers whose work he has translated are Rilke, Büchner, Lorca and Schiller.

STEPHEN SPENDER

The Thirties and After

Poetry, Politics, People (1933-75)

by agreement with Fontana Paperbacks

Published by agreement with
Fontana Paperbacks

© Stephen Spender 1978

This edition first published 1978 by
THE MACMILLAN PRESS LTD
London and Basingstoke
Associated companies in Delhi
Dublin Hong Kong Johannesburg Lagos
Melbourne New York Singapore Tokyo

Printed in Great Britain by
BILLING & SONS LTD
Guildford, London and Worcester

**British Library Cataloguing in
Publication Data**

Spender, Stephen
　　The thirties and after
　　I. Title
　　828'.9'1208　　　PR6037.P47A16
　　ISBN 0-333-25520-8

To Sonia Orwell
remembering those *Horizon* days

Contents

Contents

Introduction

I first conceived of this book as a collection of essays, some of them concerned with the political involvement of myself, as a member of the 1930s generation, with public events, others of them critical essays and reviews of purely literary interest. I hoped that this would provide a kind of case history of a thirties poet in which the connection between different documents would illustrate themes of literature and politics over a period of nearly half a century. I thought that there should be background essays connecting the sections, each of which would correspond roughly to a decade.

Later I recalled that over the years I had, spasmodically, kept journals, some of which had been published in periodicals. The journals record a continuous development throughout this whole period. They are often highly personal – in 'September Journal' too much so – but they also tend to digress into essays. The introduction of passages from the journals would, I realized, give the book a more personal and cohesive character than that of a miscellaneous collection of essays, reports and reviews.

I have tried to retain throughout the themes of the thirties – going beyond them, but relating always to them. One theme is that my own thirties generation – which seems to be identified with Auden, Isherwood, MacNeice, Day Lewis and myself as apart from that far more politically involved one represented by John Cornford – never became so politicized as to disagree seriously with an older generation of writers who held views often described as 'reactionary', fascistic even, but whom we admired this side of idolatry: W. B. Yeats, D. H. Lawrence and – most of all – T. S. Eliot. The book ends with reminiscences of Auden and Eliot which bring these generations – of so-called rebels and so-called reactionaries – together after their deaths. The development which began with Auden adopting Eliot's anti-political attitude towards literature, and which then

9

passed through the politically conscious decade of the thirties, comes full circle.

Occasionally I have cut turgid passages from the earlier essays, and occasionally rewritten sentences, but I have not altered the views expressed, and have left ones which today I would not only disagree with, but find shamefully embarrassing. I cut a paragraph from 'September Journal' which was not only mawkishly self-pitying but also extremely unjust to someone I loved. I have not completely stuck to the chronological order in which the essays were written where I thought that the general pattern of the book – cutting across the division of the four parts into four decades – would be made better by altering the order. The long essay 'Notes on Revolutionaries and Reactionaries' was written in 1966 but I think it fits better into Part Three: the Fifties, than it would later on. I have printed a poem recalling a vivid memory of Louis MacNeice, and another about Cyril Connolly when he was dying, hoping that these would have the force of illustrations. I thought a lot about Cyril Connolly when arranging and editing this material, remembering how fascinated he was by selecting and presenting his essays.

PART ONE
The Thirties

Background to the Thirties

The thirties was the decade in which young writers became
involved in politics. The politics of this generation were
almost exclusively those of the left. They were so mainly
for two reasons : first, on account of events of the time,
which I shall discuss later; secondly, because even during
the twenties when most of the well-known writers dis-
sociated themselves from politics in their literary work,
there was nevertheless an underlying left-wing orthodoxy
among writers which went back to the end of the First
World War, and even earlier, to the Fabian Society. It
is often forgotten that Osbert Sitwell, Siegfried Sassoon,
Robert Graves and Wilfred Owen – to name but a few
– were all, in 1918, socialists, though in a wider sense than
that of belonging to the Labour Party. Their socialism
was based on hatred for members of an older generation,
conservative or liberal, whom they believed to have sent
the young out to the war; on sympathy with the men in the
ranks at the Front – to an extent which meant taking
sides politically against their own officer class; on admira-
tion for revolutionary movements of various kinds –
pacifist, political and sexual – which had occurred in
Europe; on resentment at the attempts of the British
conservatives to join with those forces which were out to
crush the Russian Revolution; and on dislike of the British
Empire.

A daily newspaper, the socialist *Daily Herald*, and two
weeklies, the *New Statesman* and the *Nation*, were leftist.
Most of the writers who contributed to these periodicals
were in general agreement with the editors' politics, even
if they believed that their own creativity had nothing to
do with their political opinions. The situation is demon-
strated by the division of the contents of the *New Statesman*
and the *Nation* into the front halves, devoted predominantly
to politics, and the back halves, devoted entirely to the
arts, literature and reviewing, and maintaining a stubborn

independence from the politics of the front halves. The literary writers disdained the political journalists, but nevertheless shared the same premises, and it could be assumed that if the literary were put into a position in which they had to express a political opinion, it would, in most cases, be that of the first half of the journal.

But the gap between the literary elite and the political writers widened throughout the twenties, so that when I was a young poet and Oxford undergraduate in 1928, I came to think of the interest in politics which I had inherited from my father's side of my family, who were political journalists, as something to be rather ashamed of. When we read *The Waste Land* we thought of it as anti-political. Being, as we thought, about the end of Western civilization, we found no suggestion in it that politics, of the right or the left, might avert that end.

When I was at University College School, young schoolmasters who had been through the war reflected in their attitudes the generalized rebelliousness, based on disillusionment and tinged with a certain post-war idealism, which I have mentioned above. One of these, Geoffrey Thorp, influenced me greatly. He was a member of the avant-garde, Bohemian, leftist 1917 Club, an ardent socialist, had progressive views about education, sex, art, health foods, etc., was an atheist, derided every conformism. He brought with him the gust of a new world which blew through the schoolroom when he entered it. As a result of his being there, three or four boys who were friends of mine became politically socialist and aesthetically avant-garde. At the same time Thorp had the slightly shell-shocked dottiness of many who had fought on the Western Front.

Probably at Gresham's, Repton and Marlborough where, respectively, Auden, Isherwood and MacNeice went to school, there were, within the surrounding conformities, also one or two younger masters who had fought in the war who provided them with a view of life so different from that of the official Conservative-dominated post-war England, and which derived from the Western Front and the revolutionary hopes of November 1918. But given the fact that in the post-war era there emerged also that cynicism about public life which is to be found in the novels of Aldous Huxley, the revolutionary politics of the aesthetic avant-garde were like a damped-down fire smouldering at the centre of wet leaves. They were to burst out into flames in the thirties.

There was no orthodoxy of the right among the writers of the older generation corresponding to that of the intellectual left. Yeats, Eliot, Pound and Wyndham Lewis all held politically reactionary views. Yet although these writers looked towards the classical past of the European tradition their view of that past was medievalist and romantic. It had nothing to do with the British Conservative Party, Members of Parliament and journalists. Official Conservatives indeed considered Pound and Eliot to be Bohemians, revolutionaries, little better than socialists. It was a conservative literary critic who denounced T. S. Eliot, that ardent admirer of the French proto-Fascist Charles Maurras, as a 'drunken helot' (attempting, I suppose, a pun on Eliot's name).

Eliot was opposed to the conventionally conservative standards of reviewers like J. C. Squire and Gerald Gould who dominated literary journalism in the Sunday newspapers and who attacked whatever was experimental or avant-garde in literature. There was the period when James Joyce's *Ulysses* was banned and the luggage of the undergraduate returning to England from Paris was examined at Dover by the customs to see if it contained *Ulysses* or Radclyffe Hall's *The Well of Loneliness*. D. H. Lawrence's exhibition of his paintings was raided by the police.

The situation in the twenties and early thirties could be summed up as follows : there was an English conservative establishment, very powerful, which when it extended beyond politics into the arts was philistine, stupid, respectable and frightened, incapable of realizing that in literature the values of orthodoxy, traditionalism and reaction may take revolutionary forms. There was an orthodoxy of the left which, although rather philistine, had enough vitality, intelligence and receptiveness to tolerate work by writers who were revolutionary in their art; to do so even when they were reactionary in their politics.

To my generation, Joyce, Eliot, Yeats in his later poetry, and Lawrence stood for the modern in literature. They seemed revolutionary in their writing, which was what we cared about, and we gave little thought to their politics. At a later stage when we became anti-fascists we noticed that Yeats and Wyndham Lewis held fascist views, but the phenomenon of writers who seemed modernist in their art while being reactionary in their political opinions puzzled rather than alienated us, as I think is clear from the reviews of books by Yeats, Wyndham Lewis and D. H. Lawrence which I publish here.

Auden, at the age of nineteen, drove a lorry for the TUC during the General Strike (he was ordered by an uncle to leave the house for doing so, and, rather characteristically, asked : 'Mayn't I have my lunch first?'). But when he was at Oxford, although if pressed to state his views on politics he would say he was a socialist, he made no connection between his politics and his poetry. His whole view of poetry was that it should have nothing to do with politics or, indeed, with opinions of any kind. This was true not only of the poetry, but of the poet, who should be as detached from his material life as the scientific worker from the experimental specimens under his microscope. The poet was superior to the rest of humanity not in the manner of Tennyson's poet ('Vex not thou the poet's mind/With thy shallow wit') but in his fusion of the analytic with creative powers. To him the environment provided the 'symptomatic' phenomena which he transformed in his poetry. The poet viewed life with utter detachment, as material for his poetry.

I came to realize later that the view of the poet as detached, clinical and never expressing his own opinions or personality, which Auden advanced when I was a freshman, derived from T. S. Eliot's famous essay 'Tradition and the Individual Talent'. An extension of this view was to regard politicians as rather self-important servants laying on the arrangements of the world for the artist.

Politics, when it overtook our generation, meant for us the partial abrogation of a passive, receptive, analytic poetry – attitudes present equally in the personalism of Keats and the impersonality of Eliot – in favour of a poetry of will and the directed analytic intellect. We were aware of having renounced values which we continued nevertheless to consider aesthetically superior, in Joyce, Yeats, Eliot, Lawrence and Virginia Woolf. MacNeice, for example, even while writing poetry in *Autumn Journal*, which contained the best political commentary of the decade, would emphasize how little political poetry he had written; and I think that his colleagues if told in an accusing way that they wrote political poetry would have answered defensively that, if so, they had written very little of it. They did not enter whole-heartedly into the view which was to be adopted by poets of a later Cambridge vintage, John Cornford and Julian Bell – who took to politics with an exhilarated sense that in doing so they were shaking off the aestheticism of literary Cambridge and Bloomsbury.

The political poetry of Auden, Day Lewis, MacNeice and Spender had a temporary 'for the duration' look. It might be classified as a variety of war poetry. There was force in the catty remark, attributed to Norman Cameron and reported in Geoffrey Grigson's *New Verse*, that Stephen Spender was 'the Rupert Brooke of the Depression'. The thirties poets who had sneered at Rupert Brooke and whose feelings about war had been absorbed from the poetry from the Western Front written by Wilfred Owen and Siegfried Sassoon – and from Robert Graves's *Goodbye to All That* – were rather embarrassed to find themselves in one respect like Rupert Brooke : that is to say, writing poetry in support of war against Germans – although these Germans were not Kaiser Wilhelm's spike-helmeted Prussians but the Nazi SS. They remained, of course, repelled by the manner and matter of Rupert Brooke's famous war sonnets. In the event, what they wrote was anti-fascist poetry which was profoundly influenced by the diction and attitudes of Wilfred Owen – a kind of anti-fascist pacifist poetry. Examples of this are Auden's sonnets from China and my own poem, 'Ultima Ratio Regum'. And poets who fought in the Second World War continued to write poetry which reflected the pacifist attitude to war and expressed the same sensibility: for example, Randall Jarrell's 'The Death of the Ball Turret Gunner' and Roy Fuller's poems about the fighting in the African desert.

The Spanish Civil War was felt to be a war of light against darkness (my Oxford tutor, the idealist philosopher E. F. Carritt described it as being the only conflict in his lifetime in which the forces of good – the Republicans – seemed arrayed purely against the forces of evil – the fascists) yet just the same there was something repugnant about the whole enterprise of writing poetry supporting our side against the other side, to poets who had made a hero of Wilfred Owen.

I am not arguing that the poets of Auden's generation were half-hearted about anti-fascism. It would be truer to say that they were extremely non-political with half of themselves and extremely political with the other half. With the political half they really did try to see the world from the ideological viewpoint: this is with the idea that all those thinking and doing activities which brought one in relation with other human beings involved, consciously or unconsciously; participation in a struggle between opposed interests, those of capitalist imperialism and those of the socialist revolution. Perhaps one might not in past historical situations have seen this, but in the thirties it was so highlighted by current circumstances that if on belonged to the ruling class, not so see it was to take the side of the class into which one had been born and which had a definite interest in not seeing it; for whoever saw it was almost certain to take sides against his own class.

The thirties are often described as a literary movement,

and Auden is supposed to have been its leader. It would be perhaps truer to say that Auden was the leading influence than that there was a literary movement of Auden, Day Lewis, Spender, who later added to their number MacNeice, and who recognized Isherwood as the prose writer who was their counterpart. In a sense one might describe the thirties as a leader – Auden – with a following but no movement.

Movements have meetings, issue manifestoes, have aims in common. The thirties poets never held a single meeting, they issued no manifestoes (unless Day Lewis's *A Hope for Poetry* – a book I have never read – might be considered one). Each of them wrote a different kind of poetry from the others without his feeling that, in doing so, he was letting down the side. As I have mentioned elsewhere, the first time that Auden, Day Lewis and Spender were all three together in a room was in Venice, after the war, in 1948.

However Auden did have certain characteristics of a leader. He was in several ways very much in advance of his colleagues, he had very definite views about certain subjects of whose existence his colleagues often first heard from him, he had a tactician's sense of a map which was the time in which we were living and on which, in his mind, all the poets, past and present, had places. He was also conscious of the current condition of literature within which he and certain of his friends would belong to the winning future. He was also much cleverer than the others of us, aware of being so, and without the slightest trace of inferiority complex. (Late in life he once told me that from childhood on he was always conscious of being 'brighter than anyone else'.)

Most of all, Auden had an ascendancy over his friends which was due to his being versed in psychoanalysis and therefore in a position to diagnose their complexes. For an undergraduate poet, in 1928, this was very extraordinary. We had all of us heard, of course, of inferiority complexes, of extroverts and introverts and to some extent one could describe oneself in terms of these (I was an introvert, obviously), but that is about as far as we went. Apart from putting people in these very imprecise categories (like saying that X is an athlete and Y writes poetry) we knew nothing of the use of psychoanalysis as a means of diagnosing your friends' neurotic symptoms. Auden, however, in addition to being a strategist at the centre of a literary chart in which the positions of all other poets were determined, seemed a lone psychoanalyst at the centre of a group of inhibited, neurotic patients – us. He was not so much a leader as a doctor among his patients each of whom he treated as a distinct case, and separately. It seems to me that one always saw Auden alone. One reason why the so-called Auden group never had meetings, or even social gatherings, was that they never met together as a group. The separate analysing interview was really Auden's thing. One went to see him in his room at Christ Church where, with blinds drawn, and wearing a green eye-shade (he had a near-albino's sensitivity of the eyes to light), and with a lamp behind his chair, which showed him in shadow and shed light upon his visitor, he received his friends – or rather, one friend, one at a time. He then asked probing questions about literature, and perhaps also sexual tastes. Disregarding psychoanalytical etiquette, he talked about other patients and colleagues, but he was not happy at the idea of their getting together either with him or behind his back. Sometimes, though, he made a great thing of introducing one friend to another. I remember first meeting Isherwood with him : but this was altogether exceptional, a signal occasion. I never met Day Lewis, MacNeice, Rex Warner, or any other of our mutual friends with him.

In case I produce the impression on the reader that Auden was a conceited young man, taking advantage of the fact that he was in some ways rather sophisticated for his time, and trying to put his sense of his own superiority across his friends, let me repeat that he was in truth extremely clever. Moreover I, being two years younger than he, unsophisticated and given to hero-worship, was probably only too willing to disclaim any attempt to regard myself as his equal. To me his poetry, which he would recite from his armchair for hours on end, in his detached clinical voice which seemed to drain it of all meaning except that he emphasized certain words in a curious way as though they were objects like drowned kittens held out at arms' length – to me this poetry was incomprehensible, strange, marvellous, authoritative and absolutely beyond dispute. This willingness to accept it as impenetrable mystery defines my own mental limitations. But perhaps I was right in feeling that I was in the presence of work which could not be analysed at that time because it was entirely new.

Auden then is inadequately described as a leader. He was didactic, dogmatic even, but in no way dictatorial. He gave no orders. He was a consciousness and he heightened consciousness in others but he did not demand that they should imitate him. He was extravagant in all he said, and in his behaviour. His way was the way of excess and although this may lead to the palace of wisdom it does not demand obedience. Moreover he was extremely funny, over-acting the role of Auden and saying things in a way which caricatured them even as he did so. He had nothing about him of the pure intellectual who talks about values and recognizes none but his own. One would go into his room and see him absurdly dressed in a brown double-breasted suit, and he would say almost naïvely : 'Do you like my new suit?' He would complain about the flatness of his feet. He would boast that the Mozartian tune – of his own composition – which he played on his piano, had been whistled by the boy on the stairs – and give a knowing look as he said this. He would say that a violent attack on him in a magazine was sure proof that the author was in love with him.

Forty years after these events, it is easy to discuss the thirties as though they were a literary movement separate from the conditions from which they emanated, or simply an aberration – which is perhaps how Auden came to view most of his poetry written at this time. But this was a decade in which many assumptions previously taken for granted in middle-class democratic Europe and America seemed shaken. There were vast numbers of unemployed workers, ill-dressed, living on the dole, which was below subsistence level, standing idle in the streets or desperate on hunger marches. The capitalist system which seemed on the verge of complete breakdown and which was incapable of either employing the workers, or, if they were unemployed, preventing them from almost starving, was the same system that supported the cultivated leisured class of those whose aesthetic values seemed to have no connection with politics and social conditions. In such circumstances, many young writers came to feel that art unconnected with social conditions was 'about' this very lack of connection. This was itself a kind of connection, in being a refusal to recognize those conditions which were the consequences of the political and economic system.

As well as unemployment, there was the rise of the Nazis and, a few years after Hitler's seizure of power, the ever-growing realization that war was inevitable. Hitlerism produced concentration camps. One became more and more aware of the indescribable suffering of victims – of an incommunicable reality which was the truth of history in this decade. Compared with it, a literary movement like that called 'The Thirties' was a mockery, like a parrot imitating the screaming of a prisoner being tortured. I think that we felt this. A sensation I often had during the thirties was of there being a terrible reality which was the truth of the time experienced by people in prisons and concentration camps. To write the truth about the time one would have to enter into this cave of fire, but in doing so one would be annihilated. After all, when one reads *The Gulag Archipelago* and books about Nazi concentration camps, this perception does not seem so very far removed from how things were.

Another still mysterious and unimaginable reality was the approaching war. Doubtless to the CND protesters of the fifties, the horrors of two world wars seemed nothing compared with those they anticipated with the falling of

H-bombs. However, not knowing about atomic weapons, we anticipated the worst destruction then imaginable. In our minds, the Second World War would mean the end of civilization. By this we meant the total destruction of all major built-up areas. My own private fantasy was of emerging out of a cellar after the first air raid on London on to a scene which consisted entirely of ruins. Nor was this fantasy so far from what was anticipated by scientists. Gerald Heard, that erratic genius who used to broadcast on the BBC about the most recent scientific developments, told me of the effects of high explosives which could burn through steel girders as though they were straw. Just before the Munich agreement, Raymond Postgate showed me a map of London – with the docks, the sewage plants, the power stations all seeming defenceless and exposed – and described to me the appalling destruction which would result from the first great air raids on London. But up till the time of Munich the great majority of people in England were unaware of the reality of terror. If a small but vociferous and talented minority of what were called the 'intellectuals' (this was the decade in which this term began to be widely used or abused) were almost hypnotically aware of the Nazi nightmare, the vast majority of people – and the government and members of the ruling class – seemed determined to ignore or deny it. One had the sense of belonging to a small group who could see terrible things which no one else saw. This was the period of Stanley Baldwin's premiership, the Royal Jubilee, the British Empire Exhibition.

The writers of the thirties are often sneered at because they were middle-class youths with public school and posh university backgrounds who sought to adopt a proletarian point of view. Up to a point this sneer is justified. They were ill-equipped to address a working-class audience, and were not serious in their efforts to do so. (If their poetry strikes one as addressed to anyone in particular, it is to sixth-formers from their old schools and to one another.) But that having been said, it should be pointed out that up until the Spanish Civil War, when some hundreds of workers joined the International Brigade, the thirties writers represented a middle-class *crise de conscience*. And there is nothing despicable about this. The middle classes were the beneficiaries of the system which made victims of the workers. Moreover, some of these writers were travelled and had an awareness of what was going on in Europe, not just of the complacency of middle-class England and the apathy of most workers.

Thus the thirties was a time when, under the extreme complacency of English governments, members of the younger generation felt themselves divided by the thinnest of walls from destructive forces which seemed absolute, from terrible suffering and pure evil. Perhaps one reason for the attraction of communism was that the communists also had their vision of final crisis, though they regarded it as one involving the destruction of capitalism rather than of civilization. Considered as an apocalyptic vision, the communist view coincides with that of T. S. Eliot in *The Waste Land* or Yeats in 'The Second Coming'. To see this is to see how, looked at from a certain angle, or in a given situation, works which seem quite alien to all idea of politics can suddenly seem to be politically symptomatic and to offer a choice between complete despair and revolution. A poet of Eliot's own generation, Edgell Rickword, much influenced by Eliot, moved from a Bohemianized Waste-Landish vision of life in his poetry to communism. Another much younger poet, John Cornford, while still a schoolboy in the early thirties, read *The Waste Land* and became converted to communism.

In the mid-thirties, I published a book of critical essays partly about Henry James, Yeats, Eliot and Lawrence, and partly about writers of my own generation, called *The Destructive Element*. Taking up the famous quotation from Joseph Conrad's *The Heart of Darkness*, 'in the destructive element immerse', I read despair about Europe into the later Henry James (*The Golden Bowl*), Eliot and Yeats, and drew from this the implication in their work of

24

a communist moral. This was absurd : but the fact remains that in a crisis of a whole society every work takes on a political look either in being symptomatic of that crisis (which is itself, of course, political) or in avoiding it. This was one of those intervals of history in which events make the individual feel that he counts. His actions or his failure to act could lead to the winning or the losing of the Spanish Civil War, could even decide whether or not the Second World War was going to take place. Before going to Spain, to serve as an ambulance driver, Julian Bell, who had been interested in war games and military strategy since childhood, told me he thought this ama-teurishly directed war could be won by a great strategist. He evidently had it in mind that given the opportunity, he might win the war. Auden gave up concerning himself with the cause of anti-fascism only when he felt that the individual no longer counted in this conflict.

To say today that whoever thought that by supporting the Republic he could stop the Italian and Nazi-supported Francoists from winning the Spanish Civil War was deluded is not as great an exposure of the lack of realism of the anti-fascists as, with hindsight, it may appear to be. For one thing, the sense of personal commitment was part of the reality of the time. For another, if there had not been individualistic anti-fascism, it is doubtful whether the democratic governments would finally have decided that they had to fight Hitler with their machinery of war and conscription in which individuals seemed to count for very little.

To be modern meant in the thirties to interpret the poet's individual experience of lived history in the light of some kind of Marxist analysis. In relation to the modernist movement in the arts which began at the end of the last century and continued in the work of Eliot and Pound, this was regressive. For the essence of the modern move-ment was that it created art which was centred on itself and not on anything outside it; neither on some ideology projected nor on the expression of the poet's feelings and personality. One might say that the moment thirties writing became illustrative of Marxist texts or reaction to 'history' – and to the extent which it did these things – it ceased to be part of the modern movement. Poems like *Spain* and *Autumn Journal* work against the modern movement in that the first is an attempt to interpret the Marxist dialectic into the Spanish conflict, and the second is a record, centred on the dramatized day-to-day life of the poet, of MacNeice's reaction to events in September 1939.

From the thirties point of view, what the modernists had done was to present us with a medium in which it was possible for us to write about modern life, say whatever we chose, without taking thought as to whether language and form were 'poetic'. In writing about politics, we were using the instrument of language provided for us by our predecessors to express what they lacked in their work, an overt subject matter. We were putting the subject back into poetry. We were taking the medium of poetry which to them was an end in itself and using it as an instrument for realizing our felt ideas about the time in which we were living. Yet members of my generation continued to think that poetry should be judged by standards which were not ideological, and when a young poet writing in the fifties wrote of the thirties that 'something had been betrayed', I think that the sensation of betrayal was due to the feeling that we had regressed from the poetic aims of our predecessors by simplifying the tasks of poetry, even though we thought it necessary to do so.

It might be argued that the real thirties was that of John Cornford, Christopher Caudwell, Tom Wintringham, Ralph Fox and Julian Bell : all of them examples of men in whose behaviour ideas and actions formed a unity. But all of them were killed in Spain, and, as an exhibition of the thirties held in 1976 in London's National Portrait Gallery showed, the idea of a literary movement in the thirties continues to seem centred in England on Auden and his colleagues. In all our lives and work, there were contradictory ideas and confused actions, while at the same time the impression was produced of anti-fascist propaganda and activities being carried on energetically. The appearance of a common direction amid so much diversity is perhaps due to the fact that fascism itself gave antifascism a semblance of unity. The anti-fascists had in common that they hated it. A distressing feature of this time was that what Hitler stood for was so black that those who opposed him seemed at least pale-grey by comparison; another was that most of the English were so determinedly asleep that to be awake at all to what was going on made the wakers seem a political movement. But really poets of my own generation were full of doubts mostly due to the fact that in varying and different ways they distrusted the involvement of art with politics.

I think the essays in the first section of this book illustrate this combination of convictions and hesitations. The essay in which I announce my joining the Communist Party is rather abject and I am thoroughly ashamed of it. I persuaded myself to print it here against my strong wish not even to reread it – far less republish it – on the grounds that if I am to offer the first part of this book as a showcase of my particular thirties exhibits, I must put in the most embarrassing one.

Fortunately the publication of this essay in the *Daily Worker* led to my immediately being dropped from the Communist Party. The reason for this was that I had admitted to having had doubts about one of the sacred tenets of the CP at that time, which was that all the victims tried and sentenced in the Soviet Trials were guilty. Of course, to the reader today the very idea that anyone could have thought them to be guilty is shocking, as it is to me myself. However, to understand the thirties one ought to realize that at the time it was not at all certain that they were innocent, despite the grotesqueness of some of the accusations made against them and the extravagance of their confessions. The reader who assumes that the innocence of the accused was common knowledge forty years

27

ago should ask himself a few questions about current events to test the degree of certain knowledge about such things that exists at the time of their happening. For example : how many people were killed in China following the death of Mao? What reasons does he have for supposing three Baader Meinhof terrorists who died in prison in October 1977 to have (a) committed suicide or (b) been murdered? If he considers the available evidence on which he can answer these questions in 1978, he will appreciate how bemused we were in 1937 by the Soviet Trials. I blame myself not for having accepted the communist version of what happened but for not having insisted that I could not form any judgement one way or another on the basis of what I had read in the newspapers. A. J. Cummings, the correspondent of the liberal *News Chronicle* who reported the trials, seemed convinced of the guilt of the accused.

It was the Spanish Civil War which produced the greatest manifestations of unity on the anti-fascist left, resulting in the meetings and demonstrations of the Front Populaire. An article by Auden in the *New Statesman*, written when he was in Valencia, strikes very much the same note as I do in my journalism during the civil war :

> For a revolution is really taking place, not an odd shuffle or two in cabinet appointments. In the last six months these people have been learning what it is to inherit their own country, and once a man has tasted freedom he will not lightly give it up; freedom to choose for himself and to organise his life, freedom not to depend for good fortune on a clever and outrageous piece of overcharging or a windfall of drunken charity.

The communists were largely responsible for creating this unity but they were also the party which finally and irreparably destroyed it. The writers of my own generation experienced this process of being united and then divided as though it were a split in our own personalities. The communist ideology with its comprehension and analysis of the crisis of which we were so aware became a kind of conscience severely criticizing us in our privileged position in society. It seemed a good conscience. The demands that we should see and describe the events through which we were living in terms of a class war seen from the point of view of the working class was a different matter. It often meant writing propaganda and it sometimes meant supporting lies. I think one might sum up reasons for the disruption of the anti-fascist Popular Front of the intellectuals in a phrase : it was a refusal on behalf of all but the most convinced ideologists to tell the lies required by the Stalinist communists. In face of Stalinist propaganda and methods it was a reversion to the view that individual conscience is the repository of witnessed truth.

The lying was a process which one side of our nature watched developing within another. In reporting the Spanish Civil War this took the form of repressing evidence which was not favourable to the cause one was supporting. Gradually one came to see that the very fact of supporting this cause (which one thoroughly believed in) in some way blinkered one's perceptions. Reading my reportage on Tangiers and Gibraltar here, I feel that the young writer is set afire by the enthusiasm of the side which he supports, but I also feel that if he had seen something which contradicted this picture he might not have reported it. However, in the essay 'Heroes in Spain' his view of the propaganda of the communist-controlled International Brigade is unblinkered.

It seems to me now that for me to describe myself in an essay on D. H. Lawrence as approaching that author from the point of view of a 'socialist' is an example of wearing blinkers; made worse by the fact that I doubt whether I had the right to adopt this label. Still worse, if the article had not been written for the readers of *Left Review*, I doubt whether I would have adopted the pose of socialist.

Another kind of deception in which one caught oneself out was that of developing an argument which one be-

lieved to be true and of then discovering that it had led
one to a conclusion which one saw to be false. A striking
example of this is Auden's poem *Spain*, which is a serious
application of the Marxist view of history to the Spanish
Civil War. But in the course of developing his dialectical
argument, Auden arrives at conclusions which he later
refuted, or which were refuted for him. One of these is
the line savagely attacked by George Orwell (who took
it to illustrate the callous irresponsibility of the 'pink pansy
left' in accepting acts of violence of which they had never
seen examples and of which they had no experience):
'The conscious acceptance of guilt in the necessary mur-
der'. (Before Orwell's attack appeared, Auden had changed
this line to 'The conscious acceptance of guilt in the fact
of murder'. He argued reasonably that the line implied
no acceptance of murder, but accepting responsibility for
the fact that there were murders.) But Auden came to dis-
like *Spain* as expressing an attitude which for a few weeks
or months he had felt intellectually forced to adopt, but
which he never truly felt. Towards the end of his life he
took from Cyril Connolly's bookshelf the first edition of
Spain (which was a pamphlet), crossed out the last two
lines and wrote under them : 'This is a lie.' They are :

> History to the defeated
> May say Alas but cannot help nor pardon.

The underlying controversial issue of the thirties centred on
this one of truth, and of the attitude of the individual
to it. On the communist side there was the argument that
in stating what he thinks to be the truth the individual
is often representing the interest and point of view of the
class to which he belongs. This line of argument led to
further ones : for example, that literature which did not re-
flect awareness of a situation which ultimately could be
analysed in terms of the class struggle was 'escapist'. As
conscience-stricken members of the exploiting class, we saw
the force of both these arguments (to this day, listening

to conversations, I notice how often people, thinking they are expressing some truth, merely reflect the prejudice of the class to which they belong). But having given Marxists credit for the fact that doubts about motivations of one's views heighten one's self-critical faculties, the argument leads to other and worse falsifications and to vulgar judgements. The falsification is of the kind that occurs in all 'war' situations : that a truth which gives comfort to the enemy is a kind of lie, and that a lie which serves your own side is a kind of truth. In art the concept of 'escapism' leads one to misjudge works which, if they escape from politics, science and other branches of modern knowledge, may not at all escape from truth about life. During the thirties my own idea of a poet who was thoroughly 'escapist' was Walter de la Mare (I think I even wrote an essay saying so). In fact, if one employs at all the term 'escapist' de la Mare does seem the ideal target for it. Yet whenever I thought this, I had a sensation of being superficial and journalistic, as I was being.

The Writers' Congress held in Madrid in 1937, as I describe it here, was greatly taken up with the considerable scandal caused by the publication of André Gide's *Retour de l'URSS*. Gide, having been entertained lavishly in the Soviet Union, on his return to France published his journal which contained a few sharply critical accounts of things such as the absurd adulation of Stalin which he had witnessed in Russia. After the Madrid Congress, on my return to London by way of Paris, I left a note on Gide saying that I supported him in his desire to tell the truth about things he saw on his Russian journey. When I got back to England I told Auden that I had done this, and he said : 'You are quite right. Exigence is never an excuse for not telling the truth.' This conversation remains in my mind as a turning point in our attitudes towards politics during the thirties.

In the essay 'Poetry and Revolution' (reprinted here in an abbreviated version and with some obscurities clarified) I

31

argued the case against domination of literature by politics.
The essay was not well received by the comrades. There are
rather vivid descriptions of my relations with them at this
time in T. C. Worsley's novel *Fellow Travellers* in which
the character of Martin is a portrait of me. And in Louis
MacNeice's reminiscence *The Strings are False* there is
the following account of a confrontation at a meeting
held after a performance by the Group Theatre of my play
Trial of a Judge. It is amusing and revealing, so I quote
it in full. It conveys the atmosphere of the time :

> Then, after he had joined the Party, came S.'s play
> *Trial of a Judge*, hailed by Christopher Isherwood (this
> mutual admiration was only too understandable) as
> the greatest play of our time, but written in a verse too
> intricate and clogged for the stage. The intended moral
> of the play was that liberalism today was weak and
> wrong, communism was strong and right. But this moral
> was sabotaged by S.'s unconscious integrity; the Liberal
> Judge, his example of what-not-to-be, walked away with
> one's sympathy. The Comrades observed this and, at a
> meeting arranged by the Group Theatre to discuss the
> play, a squad of them turned up to reprove S. for his
> heresies. It was an exhilarating evening. There was a
> blonde girl, pretty and ice-cold, who got up and said
> that the play had been a great disappointment to herself
> and others in the Party; they had gone to the play ex-
> pecting a message and the message had not been
> delivered; and *yet*, she said, there *was* a message to be
> given and they all knew what it was. She spoke precisely
> and quietly, never muffing a phrase (you could see her
> signing death-warrants). Certainly, S. answered, there
> was a message and they all knew what it was; an artist
> had something else to do than to tell people merely what
> they knew and give them just what they expected. The
> heckling went on. One after one the Comrades rose and
> shot their bolts. Marx, Marx and Marx. S. began to trail
> his coat; Marx, he said, was not necessarily what Marx-
> ists thought he was and anyhow you can't feed Marx to

an artist as you feed grass to a cow. And another thing – the Comrades went on – this play gives expression to feelings of anxiety, fear and depression; which is wrong because . . . S. said if they felt no anxiety themselves, well he felt sorry for them. Lastly, an old man got up, very sincere, very earnest, toilworn. There was one thing about the play, he said, which especially worried him; of course he knew S. could not have meant it, there must have been a mistake, but the writing seemed to imply an acceptance of Abstract Justice, a thing which we know is non-existent. S. deliberately towered into blasphemy. Abstract justice, he said, of course he meant it; and what was more it existed.

After that S. gradually fell away from the Party; he had not been born for dogma.

W. B. Yeats: *A Vision*

Criterion XVII (April 1938)

Four days after his marriage, Mr Yeats's wife surprised him by attempting automatic writing. The attempt was soon very successful and the unknown communicator of whom Mrs Yeats was medium, on receiving an offer from Mr Yeats that he should spend the rest of his life putting together these disjointed phrases replied 'No, we have come to give you metaphors for poetry.'

The spirit which made this remark deserves a literary prize, for not only is it responsible for some of the greatest poetry in the English language, but also it has provided a useful hint as to the attitude which the reader fortified by that voice from the 'other world' should adopt towards *A Vision*. Whatever the merits of Mr Yeats's philosophy as such, here we have a valuable and illuminating dictionary of the symbols and metaphors in his later poems. We are able to discover what precisely is the significance of symbols such as the mask, the gyre, the lunar phases; how he employs, in his poetry, his ideas of Fate and Will. Many readers will also find that this dictionary, in common with all definitions of words for that matter, is not only an explanation and an end of inquiry, it is also a starting point in a search for new meanings and a stimulus to poetry as yet unwritten. For example, I myself am stimulated by the idea in Yeats of the Mask, which I take to be the fixed character which the will, like a chisel, sculpts on the face of man.

Later on, Mr Yeats's 'instructors' dropped their secondary role of giving him metaphors and supplied him with what can only be called an Encyclopedia of knowledge, life, death, the universe, history, etc. – an *Encyclopedia Fascista*, edited by Spengler, would perhaps be the best account of it, had not Spengler written his own. Here, I am unable to follow Mr Yeats in anything like his entirety. I can only echo the tactful words of A.E. on the wrapper : 'I am unable in a brief space' (this goes for me as well) 'to give the slightest idea of its packed pages, its division of the faculties of man, the Will, the Creative Genius, the Mask and the Body of Fate and their lunar gyrations, or of its divisions of the transcendental man, the daimonic nature and its cycles and their relation to our being, or of the doctrines of the after-life. Almost any of its crammed pages would need a volume to elucidate its meanings. It is possible it may be discussed feverishly by commentators a century hence, as Blake, . . .' etc.

The name of Blake pulls me up, for I should have thought that anyone desiring to make himself ultimately understood beyond the mere ferment of 'feverish discussion' would beware of falling into the jungles of the Prophetic Books. Like Blake, Mr Yeats is prodigiously systematic, often illuminating, clear and even precise. The difficulty is, though, to discover where his system, with its extensive philosophic claims, actually links up with reality. It is perhaps typical of Mr Yeats's whole method that although the nature of his spiritualist experiences is described, no serious attempt is made to prove to the reader that the creaking of boards in his house, the abrupt incidence of smells and so on, have really the significance which Mr Yeats attaches to them. It is a pity that people who have Mr Yeats's experiences do not attempt to establish them with proofs which are acceptable to the sceptical, because if such experiences are real they are vastly important. On the other hand, if the physical universe contains special patterns of behaviour which it reserves for Mr Yeats, it is difficult to see how to relate them to the rest of human experience.

Mr Yeats's diagrams and tables are logical and clear, in their medieval kind of way; it is when I come to his summing up of the history of civilization that everything is so generalized as either to seem meaningless or else to be matter which could only assume shape and significance in

Mr Yeats's poetry. However, occasionally the puzzle clears up, and we recognize behind Mr Yeats's lulling self-ruminating prose a voice which, whether from this world or the next, is after all not so unfamiliar. For example, in the Examination of the Wheel, the voice appears in an illuminating footnote : 'A similar circular movement fundamental in the works of Giovanni Gentile is, I read somewhere, the half-conscious foundation of the political thought of modern Italy . . . It is the old saying of Heraclitus, "War is God of all, and Father of all, some it has made Gods and some men, some bond and some free", and the converse of Marxian Socialism.' It did not altogether surprise me to read that when Yeats read Spengler, he discovered so many parallels with both the ideas and the sources of his own instruction as to suggest a common 'instructor'.

Spengler, Stefan George, D'Annunzio, Yeats : is it really so impossible to guess at the 'instructors' who speak behind these mystic veils? It is interesting, too, to speculate whether fascism may not work out through writers such as these a mystery to fill its present yawning void of any myth, religion, law, or even legal constitution, which is not improvisation.

Wyndham Lewis: *One-Way Song*

Spectator (1 December 1933)

WYNDHAM LEWIS AS POET

The career of Mr Wyndham Lewis is one of the most remarkable of our time. Before the war Mr Lewis had a European reputation as leader of the vorticist movement. Since the war, although he has painted a great deal, his painting seems to have become subsidiary to his writing. He has exploited his talent as a draughtsman to the full in his designs for covers and decorations for his books. One of the earliest of these prose works, *Tarr*, created a sensation. A philosophical work, *Time and Western Man*, produced a great stir, and when I was at Oxford it was even to be seen on the bookshelves of some of the younger and more advanced dons : but we were not encouraged to quote from it in our essays. During more recent years, in spite of the three or four numbers of *The Enemy* magazine, there has been a tendency among the critics to neglect his work.

This is perhaps explained by the fact that Mr Lewis has not hesitated vehemently to attack the critics. In spite of the strong visual quality of his prose, all sorts of excuses were offered for not reading his books. People said that they were too long, too personal, too concerned with abusing obscure literary and artistic cliques. I repeat these charges in order to emphasize that *One-Way Song* does not offer the least objective for them.

This book is finely planned. It contains five separate poems, but they are so ordered that the book has not only immense variety, but also the strength of unity. The first poem, 'Engine Fight-Talk', which is a burlesque address to an imaginary audience in the terminology of the engine

37

room, is in some ways the most striking. In order to address his audience Mr Lewis adopts their lingo : but in doing so he achieves his satiric purpose, because the use of that lingo is ironic. The seriousness of the poem seems rather cramped in the following : but the compression adds intensity to it :

But poetry came out first. So I said in my usual tones
'Let us consider next how far the Past is our pigeon !
Should we *really* drive our ploughshare without com-
    punction across its bones,
(If we have a ploughshare) or should we leave it (if we *can*)
    in its proper region?'
And every man-jack of my little chorus shouted,
Either *no* or *yes* or merely *oh!* – *no* byelaw of the classroom
    but was flouted.

The second poem, 'The Song of the Militant Romance', is a satire on the Kiplingesque school of poets, but at the same time it reveals further Mr Lewis's own poetic aims. Thus the first two poems serve as a preparation for the two long poems which follow.

'If So The Man You Are', with its Enemy Interlude, is a very personal confession, in spite of its violent satire. The subject matter of all these poems is deeply serious. The discipline of poetry has also corrected some of the excesses of which one may legitimately complain sometimes in Mr Lewis's prose. There is no repetition in this book, no element of purely destructive hatred. In the twenty-ninth canto of 'If So The Man You Are', the enemy attack is at its most personal :

I seem to note a Roman profile bland,
I hear the drone from out the cactus-land :
That must be the poet of the Hollow Men :
The lips seem bursting with a deep Amen.

This portrait would be vivid even if we did not recognize the sitter.

Mr Lewis's satire is constructive, because while it is destroying one attitude we feel that it sets up an opposing position. The political tendency of these poems is fascist. I do not see any other interpretation of these lines :

> If so the man you are, your leaders gone,
> Can you survive into an age of iron?
> In this political cockpit who can you face?
> Yours must become a very lowly place.
> Against the grain, we henceforth must discount
> This sleepy people petted and 'all found'.
> Unless, unless, a class of leaders comes,
> To move it from its latter-day doldrums.

One-Way Song is full of dislike for democracy and democratic ideas. But it is difficult to label Mr Lewis, because his scorn for the whole caravan of popular ideas and popular philosophy, for creative evolution, Progress, relativity, the expanding universe, and racial equality includes the Greater Britain.

In fact, Mr Lewis remains inveterately the Enemy : and of enemies, he seems to me the one whom it is most possible to respect. His whole book is stamped with a passionate egotism. But a passionate egotism is the only kind of egotism that is not ultimately flippant, like that of Bernard Shaw. Indeed, whilst I find myself opposed to Mr Lewis's fascist tendencies, they do not disgust me, as does the disguised fascism of those who cannot resist admiring the limelit efficiency of the corporate state.

One-Way Song is a didactic poem. That is to say, its teaching is not confined to the contexts of the poem itself. It could also carry over into prose but it gains impressiveness in verse. It is a poem of great interest even to those who do not usually read contemporary poetry. Those who like poetry will take serious pleasure in Mr Lewis's jocular and beautifully expressed claim :

I can stand toe to toe with Chapman – or
With Humbert Wolfe or Kipling or Tagore!

The Thirties and After

I link my arm with the puff-armlets of Sweet Will,
I march in step with Pope, support Churchill.
The tudor song blossoms again when I speak.
With the cavaliers I visit, with Donne I am dark and meek.

D. H. Lawrence: *Phoenix*

Left Review II, 16 (January 1937)

This heavy, unattractive volume, a collection as it is of fragments and posthumous pieces, is nevertheless the most enlivening book I have read for a long time, since a great deal of it is D. H. Lawrence at his very best. It is a panorama of the whole Lawrence at every stage of his development : as a young man, the son of a Nottingham miner, and the favourite of his genteel and sensitive mother, against whose dominating influence he was to strive long after her death; as a traveller, restlessly going from continent to continent both to escape from something and to discover a satisfactory way of life; as a dying man, aware perhaps of the failure of his own quest and yet still pouring out prophecy, an amazing analysis of contemporary middle-class society, and his gospel.

In one of these essays (on Galsworthy) Lawrence makes some remarks about literary criticism :

> Literary criticism can be no more than a reasoned account of the feeling produced upon the critic by the book he is criticizing. Criticism can never be a science : it is, in the first place, much too personal, and in the second, it is concerned with values that science ignores. The touchstone is emotion, not reason. We judge a work of art by its effect on our sincere and vital emotion, and nothing else . . .
>
> Then it seems to me a good critic should give his readers a few standards to go by . . . It is just as well to say : This and this is the standard we judge by.

I like this. Perhaps it would not apply for all the uses of criticism, not, for example, for that which tries to 'dislodge' one established poet in favour of another. But criticism which sets out to create literary fashions, and then prove that the newest fashion is unassailable, seems to me pretentious. In any case, one cannot place a prophetic, intuitional and highly emotional writer like Lawrence in any category. One does judge him really by his effect on 'our sincere and vital emotion'. If he has none, he means nothing to the reader, that is all.

My standard in judging him is that I am a socialist. Lawrence would probably not have accepted this; but then I do not believe he would have accepted any standard except his own. The penalty of being completely original is complete isolation; only Blake could really understand Blake, only Lawrence, Lawrence. The rest of us have to take from his work whatever is useful to us.

Lawrence's isolation and his desperate originality of thought were forced on to him by his social position. Born of a working-class family, he spent his life amongst the bourgeoisie, partly because intellectual life in England is predominantly bourgeois, partly because the sheer ugliness and hopelessness of the surroundings from which he emerged, depressed him. Yet he was acutely self-conscious socially. As a worker he despised the middle class, but at the same time, he could not bring himself to believe that the proletariat could offer any better solution either for his or the world's problems. He did not fit into any social group or class. The solution which offered itself was sex; the meeting of two individuals, a man and a woman, compensating for his own lack of any fixed social background; so that an enormous amount of his work is devoted to invoking ways in which the sexual relationship may prove to be the means by which man will rediscover his soul and his integrity. It is not too much to say that Lawrence saw sex as the pivotal point on which would turn a social revolution.

It is becoming rather fashionable to sneer at Lawrence's obsession with sex. Perhaps it became an obsession because sex did not take Lawrence far enough, so that at the end of his life he was left simply reiterating and insisting on

the truth of his vision that the sexual relationship was
wrong in contemporary society, and should be altered. I
believe that Lawrence's intuition was right : the corrup-
tion of a society which sets commercial values above human
values is most evident in the sexual relationship. I think
Lawrence has gone further in describing the symptoms of a
sexually neurotic society than Freud, whose observations
are necessarily confined to pathological examples. What
Lawrence saw very clearly was that the bourgeoisie has
really come secretly to hate and trample on sex; idealized
love and prostitution are only two different ways of de-
basing the unpopular sexual act. He saw, too, that
older civilizations had a healthier and less inhuman atti-
tude.

Whatever else Lawrence may be, he is first and last a
revolutionary. Politically he was nothing, or, if you like it,
anything. For his opinions when they are stated, are wildly
inconsistent and can be fitted into several political philo-
sophies. The Nazis, with some justification, have claimed
him as their own : for, when his intuitions failed him, he
gave way to mystifications about Dark Forces, and even, in
The Plumed Serpent, about leadership. But the differences
between Lawrence and Nazi philosophy is that the Nazi
philosophy begins and ends with deliberate mystification;
Lawrence only began to mystify when his intuitions did not
lead him as far in solving a problem of human or social rela-
tions as he would have liked. Strip away the mystification
and one gets back to the truth of his analysis of modern
life.

Lawrence hated politics because he saw them as forms of
idealism, self-seeking materialism, egotism. In his own life
he had abjured class, country, civilization even, and tried
to rediscover his lost social background in his relation-
ship with one woman. Therefore he hated any movement
that involved masses of people. The revolution was for him
the revolution of the individual in himself, then of the
man and woman in their relationship with each other,
radiating outwards.

Here, again, we can hardly accept his teaching, even

though we recognize the truth of his vision. Until their material conditions are altered, the vast majority of people are prevented by upbringing, environment, lack of opportunity and a hundred other things from leading the kind of experimental life which was possible to Lawrence.

Lawrence saw that human relationships were wrong, the standards of capitalist society false; he said change the relationships, abolish the standards, and then the evils of the social system will crumble away.

> When men become their decent selves again, then we can so easily arrange the material world. The arrangement will come, as it must come, spontaneously, not by previous ordering. Until such time, what is the good of talking about it? All discussion and idealizing of the possession of property, whether individual or group or State possession, amounts now to no more than a fatal betrayal of the spontaneous self. All settlement of the property question must arise spontaneously out of the new impulse in man, to free himself from the extraneous load of possession, and walk naked and light.

What he forgets here is that those who already, by their birth and condition, are freed of the 'extraneous load of possession' – by having no possessions – are in no position 'easily to arrange the material world', nor even to 'become their decent selves again'. Lawrence refused to recognize this. If he went to Nottingham, the countryside 'plastered with slums' depressed him unutterably, and he came away again. He saw ugliness as an expression of man's soul; not as an expression of the soul of one class which conditioned the slavery of another.

In the remarkable essay on Democracy, from which I have quoted the remarks above, Lawrence comes into the open about communism.

> The one principle that governs all the *isms* is the same : the principle of the idealized unit, the possessor of property. Man has his highest fulfilment as a possessor

44

of property : so they all say, really. One half says that the uneducated, being the majority, should possess the property; the other half says that the educated, being the enlightened, should possess the property. There is no more to it. No need to write books about it.

There is, in fact, just this more to it : that communists would abolish private property. If Lawrence had realized what this means, he might have seen that one of the implications of the propertyless society is a new relationship between men and between the sexes. Since he did not, we can accept his premises about society, even though we do not agree with his conclusions. For the revolt of his genius against bourgeois society was complete.

Louis Aragon: *The Red Front*

New Verse 3 (May 1933)

This is a translation of a propagandist poem. The poem is divided into four sections. The first section describes the corrupt state of capitalist society which has only vaguely heard the rumour of

> Unhappy Russia
> The URSS
> The URSS or as they say SSSR
> SS how is it SS
> SSR SSR oh my dear
> Just think SSR,

like a far-off train. The second section is an exhortation to the proletariat to unchain its forces and to fire on M. Léon Blum. The engine, whose pistons go SS RR and SSR SSR SSR, is now nearer. The third section describes the building of the new state, to an accompaniment of the bursting gunfire which 'adds to the landscape a hitherto unknown gaiety'. The fourth section is exalted, metaphysical exhortation, in which the proletariat is told that

> Each of your breathings begets
> Marx and Lenin in the sky.

The express has now reached its destination.

It seems to me that in spite of its effective cinematographic technique this poem fails, because it does not convince one that the writer knows why the proletariat should kill and oppress the bourgeoisie except because the bourgeoisie is now oppressing the proletariat. He assumes that there is some absolute virtue in the proletarian which makes

his atrocities glorious whereas the atrocities of the bour-
geoisie are sordid. Yet M. Aragon is much too good a
materialist to explain what this absolute virtue of the
proletarian really is. The only reason for getting into the
train seems to be that

> No one remains behind
> Waving handkerchiefs Everyone is going,

that is to say Everyone except those who are shot for not
going. This poem is really as much a threat as propaganda.
The young communists are told :

You hold in your hands a laughing child
A child such as has never been seen
He knows before he can talk all the songs of the new life.

And he had better not learn to talk.

If this type of propaganda has any effect at all, I do not
see what that can be except to breed in people a super-
stitious belief in the necessity of murders and reprisals. This
seems to me an excessive simplification. It is so simple that
unfortunately it is effective. Before the revolution the
intellectuals preach violence which to them has a merely
pictorial significance, but after the revolution they are
horrified at the forces they have let loose. If bloodshed
is a criterion of communism, Hitler is as much a com-
munist as M. Aragon, and his rhetoric is even more effec-
tive. The intellectual capacity of Hitler and this poet seems
about the same. Readers of the poem should compare it
with any speech by Hitler.

Poetry and Revolution

New Country (March 1933)

I

Of human activities, writing poetry is one of the least revolutionary. The states of being a rentier, a merchant, a capitalist, contribute their bits to revolution : they actively crumble. But the writing of a poem in itself solves the poem's problem. Separate poems are separate and complete and ideal worlds. If a poem is not complete in itself and if its content spills over into our world of confused emotions, then it is a bad poem, and however much it may impress people at present, soon it will be forgotten and will cease to be a poem at all. This is what people mean when they say that it is impossible to write good propagandist poetry. A work of art cannot reach out into everyday life and tell us whom to vote for and what kind of factories to build, because injunctions how to act in a world that has nothing to do with the poem destroy the poem's unity.

II

Apart from the remote possibility of a kind of poetry being written which would incite people to action as effectively as the propagandist film, poetry remains an intellectual activity which is idealist in the sense to which revolutionaries most strongly object. That is to say the poet, often a potential revolutionary, is able to escape from the urgent problems of social reconstruction into a world of his own making. This world is a world of the imagination only bounded by the limits of the imagination. Music is an even more powerful means of escape than poetry, in fact perhaps it is the most powerful of all the idealist drugs except religion. In the elements of tune and rhythm which poetry and music have in common, rather than in the thinking element, lies the power which withdraws the artist from the world.

It is conceivable that an artist might write from the standpoint of a consistently materialist philosophy, but even then his occupation of writing poetry would remain the very type of idealist activity which is tactically dangerous to communism. The people who read these poems would linger over certain aspects of materialism, they would forget, in the course of their meditations, the social revolution, and here, in the very heart of materialism, idealism would creep offering its dangerous delights and consolations.

From the point of view of the revolutionary propagandist, art plays amongst the more intelligent and less satisfied members of the leisured classes the same role as charity plays among the poor. Where there should be friction leading to a final breakdown, it oils the machine and enables it to go on running. Dissatisfaction is sublimated into art which can only be enjoyed by a cultivated and endowed minority. The creators of that art are isolated, potential rebels, individualists, who, instead of turning against the society that cannot make them happy, have withdrawn into themselves and built up their little worlds of the imagination. The existence of such individuals is dependent on such a state of society, but insofar as these people justify their own existence they may be said to be in effect counter-revolutionary propagandists.

The art which is being and which can be created today is not in any sense proletarian art. It is not easy to think of any writer today who is an artist and whose work appeals to a proletarian audience. A writer like D. H. Lawrence, who was the son of a miner, in the process of becoming a poet and novelist was educated into another class. The readers for whom he wrote were inevitably members of that other, superior, cultured class, however much Lawrence himself might write about his own people. Our modern poetry, even poetry about communism, or even the war poetry of Wilfred Owen 'about men, not heroes', and certainly not about officers either, if it is read at all by proletarians is only read by those who have obtained scholarships so that they can enter the cultural tradition of the middle classes. Moreover, except for the music hall, there is no tradition of working-class art which can compare with the individualist art of the middle class in the same way as one can compare peasant art or the ballad with the work of the Italian masters.

The contemporary writer who sympathizes with communism is faced with this primary difficulty : whether he is a member of the middle class or is a worker by origin, in order to reach a public he has to enter into the tradition of bourgeois art. Bourgeois art includes the art of rebels against the bourgeoisie, such as Rimbaud; in fact, to the communist, Rimbaud seems supremely bourgeois and individualist. On the other hand, if it be disputed that the art written by proletarians is in the bourgeois tradition, it is only necessary to mention the fiction produced by Soviet writers in such quantities. The subject matter of these books (or of such as I have read in translation) is certainly new, being about the revolution, and there is certainly sometimes a naked directness from which a proletarian tradition may eventually emerge, but perhaps the most surprising characteristic of these stories and novels is their lack of originality in form. If they are read by proletarian audiences, it must be because the Russian proletariat is rapidly being educated to become middle class.

So the artist today feels himself totally submerged by bourgeois tradition, he feels that nothing he can write could possibly appeal to a proletarian audience, and therefore he finds himself becoming simply the bourgeois artist in revolt, in short, the individualist. He feels that nothing of revolutionary interest can be produced within this tradition, and yet there is no way of getting outside it. All his judgements are ruled by it, and to be an exception is only a way of emphasizing his individualism. For these reasons he is tempted to feel that the artist should go into active politics now as the revolution has no need for art.

III

The artist cannot renounce the bourgeois tradition because the proletariat has no alternative tradition which he could adopt. The remedy of communists for this is to encourage individual writers to write communist propaganda and books about the life of the proletariat. It is supposed that all bourgeois art is in effect propaganda for bourgeois ways of thinking, and therefore that if communist propaganda is written it will turn into proletarian art.

It is certainly probable that when the workers have been in power for some time, the proletariat will develop a literature which is very different from that of today. But to suppose that for this reason it is necessary to renounce all literature that has been written up to the present day, is absurd. The root of the communist dislike for bourgeois art is the misconception that bourgeois art necessarily propagates the bourgeois 'ideology'. The proletariat, when it has produced a literature of its own, will of course rediscover the literature of our period. It will then be seen that bourgeois literature is not bourgeois propaganda but simply the life history of the phase in our society when the middle classes were cultured. Naturally this art was the product of a middle-class environment, because the middle classes then enjoyed power. But just because art was produced for a time by the middle classes, this does not mean that artists are dependent for their existence on the survival of the capitalist system . . .

It is true that bourgeois literature has been written by the bourgeois about the bourgeois for the bourgeois, but it is not true that this art has all been counter-revolutionary propaganda. Indeed, it would seem far truer to say that bourgeois art has contributed extensively to the breaking up of capitalist society; but this is not the case either, art has simply communicated the elements of disruption which were already present there. Propaganda has not been a function of art in society, but psychoanalysis has been one. For this reason it is still very important that we should have good artists today and that they should not be led astray into practical politics. Art can make clear to the practical revolutionaries the historic issues which are in the deepest sense political.

IV

People sometimes talk about poetry as though it were dead, and they will point out that the type of mind which in an earlier age would have expressed itself in poetry now turns to science. If this be true, it is surely a disaster. For as long as we can speak and feel, poetry should remain a most important function of speech and emotion. Poetry records the changing uses of words, it preserves certain words in their pure and historic meaning, it saves the language from degenerating. Poetry also is a function of our emotional life. It is the language not necessarily of our highest or lowest moments (if these terms mean anything), but it is the language of moments in which we see ourselves or other people in our or their true relation to humanity or nature. Poetry is certainly 'counter-revolutionary' in the sense that it expresses compassion for all human beings, regardless of class or race.

Poetry may be taken as the type of all art, and to censor it or any other art is like censoring those functions of the body which purify the blood or give us our sense of balance. Revolution is to be accomplished by an act of will on the part of some, a paralysis of it overtaking others, but it cannot be assisted by censoring the truth of artists. Artists always have been and always will be individualists. When we admire qualities in the carving of the altar of a church of the Middle Ages which are beautiful and yet seem anonymous, and when we say that art of this kind is not individualist, we do not mean that every member of the village took a chisel and had a cut at the altar, but that one artist, whose work reflects social conditions in which everyone is not primarily concerned with expressing his individual personality, made it. The majority of artists today are forced to remain individualists in the sense of the individualist who expresses nothing except his feeling for his own individuality, his isolation. The writer who sympathizes with communism suffers because it is economically impossible for him to be a communist in a complete sense before the world revolution; he must be a rentier or a capitalist hireling. Therefore the majority of artists today are forced into isolation. But by making clear the causes of our present frustration they may prepare the way for a new and better world.

The Poetic Dramas of W. H. Auden and Christopher Isherwood

New Writing, new series I (Autumn 1938)

> The Elizabethan drama was aimed at a public which wanted *entertainment* of a crude sort, but would *stand* a good deal of poetry; our problem should be to take a form of entertainment, and subject it to the process which would leave it a form of art. Perhaps the music-hall comedian is the best material. I am aware that this is a dangerous suggestion to make. For every person who is likely to consider it seriously there are a dozen toymakers who would leap to tickle aesthetic society into one more quiver and giggle of art debauch.

So wrote Mr T. S. Eliot in *The Sacred Wood*, outlining a tactical programme for writers of poetic drama which has been carried out more exactly by Auden and Isherwood in *The Dog Beneath the Skin* and *The Ascent of F6* than by himself in *Murder in the Cathedral* and *The Rock*.

The problem was to write plays in verse which would interest an audience large enough to justify their presentation on the stage, and attract this audience by entertainment rather than by the sense of piety which still commands people to pay a bored homage to the holy muse. In this, these writers have succeeded; and one can consider their plays successful. The faulty Group Theatre productions have shown that it is possible to interest a growing audience in a type of play rather resembling the revue or even the musical comedy, but which has a serious subject and contains excellent poetry. *The Ascent of F6* had a successful run in London at the Mercury Theatre throughout the 1937 Coronation season. There is little reason to

54

doubt that, given sufficient commercial backing, plays of this kind could be as successful as any popular revue, and would command a great deal more attention from their audiences.

The victory has not been gained without a certain number of concessions which amount perhaps to a loss to poetry. Most of the poetry in these plays is inferior to the poetry of Auden's single poems. More noticeably no character in them has the subtlety and profundity of characters in Mr Isherwood's novels. The fact that a collaboration produces results inferior to the separate works of either collaborator is rather disappointing. Lastly, I doubt whether, considered as purely literary influence, the effects of these plays have been altogether good on writers younger than Auden and Isherwood who imitate them. What a relief it must have been to the undergraduate admirers of Auden's difficult *Poems* to discover that Mr Auden had started writing in the manner of Cole Porter! How easy to imitate him! Backed up by a misunderstanding of Mr Auden's statement that he considers *Lear*, jazz lyrics and rhymes in Kennedy's Latin Grammar all as 'poetry', his influence has produced a kind of Lowest Common Denominator of his own work written by his followers who find that after all it is not so difficult to write Auden – at any rate at certain levels. The magazines devoted to new verse are full of his imitators.

Still, Auden's jazz lyrics are extremely effective. Isherwood, on the other hand, when he depreciates his style is not so successful. In the parody of various public figures in *The Ascent of F6*, he fails, because he does not succeed in making one think that any set of people talk so exactly like parodies of them, which, in 'real life' they may, of course, well do. Colonels, newspaper proprietors, Lady Houstons, cabinet ministers, are so unconvincing if one hears them speak (for example, I have heard Sir John Simon give a perfect Auden-Isherwood talk in his club, on Red Gold) that if they are presented on the stage something has to be done to prevent them appearing as the stuffed dummies which, in fact, they are. C. K. Munro's play, *The Rumour*, fails for the same reason as Isherwood's dialogue in *The Ascent of F6*; huge maps are put on the wall, everything is made as important and public as possible, all the elements of publicity are exaggerated to an extent which is incredible in real life (although true) and therefore doubly incredible on the stage. For that matter, I have failed in the portrait of Hummeldorf and in Act II of *Trial of a Judge*, for the same reasons. There is one example of a completely successful solution of the problem; and that is Bernard Shaw's portraits of Asquith and Lloyd George in *Back to Methuselah*; they provide a wonderful combination of private motives with public ridiculousness. The absurdity of the public man's position lies in the perpetual interplay between the littleness of the man and the greatness of his position. Most successful publicists have succeeded in concealing their private personalities and in becoming entirely public; the clue for the satirist lies not in emphasizing the public qualities of public figures, but in stripping them away so that one can see the private weaknesses behind.

Other critics have remarked on adolescent qualities in the satire of the Auden-Isherwood plays. I think we have a clue to it here. They have fallen into the trap of making the absurd absurd, of setting down what is ridiculous or horrible in real life, copying it directly, just as a schoolboy caricatures the most obviously ridiculous defects of his masters. The schoolboy's caricature appears ineffectual because it is fainter than the characters caricatured and it therefore remains merely spiteful. It draws our attention to the schoolboy's own weaknesses in being subject to the absurdities of others. Isherwood produces a mere flat representation of Lord Stagmantle the newspaper proprietor, without analysing his motives. In *The Dog Beneath the Skin*, both writers present pictures of a world in decay, which are not nearly as frightening as that world itself. The scene in which the inmates of a lunatic asylum of Westlanders applaud a broadcast speech by the Leader and behave in the way that Nazis behave is inept because the alarming fact about Nazi Germany is that the Nazis are *not* lunatics. Merely to say, 'Oh, the Germans are lunatics' (which is the effect of this scene) so far from being satire is complacent; it is like the schoolboy calling the master who sneaks 'Slimy' or the French master 'Froggy'. On the whole, the effect of such a scene cannot be to increase the spectator's realization of what fascism signifies, but to make him reflect that after all his compatriots are not lunatics like the inhabitants of Westland. The satire of *The Dog Beneath the Skin* suffers through the approach of the writers to European problems being much too direct. You cannot reproduce chaos by buffoonery chalked on a school blackboard.

This is not to say that all – or nearly all – of the satire in *The Dog Beneath the Skin* fails. For example, the satire on the invalids in the hospital where an operation is performed by a famous surgeon is extremely successful. With a sure touch, it probes beneath the hygienic surface of the whole atmosphere of the sick bed and reveals an egotism on the part of the patient and a superstition attached to the medical profession, which are not generally recognized, but which, once pointed out, the audience recognizes are true. Satire must probe, it must present new and striking surfaces; that is why the obvious objects of satire – ludicrous public men behaving ludicrously – are difficult to satirize, whereas there is always something new to learn about the 'manners' of an age – the fashionable vices and diseases – which are skins grown over vanity and egotism.

The Dog Beneath the Skin succeeded, in spite of its faults, by its high spirits and great energy. Although some of the visits of Alan, the hero, to different parts of Europe in search of the long-lost heir Francis, who is disguised in the skin of the dog which accompanies him, are like the visits of a schoolboy to an International Exhibition, the total effect of a long and exhilarating journey made and a large and varied scene created, does get across. It is at the end of the play, when we are presented with a moral, that misgivings arise. The dog, having returned home with Alan, whose search seems to have proved fruitless, reveals himself to the villagers of his home estate Pressan Ambo as their long-lost heir and makes a sermon. Hearing this sermon, one wonders whether after all this enormous journey and this animal disguise was not rather a circuitous route by which to have arrived at conclusions which the Vicar of Pressan Ambo himself could scarcely have regarded as astonishing. 'As a dog,' says Francis to the villagers, 'I learnt with what a mixture of fear, bullying, and condescending kindness you treat those whom you consider your inferiors, but on whom you are dependent for your pleasures. It's an awful shock to start seeing people from underneath.' The real moral then emerges. Francis renounces all claim to his inheritance because he has decided that the inhabitants of Pressan Ambo are part of an army. He belongs to another army – the Workers – which he is now going to join. As this is the first we have heard of the army 'on the other side' throughout the play, this conclusion may seem rather surprising. But it is not really so, because the satire has been directed from 'the other side' throughout the play. The reason why the writers fail to present that 'other side' whose point of view they implicitly accept is because whereas they know a great deal about the side of the bourgeoisie – from which they consider themselves disinherited – they know far less about the workers' side which they believe themselves to have joined. *The Dog Beneath the Skin* is a picture of a society defeated by an enemy whom the writers have not put into the picture because they do not know what he looks like although they thoroughly support him.

The Ascent of F6 is the most successful of these plays, partly because the characterization of the members of the mountaineering expedition is convincing, partly because of the fable of the expedition which is at once a pure attempt by Ransom the hero to excel and at the same time an important turning point in the struggle between two imperialisms, is largely plausible. Ransom is, of course, a prig; but the struggle which takes place in his mind is a serious and important one. This struggle is implicitly religious, though it is set against on the one hand the background of politics and commercialization, symbolized by the struggle between two imperialisms to ascend the mountain first, and on the other hand, Ransom's own psychology – his rivalry with his brother James, the successful politician, for the love of his mother. But when the mother turns out to be the demon at the top of the mountain who is the final goal of Ransom's achievement at the moment of his death, one feels that the religious theme of the struggle going on in Ransom's own soul has not been fully worked out. The conversations with the Abbot on the mountain do not lead to a satisfactory solution, and a cliché of modern psychological ideology is substituted for some ending to the play which the authors have not been able to find.

If one looks closely at the actual writing of the play, one wonders whether there is not a lack of organic structure in the speeches themselves. A very ingenious framework has been contrived, some natural characterization and dialogue written, and into this a number of speeches are fitted which are not always closely enough related to the action of the play. Here Auden particularly seems content to throw in too much 'stuff' which is what Mr Geoffrey Grigson would call 'good Auden' but which does not have an essentially dramatic bearing on the action and thought of *The Ascent of F6*. More than any other form, a play must be coherent with itself and be impregnated with its own unique and confining atmosphere; but the following might be an extract from *The Orators* or any other of Auden's prose speeches : 'Virtue. Knowledge. We have heard these words before; and we shall hear them again – during the nursery luncheon, the prize-giving afternoon, in the quack advertisement, at the conference of generals or industrial captains : justifying every baseness and excusing every failure, comforting the stilted schoolboy lives . . .' etc. Now this speech – which should certainly create an atmosphere, since it opens the play – lives within the body of Auden's *Collected Works*, but does nothing to suggest the key symbols of the play. There are far too many references to a scene of activity outside the theatre, which have nothing to do with the evening's performance. Of course, I am not suggesting that a play's imagery should be en-

The Thirties and After

tirely self-enclosed, but I think that there is a tendency
in this play to invoke far too wide a range of references. It
may be said that it is impossible to write poetic prose
speeches without a very wide range of reference to an
emotional background outside the play. If the reader thinks
this, I beg him to read *Dantons Tod* by Georg Büchner
which, although written in the early nineteenth century, is
a play suggesting a solution of nearly all the problems of a
modern poetic drama.

The blank verse speeches suffer from being Shake-
spearean. The speeches by Mr and Mrs A. do produce ex-
actly the suburban atmosphere which Mr Auden intends;
but Michael Ransom slides off into patches of *Lear* which
are even more disconcerting to hear on the stage than to
read :

　　O senseless hurricanes,
That waste yourselves upon the unvexed rock,
Find some employment proper to your powers,
Press on the neck of Man your murdering thumbs,
And earn real gratitude !

An encouraging start has been made by Auden and
Isherwood to solve the problems of creating a contem-
porary poetic drama. The most important of these prob-
lems – that of finding an audience – they have solved better
than anyone for a generation. They have concentrated –
quite justifiably – on providing entertainment, but since
they are also creating a form and presenting a view
of the world, one has to realize how many of the problems
of presentation they have evaded. The most obvious failure
is the failure to write satisfactory endings to their plays :
but, where an ending cannot be found, one may suspect
that there is a lack of organic growth throughout the play
and something is wrong from the start. One may suspect
that the collaboration itself is responsible for some of these
faults : each writer hopes that the other is going to try
harder than himself; when a difficulty is encountered by
one writer the other suggests a solution which is really an

60

evasion; neither writer feels as responsible for the criticism which the play may arouse as he would if the work were entirely his own. More important, it must be very difficult in a collaboration to construct the unique, hemmed-in and claustrophobic atmosphere which is essential to a play.

So far, these writers have been content to throw fragments of good stuff into a loosely constructed play, without concentrating their abilities on making the whole conception rank with the most serious work of each. For them, the problem is largely an aesthetic one – to write a play which is as good as *Mr Norris Changes Trains* or any single poem in *Look, Stranger!* For their audience the problem is neither simply aesthetic nor simply a question of increasing the prestige of poetry by restoring the spoken word on the stage. It is really a question of reviving the drama itself, which has fallen into a decadent 'naturalistic' tradition, confining itself, for the most part, to the presentation of faked-up photographic vignettes of the life of a small section of the rentier class. If we think of the realities of the world today – using the word reality in a sense little known to the West End London stage – we see that there are great conflicts and a moral and material struggle involving the birth of a new world, which poetry is peculiarly qualified to deal with, since a poetic use of language is the only literary medium which can deal realistically with a wide and generalized subject without being overloaded with details of naturalistic representation. The Auden-Isherwood plays are only the beginning of a movement far more significant than any 'revival' of the poetic drama or even any sudden flourishing avant-garde poetry; for what is required and what we may get during the next years is a revolution in the ideas of drama which at present stagnate on the English stage, and the emergence of the theatre as the most significant and living of literary forms.

Tangiers and Gibraltar *Now*

Left Review III, 1 (February 1937)

Only a few months ago Mussolini upset one end of the Mediterranean, and now the Spanish Civil War, with German and Italian intervention, is upsetting the other end. I have had an opportunity of observing this commotion; for having failed to obtain a safe conduct to Cadiz and rebel Spain, I have been staying for a few days in Tangiers and Gibraltar, interviewing emigrés, consuls and journalists.

The tourist who goes south in winter with the swallows is the least hardy of all birds, and has almost deserted Tangiers this winter. The few who remain congratulate themselves on their hardihood and twitter vaguely about the troubles over the water, of which they are reminded by select specimens of the German, Italian and British Navies, anchored in the international harbour. There has been violence, too, of the discreet, artificial, bullying kind in which the fascist countries excel. Some bands of Italian sailors, giving way with impulsive generosity to feelings of indignation against international Bolshevism which their officers found themselves unable to restrain, 'spontaneously' wrecked the offices of a socialist newspaper, attacked socialist cafés, etc.

The extremely mixed population of Tangiers – a third of which is Jewish – is a wonderful soil for fascist propaganda and every kind of intrigue. The Spanish war has, of course, dramatized this situation. A part of the population refuses to recognize the Spanish consul, who is not only consul, but also a member of the governing commission. Yet in spite of intensive German, Italian, and Franco-ist propaganda, the theme song of Tangiers which one hears sung and whistled in all but the wealthiest streets of the town is the 'Internationale'. Whilst I am writing these lines I can hear someone whistling it in the street outside.

The very large working-class section of the Spanish population which supports the government, does so with a nervous enthusiasm which is astonishing. Last night (January 17th) I attended a meeting of the Spanish and French supporters of the popular front in the largest theatre here. The theatre could have been filled several times over, and was crowded to suffocation. The most moving part of the evening was not the speeches – which were disappointing – but the fervour of the crowd as they raised their fists in the socialist greeting to the Spanish consul, and sang the 'Internationale'. Workers stood up and shouted slogans, which the entire crowd immediately and fiercely responded to. One speaker ended his speech with the words 'No Pasaran', and immediately the whole audience stood up and cheered. These people listened attentively to speeches, which were immensely long and delivered mostly in French, a language which many of them could not understand.

At this meeting I realized as I had never done before how completely the will and aspirations of the Spanish people are identified with the Valencia government. It is not often in the history of a nation that the phrase 'the people' has any meaning : but there are moments when suddenly the masses acquire a conscious will. Such moments occurred during the French and the Russian Revolutions; and are now in Spain.

The Spanish governing classes even within the Valencia government are predominantly bourgeois. Yet when one meets the representatives of the Spanish Republican Government one realizes that they, too, have made their choice, involving perhaps their death, and in any case the loss of their property. In this part of Europe it is impossible not to recognize that those who support the Spanish Republicans realize that their common enemy is property; whilst the English governing classes in Gibraltar sympathize with the rebels because property calls to property even when reason tells them that the victory of Franco would endanger the Empire and the Rock. As one retired English official said to me : 'This is the old struggle of the Have-nots and the Haves. The workers want to take over that which belongs to the aristocrats. They used to be content with their spiritual solace – religion – but the damned communists have stopped all that and made them dis-contented.'

This same official embellished his interpretation of the struggle which the English governing classes appreciate when it happens abroad, whilst pretending that it does not exist in England, with atrocity stories told against the Reds. Gibraltar is now the chief centre in the world for the export of such propaganda. The Governor of Gib-raltar generously entertained and put up numerous aristocratic exiles after the outbreak of the revolution. These people repaid his hospitality with piteous tales of the sufferings they had undergone, which sent a shudder of righteous indignation and pious self-satisfaction through official circles. No doubt some, or even many, of these stories may be true; yet it seems to me that atrocities are a measure of the ignorance and suffering imposed on the isolated people who commit them, and thus they are only a by-product of the monstrous Spanish system which is now being abolished.

Yet other bonds than pity and indignation endear the English in Gibraltar to the rebels at La Linea. For 'life' in that austere garrison, where all the cafés are closed and everyone is sent to bed at 11 o'clock, has outlets only in polo and fox-hunting. Friendly agreements have therefore been made with the rebels at La Linea for the English to pursue their sports in rebel territory.

The largest and grandest hotel in Gibraltar is The Rock, owned by the Marquis of Bute, who also owns the Hotel Minza in Tangiers. One of his guests is the English wife of the young Spanish fascist nobleman who is General Franco's chauffeur. This young man, until recently, used to pay his visits to his wife at The Rock, dressed in rebel uniform. He has been reprimanded; now he changes into mufti at the frontier.

The secretary of the Marquis of Bute is the Count de Reventera, an Austrian married to a Spanish wife. De Reventera is the chief organizer of the Spanish fascists in this zone. I first heard of him in the course of a conversation at the Hotel Minza. His English friends admire him greatly, and boast that he owns an armed trawler with which he attacks and confiscates Russian traders. A few weeks ago he suffered two slight set-backs : he was not allowed to bring his trawler into the harbour at Tangiers, and he was forbidden to go to Gibraltar. Now, however, this unpleasantness has been overcome, and he is again to be seen in his leisure hours discussing his latest haul of Russian caviare in the bar of The Rock.

Journalists in Gibraltar are in a peculiar position. Their chief source of news is either rumour or that which is issued by the Naval Intelligence Department, the Army Intelligence Department and the Colonial Secretary. Owing to the delicate situation in the Mediterranean, the Naval Intelligence has made the simple decision of giving the local correspondents practically no information. Often they are in the humiliating position of hearing on the wireless or reading in English papers two days old, news from Gibraltar which has been given out by the London Admiralty before it is issued by their own department.

Gibraltar is a garrison town, and one cannot be surprised that it exists under a permanent martial law. But it is undergoing a crisis. For it is still, in spite of the presence of the British, a Spanish town, and the Spanish workers support the Frente Popular. The Labour Movement – unassisted by the British party who appear to have ignored reports sent to them by the Transport Workers' Union – is growing rapidly. As one of my English informants said : 'Go into the streets here; talk to the people and you will find that eighty per cent of them are damned Reds.'

Heroes in Spain

New Statesman & *Nation* (1 May 1937)

George, a driver in the convoy of the Unit to which I managed to attach myself from Barcelona to Valencia, was formerly a cellist in a Corner House orchestra. Fat, frank, spectacled and intelligent, he had learned to drive a lorry on the day of his arrival in Barcelona : he drove with too much concentration, leaning over the wheel to fix his attention short-sightedly on the road. In a moment of emotion, when we were driving along the moonlit coastal road between Tarragona and Tortosa, he told me that he had only wept three times in his life : once, at the Wembley Tattoo when the whole crowd was hysterical with imperialist fervour, and looking round he had a sudden vision of what it all meant and was leading to; once, when after playing musical trash for months in the restaurant, he went to Sadler's Wells, and hearing *Figaro* performed, realized what music might be and what the standards were by which he earned his living; once, that very morning in Barcelona, when he realized, as he put it, that 'the people in this town know they are free.'

All the time I was in Spain I remembered these three occasions on which George had wept; they seemed to me a monument of personal honesty, of the spirit in which the best men have been able to live not for themselves but for a principle. One man goes out to Spain because his dislike of the Corner House orchestra and his love of Mozart suddenly becomes a rule of action with which his own life is identified. A young girl, who happens to be an Anglo-Catholic, and who is politically ignorant, goes out to nurse the wounded because she wishes to alleviate human suffering. Her patients, as soon as they are convalescent, bully her for her lack of 'ideology', and she suffers more than they are able to imagine.

The unity which exists today in Governmental Spain is the unity of a people whose lives are identified with a principle. This unity is real, though it is something far more difficult to put one's finger on than the obvious differences of the political parties. Talk to people and they are best able to express their differences of opinion, and these differences soon produce various degrees of feeling. Read the editorials of the newspapers in Valencia and the differences which are labelled under such initials as UGT, FAI, CNT, POUM, soon appear alarming indeed, especially when 'unity' is being discussed. As one newspaper correspondent said : 'The more they speak of unity, the more they seem to quarrel.'

Yet the unity which was George's and my own first impression of Barcelona is a reality which is probably moulding Spanish democracy more quickly than those who deal in journalism and political controversy realize. The attitude of the Spanish people to members of the International Brigade is a good test of their fundamental agreement. In the first place, propaganda about the Brigade has perhaps not been handled as tactfully as it might have been. For example, the battle of Morata was a turning point in the war because the Spanish troops rallied instead of fleeing at a critical moment. When I went along the lines at Morata, in March, I found that the Spanish Lister battalion was entrenched in positions nearer the enemy lines than any trenches of the Brigade. Yet almost all the credit for Morata has gone to the Brigade. Again, quite apart from the decisive action of the Republican Air Force, which is now ninety per cent Spanish, Spanish troops fought courageously at Guadalajara, yet all the glory went to the Italian Garibaldi battalion.

Tactless propaganda about the International Brigade might appear humiliating to the Spanish people, so it is sometimes suggested that the Brigade is rather resented in Spain. Yet during my six weeks of travelling in Spain I was almost invariably mistaken for a member of the Brigade and treated with extraordinary generosity on that

account. Again, it is suggested that the anarchists are afraid
of what the Brigade may do after the war is won. But
in practice, anarchists and members of the Brigade work
and fight side by side and the boundaries between political
movements are broken down at the front.

I went to Barcelona, Valencia, Madrid, Morata,
Alabacete and Tortosa (where thousands of people had
camped out on the hills at night for fear of an air raid);
and I travelled a good deal between these places, going
in trains, lorries and private cars. My first and last im-
pressions were not the struggle for power amongst the
heads of committees in the large towns, nor inefficiency
and bureaucracy, common as they are during a revolution
which is also a war; but the courage of the people in
Madrid, the enthusiasm of eighty per cent of the people
everywhere for the social revolution, the generosity of the
workers wherever I met them, in the streets, in trains, in lor-
ries; the marked difference between the awakening younger
generation of Spanish workers and the stupefied older
ones. Every observer who stays in Republican Spain comes
back again and again to a realization that it is the people
of Spain who count.

At first the war strengthened and unified the social
revolution, but in the long run war demands its own
measures which threaten to engulf the whole social sys-
tem. I set beside the story of George, the lorry driver, the
story of Harry, a member of the International Brigade,
who first came out as correspondent for one of the most
reactionary English newspapers. Harry fought in the battle
of Morata, where there were four hundred casualties in
three days out of a battalion of six hundred men. The
worst part of this battle was fought without trenches or
other protection, except olive trees, in hilly country amongst
the fields and olive groves. On the first day of the battle a
friend of Harry died of a stomach wound, bleeding to
death. Harry stayed by him, under fire, until he died.
That night Harry disturbed his comrades, who were try-
ing to sleep, by walking along the lines shouting out that
he was thirsty and must have water . . . The next morning

he happened to be fighting next to a friend of mine in the olive grove. He repeatedly said to my friend : 'You see that wall over there? How far do you think it is?' My friend answered, 'One hundred yards.' 'Well, you take a range of 120 and I'll try one of 100,' etc. . . . That evening he appeared in the lines holding a bundle of telegraph wires which he waved above his head. He said 'Look, I've cut Franco's communications.' He had gone mad.

I tell this story in order to counteract the propaganda about heroes in wars. The final horror of war is the complete isolation of a man dying in a world whose reality is violence. The dead in wars are not heroes : they are freezing or rotting lumps of isolated insanity.

People try to escape from a realization of the violence to which abstract ideas and high ideals have led them by saying either that individuals do not matter or else that the dead are heroes. It may be true that at certain times the lives of individuals are unimportant in relation to the whole of future history – although the violent death of many individuals may modify the consciousness of a whole generation as much as a work of art or a philosophical treatise. But to say that those who happen to be killed are heroes is a wicked attempt to identify the dead with the abstract ideas which have brought them to the Front, thus adding prestige to those ideas, which are used to lead the living on to similar 'heroic' deaths.

Perhaps soldiers suspect this, for they do not like heroic propaganda. When I was at the Morata Front several men complained of the heroics in left-wing papers. Some praised very highly the report of the battle of Morata, written by Philip Jordan, which appeared in the *News Chronicle* : but they complained that even that, restrained as it was, was too heroic. I had the impression that soldiers in a war have an almost pathetic longing to know the truth.

I returned from Spain feeling more strongly than I have ever felt before that I support the Spanish social revolution. Since the war must be won if the revolution is to be retained, there is nothing to do but accept it as a terrible necessity. Shortly before he died, the poet García

Lorca is reported to have said that he would write in time of war the poetry of those who hate war; and when the Indian writer Mulk Raj Anand asked the soldiers fighting in the trenches at Madrid what message they would send to the Indian peasants and workers, they answered: 'Tell our Indian comrades that we hope that when the time comes, they will not have to fight for their freedom as we are doing.' I like Spanish people because it seems to me that they are emotionally honester than other people. There are few heroics, no White Feathers, and genuine hatred for the necessity of the war in Spain. A war such as the present one may be necessary: but it seems to me that the left-wing movement in this country can never afford to forget how terrible war is; and that not the least of its crimes is the propaganda which turns men into heroes.

Spain Invites the World's Writers

New Writing 4 (Autumn 1937)

NOTES ON THE INTERNATIONAL CONGRESS, SUMMER 1937

From the moment of our arrival in Spain, our congress was overshadowed by the wonderful country, the Spanish people and the civil war. Port Bou itself makes the strangest impression – a town in which the people are particularly friendly, in which a third of the population seems to be occupied in military training in the hills, a third bathing and sun-bathing in the harbour, while the rest sit at cafés or stand about, impressing us with that peculiar feeling of a war, that the people are not so much living in the town as haunting it; they are spirits obsessed by their idea, easily transferable to some other scene of war; and their relation to their homes, their material surroundings, is very slight. I have been at Port Bou three or four times during the past few months, so this was not new to me, but I was very conscious of its effect on the South American delegates. We were shown parts of the town which had been destroyed in the course of several unsuccessful attempts to bomb the station. The South Americans were upset, and their usual gaiety seemed rebuffed. They noticed with a certain anguish the thing that is surrealistically *amusing* about bombardments : the single piece of furniture left quite undisturbed at the edge of a room which has been cut down, as though by a knife. But all this time we were preoccupied by two other things which are Spanish : the heat, and the monumental delay in the preparations for our midday meal.

After that excellent meal, we set out in a fleet of cars

along the beautiful mountainous coastal road to Valencia. The English delegation were given a Rolls-Royce and a chauffeur whose one idea of driving was to 'show her paces'. The wheels screamed round corners, he never changed down up hills. In the early months of the war the banks of the Valencia-Madrid road were littered with wrecked motor-cars. Even now in the course of our journeys, we saw a great many wrecks on the sides of roads, and so much dangerous driving that I wondered there were not many more.

By the time we reached Gerona I was on back-slapping, embracing terms with most of the Spanish-American delegates – magnificent, bronzed, emotional speakers, most of them. André Malraux seemed slightly disappointed with the Mexican delegates : he said that our massively-built, jet-eyed, warm colleagues – impressive for their immediate responsiveness and their directness of manner – were mere university professors compared with what Mexico could provide. Mexican poets should be utterly mad; they should be dressed like cowboys, carrry hide whips and fire off revolvers from each hand.

We reached Barcelona at eight or nine in the evening. We were received by the Minister of Propaganda who asked us whether we wished to stay the night in Barcelona. Sylvia Townsend Warner, who was dead tired, amused us all by saying, on behalf of the English, 'Of course we are quite willing to go on, but I think that out of consideration for this Mexican comrade,' dragging one of the Mexicans forward, 'who has been travelling for ten days, we *ought* perhaps to stay the night.'

We were entertained by the Catalan Government at The Majestic, the best hotel in Barcelona. Next morning, we got up at six and waited for the usual two or three hours, before starting for Valencia. We were no longer in the Rolls-Royce, as that had belonged to the Catalans, and the new fleet of cars was from Valencia. I travelled with Malraux and Aveline. During the congress, Malraux, with his youthful appearance, his close-set greenish eyes, pale looming face, with one lock of hair overhanging his forehead, his hands in the pockets of his rough tweed suit, his slouching walk, and nervous tic, had the air of being a senior, if not altogether respectable boy. But for me he was and is a hero. We talked a good deal during the journey to Valencia. I believe that for Malraux the creation of his own legend – his political activities, the 'Malraux squadron' – fulfils a spiritual need which is essential for him as an artist. The writer must create from a centre which is his environment : and it sometimes happens (as it has happened repeatedly with bourgeois writers during this generation – and that indeed is the root of the interest of so many contemporary writers in politics) that the writer does not fit into his environment. He is then driven to discover some other environment, or, if he is intensely individualist, to create one, all his own. He must first create his environment, and then create literature out of his personal legend. That is the task of a T. E. Lawrence or an André Malraux. For them, their environment is not static, the background, but the life of action. 'If you ask me what it is necessary to do, *il faut agir* – it is necessary to act.'

I remember one conversation in which we discussed politics and poetry, when he emphasized the influence of environment on the poet's symbolism. Set the poet in simple surroundings of the earth, the ox, the woman and the mountain, and the imagery suggested by this environment will recur in his poetry. To the modern poet who does not accept the bourgeois environment and the bourgeois ideology, a problem exists which is not merely one of style but a problem of will. He must deliberately change his environment.

When we reached Valencia, on 5 July, we were immediately taken to a session of the congress, where we met Ralph Bates, whom we elected leader of the English delegation for as long as we were in Spain. The session was held in a council chamber of the bombed town hall. All except this wing of the building had been gutted out, and the marble stairs leading to our meeting place had been filled with concrete where the marble was destroyed, like the fillings of teeth. In the congress it was exceedingly hot, and made still hotter by the blaze of lights for the cinematographer. Ralph Bates spoke in Castilian, welcoming us. He was in a very dynamic mood and hammered a lot with his fist. He had been inspired by a speech made by Del Vayo that morning, which we missed. Del Vayo was there with his broad, red, intelligent face, amiable and gleaming as always. Alexei Tolstoi made a speech attacking Trotsky. Tolstoi is a robust, clever, immensely prosperous man who yet does not seem to belong to the new order. Whenever I saw him he was perspiring profusely and, perhaps for that reason, I have an image of him in flannels and a silk shirt, handkerchief in hand, panting strenuously at the end of a successful race to keep up with the time. José Bérgamín made one of his paradoxical, careful and sincere speeches; as president of the congress he was its most popular member. With his slight, beautiful face, one always listens to him because he never intrudes, one always watches him because he seems almost invisible.

That evening I saw a performance of a play by Lorca and got to bed, as usual, very late. We were woken up at 4 a.m. by the air-raid alarms, and the pale morning sky was shot across with the red stains of anti-aircraft shrapnel, the guns making a rather hollow pleasant popping noise like the drawing of corks. Frank Tinsley, Reuter's correspondent, who had put me up in his room of the Hotel Victoria, said that we ought to get dressed and go downstairs. There I met Fernsworth, *The Times* correspondent, who is afraid neither of bombs nor shrapnel. He invited me to walk down to the hospital opposite the British Embassy with him to see if we could gain any news of the seriousness of the raid. We went, but there was no news. The only danger we ran was from the anti-aircraft shrapnel, which has to come down somewhere.

At ten o'clock our caravan of cars left Valencia for Madrid. By this time most of us were very exhausted. In Spain I have found my tiredness taking an entirely different form from the routine tiredness I often feel at home.

One can, I think, become so tired that one is actually more receptive than normally — because fatigue breaks one's ordinary habits of resistance down. For example, I am bad at listening to public speeches. But, in Spain, at the congress, I have at times had the experience (or the delusion), when excessively tired, of understanding every word that was said, even of difficult speeches in French, German and Spanish : where ordinarily the fact that the speech was in a foreign language would have persuaded me that I could not understand it, and thus set up my machinery of resistance.

I mention this because anyone who has been in a war — or even at the edge of it — will realize how important an element fatigue is in war psychology.

On our way to Madrid we stopped for lunch at a village called Minganilla — memorable to every delegate of the congress. It was a very hot, dazzling day. I remember walking up a straggling, dusty village street, with charming children and peasant women picturesquely dressed, whom Alexei Tolstoi photographed, with their donkeys. We drank lemonade in a guest-house, while we waited for our meal to be prepared. After two hours — or so it seemed — of waiting and talking we were told that lunch was ready and we adjourned to the long, low, first-storey room of the Fonda, where we sat down at long tables to eat omelettes and flat, white hunks of Spanish bread, followed by slabs of raw bacon. Whilst we were eating we were interrupted by the singing of all the children of the village outside our windows. First they sang the 'Internationale', then they sang other songs of the Spanish Republic. We got up and stood at the windows to thank and applaud them. When we had finished eating we went down the stone steps of the Fonda where the children had cleared a little space in their crowd in the square and they were dancing a dance which consisted of running up and down from one end of this oblong space to the other. There were no men in the village — they were all either in the fields or fighting — and the women, who stood watching their children dance, suddenly started weeping. When we went into the square to get back into our cars, the women began talking to us about the war and they asked that one of us should speak from the balcony of the Fonda in order to show that we understood their fate (these were their words). One of the Mexicans (Octavio Paz) spoke, very effectively. After that one of the women took Pablo Neruda and me back to her house, which was beautifully clean, and showed us photographs of her two sons at the Front, and, in spite of our earnest protestations, insisted on our taking about half of all the sausages she had, because we would be hungry on the rest of our journey. We were all of us more moved by our few hours in Minganilla than by any other single incident of our stay in Spain.

A happy evening after dinner in the Hotel Victoria at Madrid, with the Spanish singing Flamenco songs, clapping their hands rhythmically. They sang the traditional tunes for which the modern poets have written new words about the civil war. Rafael Alberti sang a ballad which he had written about Franco. Later the growing din was interrupted by Alberti, a massive, leonine figure, dressed in blue dungarees, with flowing hair and Michelangelesque features, leaping on to a chair and shouting with passionate fury to everyone to be quiet. Then he told us that a bombardment had started. Frank Pitcairn [the pen name of Claud Cockburn], Edgell Rickword, René Blech and I walked to the Puerta del Sol and watched the upper storeys of the Ministry of the Interior blazing, where they had been struck by an incendiary shell. René Blech walked out into the centre of the square, looked up, came back and shrugged his shoulders with one word *'ignoble'*. Then we returned to the hotel.

The impression made by Madrid today is sublime; the great, tall ugly town, whole quarters of which are silenced and destroyed, yet through which the stream of life still flows; Madrid with its blue summer sky torn open by the sound of aeroplanes machine-gunning, as they battle above the streets whilst the people stand in their doors, at windows and in the open street, watching; Madrid drummed all day by the roar of artillery from the city fronts, and sullenly illuminated at night by the red glow where incendiary shells have struck; above all, the city defended by the people who have already begun to live there the life of communal ownership which will be their future if they win the war. In this environment the endless stream of our oratory continued rather ineffectively.

What we said in public was of little interest, besides which it has been published elsewhere, and for that reason I have thought it worthwhile to record some of the things which were said in private and which were, in fact, attempts to discuss problems which the congress should have discussed. There was André Chamson, pale and furious with the congress because we had stayed longer than three hours in Madrid, and because, having stayed there, all the delegates didn't feel as he did about it. *'Le devoir d'un ecrivain est d'être tourmenté'* – and none of us was tormented. *'Moi, moi je suis responsable.'* One of us would get killed by a Franco 'obus' and then the world press would shriek that the Reds had assassinated him – and Chamson, as secretary of the French Association, would bear the responsibility. Every morning I would go up to Chamson to inquire how he was and he would reply, *'Mal, mal, MAL!'* He would go on to say that the intellectual level of our congress was appallingly low, that we were light-hearted, irresponsible, we did not *feel*. I think that in a way he was right. Along paths which I can scarcely follow, Chamson had arrived at a truth which few of the congress – fêted, banqueted, received enthusiastically, the women bridling with excitement at Ralph Bates's or Ludwig Renn's uniform – had even glimpsed, that the war is terrible, that the mind of Madrid, if it is sublime, like Shakespeare's, is also terrible, like Shakespeare's. I myself had learnt this through painful experiences some months before, not at the congress.

From reading the romances of the civil war by Spanish poets, one might conclude that the whole of Spanish poetry on the government side has adopted an uncritical, heroic attitude towards the war. Yet this is not so. I myself, because I am not a writer of heroics, have felt rather isolated from the cause and the people I greatly care for, because I could not share this uncritical attitude, but when I spoke to Alberti, Altolaguirre and Bergamín, I found that they felt about the propagandist heroics of the war much as I did myself. Alberti, a brilliant, arrogant, passionate individualist, is himself rather isolated, I feel. He is in a peculiar position as the recognized successor to Lorca, who yet is not a great influence on other contemporary Spanish poets.

On 13 July we sat once more in the little port of Carbère, very tired after a banquet in Barcelona and a terrific day of sight-seeing. A few of us had crossed the frontier before the other delegates, and I found myself next to Bergamín. We began talking about the poetry of the Spanish war, about Gide, about some personal tragedies occasioned by the war, about Bergamín's own family, about the assassination of Ramón Sender's wife by the fascists. Bergamín has a paradoxical involved mind which at times surprises one by its whimsicality not unlike E. M. Forster's, but, also like E. M. Forster's, surprises one even more by its combination of paradox with penetrating honesty and a concrete unevasive grasp of every problem. Bergamín knows what the tragedy and horror of war are : he knows also the lies which war produces, and yet his mind seems to penetrate through all these obstructions to a position where he is absolutely secure, where he accepts the tragedy and horror, relates the lies to the forces which render them inevitable. In a word, he was the only member of our congress who was entitled to rebuke Gide, because he does not resent that which is honest in Gide (as far too many of his detractors seem to do), but because he, Bergamín, has a mind of even greater honesty, a mind which sees not merely the truth of isolated facts which Gide observed in the USSR, but the far more important truth of the *effect* which Gide's book is going to have.

During this conversation, one question troubled me – Bergamín's Catholicism. At last I dared to ask him : 'Are

you still a Catholic?' He held up his hand, placing to-
gether the index finger and thumb, thus forming a small
circle, and said in his thin, nasal French :

> If you ask me do I believe in the Articles of Faith, I
> say, yes, yes, yes, I accept all of that. But if you ask
> me do I believe that the Church has the right to inter-
> fere in the political life of the people and to represent
> the interest of one possessing class, I say no, not at all.
> Indeed, I go further than that. I say that the Church
> should have no influence in public affairs at all. I even
> say that there should be no public ceremonies and demon-
> strations which the Church is able to use for religious
> propaganda, there should be no system of religious
> education, the end of which is to make men and women
> good members of the Church. Religion is a question
> for the private conscience of the individual and for that
> only. Now, I am writing a book in which I state my
> own position, and I cannot doubt but that this book
> may be placed on the Index. Good. In that case, I
> confidently make my appeal not to the Pope, but to an
> authority greater than the Pope's on the Day of Judg-
> ment. In doing this, I maintain that I stand within the
> great tradition of Spanish Catholicism. I am fighting
> for the spiritual life and the spiritual freedom of
> Catholic Spain. But, unfortunately, the Church has
> used its power to support propertied interests, to repre-
> sent materialism and to oppose the spiritual growth of
> our people.

It has been said that a revolution corresponding at once to
the French and the Russian revolutions is taking place in
Spain. But there is yet another great change taking
place; it is Spanish Protestantism and the Spanish Reforma-
tion.

I Join the Communist Party

Daily Worker (19 February 1937)

In January Victor Gollancz chose my book, *Forward from Liberalism*, as the book of the month for his Left Book Club. My aim in this book was to portray an attitude of mind which would be a common denominator among people who really care for progress rather than reaction, peace under international control rather than imperialist aggression, government in the interests of the whole people rather than fascism.

I believed that if the implications of this attitude of mind were clearly stated many liberal individualists would find themselves set on a path which would lead them ultimately to the idea of the classless international society and to an acceptance of the action necessary – such as the formation of a United Front – to achieve that society.

This book produced various reactions among the reviewers of the capitalist press, from the patronizing coos of *Punch* to the sadistic fury of Mr F. A. Voigt, of the *Manchester Guardian*, who found that I am lacking in all generous feeling and implied that I should be put in one of those fascist concentration camps which he has made his speciality, and now, it seems, his spiritual home.

But most of the reviewers confined themselves to pointing out that my prose is bad, just as when a boy stammers the schoolmaster has an excellent excuse for pointing out to him that he stammers and ignoring what he is saying.

It is not necessary to answer this criticism, which is simply fault-finding, but I think it is necessary to answer the article on my book by Comrade Campbell, which appeared in the *Daily Worker*.

First, it is very important that I should remove the misapprehensions for which I am alone responsible in my attitude to the Soviet Trial. When I wrote this book the Soviet Trial had only just begun; I realized that if I ignored it the critics in the capitalist press might use it as an argument to refute the latter part of my book about the new Soviet constitution. I therefore thought that it was necessary for me to prejudge the whole issue and prejudge it against the USSR as far as possible.

Some time before my book had appeared I had read the rest of the evidence and I became convinced that there undoubtedly had been a gigantic plot against the Soviet Government and that the evidence was true. However, it was too late for me to alter my book.

Some comrades will think that I ought to have assumed immediately that all actions taken by the Soviet Government were justified; but I explicitly stated at the beginning of my book that I was portraying an attitude of mind which was not communist but that of a liberal approaching communism; and I determined to make this portrait consistent throughout.

In the latter part of his article Comrade Campbell interpreted one of my remarks to mean that I was the sort of person who is unable to work within a political movement.

It is possible that there are inconsistencies in my book which would lead critics, who want to think the worst, to this conclusion. However, I made one remark which I myself imagined to be conclusive : that the only genuine criticism of a socialist movement is made by those who give their life to it, thus modifying it with the structure of their own being.

Anyhow, I do not think that there is much point in arguing about past words. In order to make my attitude as clear as possible, I have now joined the Communist

Party, before going to Valencia in order to broadcast anti-fascist propaganda from the UGT station. I think a good many readers of my book will see that both these actions are a consistent development of my thesis there. Admittedly, to join the Communist Party is one thing, to be a good communist another. And I do not imagine that I can do anything – nor do I desire to do it – which will put my own political actions and writing beyond the pale of criticisms by other party members.

It was not merely as an answer to Comrade Campbell's review that I joined the Communist Party. A few weeks ago I went on a political tour which took me to Gibraltar, Tangiers, Oran and Marseilles – all of them towns on the border of the Spanish conflict.

Nothing could be clearer to me from seeing these towns than that the Spanish Civil War is the class war played out on an international scale, in which the small capitalist class is backed by international imperialism against the democratic will of at least 80 per cent of the Spanish people.

Everywhere I found that the sympathies of the official, ruling capitalist class were unconcealedly with Franco, while the Spanish population of all these towns passionately identified itself with the government. Everywhere I found that the best workers in these towns, the people with the most dignified standard of life, were Communist Party members.

I felt that is was necessary to make a choice between one international class representing imperialism, and the workers' international.

It seems to me that the most important political aim of our time should be the United Front, organized so that it has a common interest with the Soviet and the Popular Fronts of Spain and France. I wish to belong to the party which is most active in working towards this end, and so I have joined the Communist Party.

PART TWO

The Forties

Background to the Forties

With the ending of the Spanish Civil War it became clear that the thirties was being wound up like a company going into bankruptcy. The departure of Auden for America in 1939, whatever personal feelings it aroused considered as a public act only underlined what most of his colleagues already felt : that the individualist phase was over. From now on, people did not join anti-fascism as individuals who might influence history. They joined armies in which they were expected to forget that they were individuals. It is characteristic of the change that militant anti-fascists of the International Brigade, like Tom Wintringham and Humphrey Slater, were considered suspect by the authorities of the British Army. American authorities were later to invent the phrase 'premature anti-fascists' to describe such people.

The getting together of Stalin and Hitler, two monsters out of the Book of Revelation, was an apocalyptic event. One imagined the vast armies and air forces of these beasts over-running the land and darkening the skies, raining down bombs on the cities of the West. Part of the creed of the anti-fascists had been that we were defending civilization, keeping Apocalypse at bay, so, when war broke out in 1939 one expected the total destruction of London.

From the point of view of an anti-fascist like myself, those who actually conducted and fought the war were – with the exception of Winston Churchill – curiously unconcerned with the evil of Hitler. The war was started after all the positions for which the anti-fascists had been fighting were abandoned – Republican Spain and Czechoslovakia – in support of the least guaranteeable and least democratic of Hitler's victims, the Poland of 1939. There was something magnificently arbitrary about Britain's reasons for fighting : it was not so much that Hitler was evil as that he had gone too far.

The attitude reflected the mood of the British public. Four years in which the Nazis had been given all – indeed far more than – that which was denied to the Weimar Republic, had led to increasing demands from Hitler and the increasing demoralization on our side which was the result of always giving way. There was a certain pleasure to be derived from the British unreasonableness over Poland – which Hitler was prepared to be reasonable about. It was very characteristic of the British, having given way all along the line, at the very end of it, when all seemed already abandoned, to say 'No'. This was the exercise of a British logic which, like our attitudes between 1918 and 1939, did not appeal to the French.

The attitude of the English towards Germany in the Second World War differed amazingly from that which they had shown in the First, when anti-German feeling, whipped up by the Rothermere Press, was as hysterical as its manifestations were philistine. In the First World War people who had German connections were persecuted and the greatest achievements of German philosophy and music were lambasted for 'hunnishness', even by journalists as famous as Chesterton and Belloc. In the Second World War, while England stood out with fatalistic determination against the onslaughts of the Nazis, the British showed an almost touching refusal to hate the Germans and German thought and arts. My fellow firemen in the National Fire Service (which I joined early in 1941) regarded the ordinary Germans simply as people like themselves, dragged into a war which was none of their making. During an air raid one of them said to me : 'You know Germany, don't you? I suppose they hate being bombed just the same as what we do.' In his mind the bombing created a camaraderie between the bombed in both countries. In a train an RAF pilot, seeing me wearing my NFS uniform, looked at me ruefully and said : 'You're the chaps I feel sorry for when we're on a raid,' as though I were a fireman in Berlin or Hamburg.

❈

Before joining the NFS, I assisted Cyril Connolly in editing the magazine *Horizon* which was published from my flat in Lansdowne Terrace W.C. where I was living alone having been left by my first wife, who married Charles Madge. The appearance there every weekday of Cyril Connolly, Peter Watson – the adored, handsome and rather enigmatic young man who paid for the magazine and was its art editor – and of the editorial secretaries, Sonia, Lys and Diana – helped me over this difficult period of my life.

To start a literary magazine in September 1939 at first sight seemed an act of mad defiance of historic circumstances. But in fact *Horizon* relieved for its readers the tedium and anxiety of the war. Starting it then also had the advantage that Cyril, a great traveller and Francophile, had to stay put in England. His concern with the diminishing role of the individualist and the aesthete after the collapse of the Spanish Republic and at the beginning of the officially anti-fascist war, is apparent in the opening paragraphs of Cyril's first 'Comment' :

A magazine should be the reflection of its time, and one that ceases to reflect this should come to an end. The moment we live in is archaistic, conservative and irresponsible, for the war is separating culture from life and driving it back on itself, the impetus given by Left Wing politics is for the time exhausted, and however much we should like to have a paper that was revolutionary in opinions or original in technique, it is impossible to do so when there is a certain suspension of judgement and creative activity. The aim of *Horizon* is to give to writers a place to express themselves, and to readers the best writing we can obtain. Our standards are aesthetic, and our politics are in abeyance. This will not always be the case, because as events take shape the policy of artists and intellectuals will become clearer, the policy which leads them to economic security, to the atmosphere in which they can create, and to the audience by whom they will be appreciated.

At the moment civilization is on the operating table
and we sit in the waiting room. For so far this is a
war without the two great emotions which made the
Spanish conflict real to so many of us. It is a war which
awakens neither Pity nor Hope, and what began as a
routine police operation, a military sanction, is now
hardening into the grim historical necessity of Keeping
Alive.

These sentiments can hardly be described as patriotic or
heroic. But there is a kind of defiance about them, a bit
absurd, of the aesthete in the last ditch, with his high-
brow worm's-eye view that needs to be expressed. The
writer seems to take it for granted that the creativity of
writers is the product of the historic circumstances in
which they find themselves placed. It is up to history to
arrange itself in such a way that they can write their best,
otherwise the politics of writers will be kept 'in abeyance'.
These politics turn out, rather oddly, to be those that 'lead
them [the writers] to economic security, to the atmosphere
in which they can create, and to the audience by whom
they will be appreciated.'

It would be a mistake to think that the success of *Horizon*
was due to the fact that readers took Cyril's editorial views
seriously in the manner in which the readers of *Scrutiny*
undoubtedly took those of F. R. Leavis (which, presumably,
never raised a laugh). It would be truer to say that they took
very little of what he wrote uncritically, finding it sometimes
amusing, sometimes irritating, but also sometimes flashingly
truthful, and sympathetically vulnerable, honest. They
looked beyond what he wrote to the personality behind
the printed page. Peter Watson and I, *Horizon*'s co-editors,
felt very much as its readers did. Peter once remarked to
me, perceptively, I think: 'Cyril's a brilliant editor be-
cause he's like a brothel keeper, offering his writers to the
public as though they were the girls, and himself carrying
on a flirtation with them.' Readers were often maddened
by what they were offered, and rejected it in disgust, but

they were delighted with other offerings (Evelyn Waugh's novel *The Loved One* for example) and they bought *Horizon* every month to have the pleasure of enjoying or being disgusted by it.

The war was probably the best period in Cyril's life for his work, and it is worth asking why this was so. Partly, I think, because, as I remarked above, it kept him in England; partly also because he was a born editor. He took a vicarious pleasure in publishing the best works and the best writers as though they were by him, and he was bold in choosing things which interested him simply because of their content, without attempting to iron out faults of style which were idiosyncratic to their authors. In his own personality he combined quite opposed characteristics. On the one hand he was disloyal to, satiric about his friends, unable to avoid telling a good story about them or make a spiteful remark, if it seemed amusing. He was envious and not unmalicious. But on the other hand he had affection for his friends which transcended the disloyalty and he was as good at finding indulgent excuses for their behaviour as at exposing it to ridicule. He loved his friends and he loved to be loved. His disclaimers when he was caught out in some act of seeming treachery could be wholly disarming. During the war the BBC had a wavelength which (in theory) reached India. George Orwell, who directed this programme and who soon realized that the broadcasts were heard by no one on the sub-continent, took advantage of this to commission writers to say whatever they liked. On one occasion it came back to me that Cyril, speaking on this wavelength, had made a particularly wounding personal attack on his fellow editor on *Horizon* – myself. After hearing this, I took care not to see him for a few days, knowing that mutual friends would tell him why I was not doing so. Soon I received a letter from him in which he explained that he had been puzzled by my silence; but now that he had been told the reason for it he could not understand my avoiding him because he had assumed that I would realize that his remarks were 'only for India'. The injury dissolved, as it were, into an anecdote which could amusingly be turned against himself. Soon after the war I was walking with him in the Piazza San Marco in Venice when an angry bearded figure came striding up to us and called out accusingly : 'Are you Cyril Connolly?' Connolly looked terrified and murmured, as though admitting it only to himself : 'Yes.' The bearded figure asked : 'Why did you accept for *Horizon* a story I wrote, send me the proofs and then never publish it?' Cyril looked still more scared and then said in a quavering but somehow also consoling voice : 'Because it was good enough to accept and set up in proof but not good enough to publish.'

Cyril was able to see others satirically and yet feel affection which enabled him almost to identify with them. In conversation he constantly turned on a stream of parody which would take off as illustrations of some point made. Once he joked that when two women were first introduced to one another they should instantly exchange handbags, and each explore the contents of the other's. Instantly he was transformed into a woman going through another woman's handbag; finding the eyelash powder, spitting on it, brushing her eyelashes. This capacity for identifying with others made him a brilliant parodist. In his parody of Aldous Huxley's *Eyeless in Gaza* he enters so completely into Huxley's mind that it produces the effect of Huxley himself parodying Huxley and makes it difficult afterwards to read that novel except as a self-parody.

During the war, Connolly-*Horizon* (for Cyril became identified with the magazine) was to be a kind of anti-toxin produced by the war itself. Connolly-*Horizon* was no more against the war than Falstaff or Thersites were against wars they were involved in. In fact, *Horizon* contained essays by Orwell discussing war aims and by retired generals on strategy (Cyril wrote a Comment advocating his own secret weapon – Colonel Connolly's Tank Trap). While keeping up the notes of absurdity and derision, *Horizon* also showed that values of civilization, literature and art could be sustained at a time when everything seemed shrouded by the austerities and exigencies of war.

Looking back now, it seems to me that in England the war period was a little island of civilization in our lives. Civilized values and activities acquired a kind of poignancy because they were part of what we were fighting for and the reasons for which we were fighting. It could make us feel humble that there were pilots in the Battle of Britain who came into our offices to say that they felt they were fighting for whatever *Horizon* represented. (There were still more who were ready to fight for John Lehmann's more widely circulated *New Writing*.) Thinking of the war as viewed from London, I remember not only streets full of shattered glass the night after an air raid; flames and the smoke of gigantic fires from the docks seen against the silhouetted foreground of Bloomsbury eighteenth-century squares; and a dinner party at Elizabeth Bowen's house in Regent's Park and walking out into the street afterwards to find it lit whiter than daylight by dropped flares : but also of concerts at the National Gallery with pro-grammes played by Myra Hess, Clifford Curzon, or some famous quartet; magical Shakespearean performances with John Gielgud and Peggy Ashcroft; the series of 'Shelter' drawings by Henry Moore; paintings of burning buildings by Graham Sutherland and John Piper; poetry readings and lectures at the famous Churchill Club at Westminster; T. S. Eliot's poignant *Four Quartets*; the grim and realistic poems of Roy Fuller; the apocalyptic ones of Dylan Thomas and the unaccountable, weirdly inspired ones of Edith Sitwell. A little island of civilization sur-rounded by burning churches – that was how the arts seemed in England during the war. And looking back they retain their strange aura which was also that of the last flicker of the England which began with the reign of Queen Elizabeth I and which ended with the war and the diminution of England to our Welfare State.

The first section of 'September Journal' was published in

the second number of *Horizon*, in February 1940. It was
begun in September 1939, a date which, as I explain rather
embarrassingly in a paragraph which I have here omitted,
corresponded with the 'shattering' of my own life. 'It so
happens that the world has broken just at the moment
when my life has broken.' This is a bad beginning, but
fortunately the mood quickly shifts and I become the
observer, albeit a rather self-observing one.

An essay published in *Horizon* in September 1940, en-
titled 'A Look at the Worst', is too diffuse to reprint in full.
Written at a moment after the fall of France when Britain
seemed waiting for the much-heralded invasion, it is for
the most part an attempt to translate the spirit of anti-
fascism into a programme for democracy in the post-war
era. Democracy is seen as a mixture of forces, some sym-
pathetic to the Nazis before the war, some Christian, some
materialist, some socialistically idealist. The writer, looking
at what has happened in various European countries, feels
that there is a danger of cynical materialists in Britain still
doing a deal with the Nazis :

> But while in the democracies people talk about, and
> even practise, ideals, at the same time they are at the
> mercy of the anarchic and ruthless and irresponsible
> materialism of business interests controlled by 'in-
> dividualists'. These respect the interests of their country
> and of democracy no more, when business is threatened,
> than they do those of the workers. The war has shown
> how democracy, unable to choose between the good
> and evil within itself, tends to be weakened by both.
> Ideals, traditions, Christianity, inhibit it from using
> the barbarous methods of its opponents. Nevertheless,
> it has not expelled poisons from its system. In fact, it
> contains great lumps of ruthless and cynical and
> arrogant materialism sympathetic to the forces abroad
> which have overthrown democracy in their countries.
> This . . . has happened in all those countries
> with Quislings and Fifth Columnists and reactionaries,

ready at any moment to seize power and 'restore order'
by handing their country, with 'business' intact, over
to the enemy.

Democracy, then, confused and not completely committed
to the individual freedom and social justice which are its
essential virtues, exists in a world of dictatorships and
police states, in which it sometimes seems designed for the
role of sacrificial victim. Although attacking communism, I
distinguish between communist and fascist tyranny, seeing
in communism a kind of Christian heresy which, whatever
the character of the dictatorship, still maintains socialism
as a fundamental criterion by which its success or failure
will be judged, whereas Nazism has no values except the
furtherance of the power of the state :

> Although it is a mistake to assume . . . that communists
> have charitable, humanitarian or Christian motives . . .
> the motive of their hatred for religion is at root an
> ethical one. But in Nazi Germany, anti-religious feeling
> is not based on a desire to right a wrong and reverse
> a historically unjust process : it is based on hatred of
> spiritual values as such, and a desire to destroy an
> organization which competes with the single-minded
> allegiance of the individual to the State . . . Russia can,
> and will, be judged eventually by its success or failure
> in achieving socialism. There is no principle by which
> we can judge Nazi Germany, where power is an end in
> itself and where culture and family life and philosophy
> and religion have all been made subservient to the
> tyranny.

I go on to consider the situation of the 'artist' within the
present conflict. The events of the thirties have made it
clear to me that even if a writer is concerned with politics
and holds the views which are the orthodoxies of some
political party, he must in his imagination be free of the
party and, in what he writes, take a longer view than its
programme :

Politics have necessarily a very restricted view of life. By comparison with the greatest subjects of art . . . all politics seem like provincial struggles for booty between dusky tribes . . . Political causes have defined aims which are either attained or abandoned. The artist who commits his imaginative life to some political end is making it subject to an external fate by which it will either be robbed of its impulse when that end is achieved, or else destroyed when it is abandoned.

During the prolonged lull in the Blitz when Hitler was preparing to invade Russia, I was one of those who started an education scheme of discussion groups in the Fire Service, corresponding to those that already existed in the army. Post-war planning was the subject most discussed and representatives of the London County Council would come and tell us about Herbert Morrison's plan for a rebuilt London (whatever happened to that? – we were shown architects' drawings of it), and we discussed the Beveridge Report and the milk and honey soon to flow from the Welfare State.

I have no doubt that the utopian ideas disseminated by army and civilian defence education schemes of this kind were influential. They contributed considerably to the success of the Labour Party in the 1945 General Election. There was, really, during the war, despite all the horrors, a vaguely disseminated spiritual atmosphere of hope and faith, something out of which a new England might really have been born and which might have provided a great opportunity to the Churches.

By coincidence, while I was putting together this volume of essays, Mervyn Stockwood, now Bishop of Southwark, found among some papers and very kindly returned to me, a letter I wrote him in September 1944. This was occasioned by an article he had written for *Horizon* and that Cyril Connolly had asked me to discuss with him. Evidently the article was concerned with the role of the Church in politics. In my letter I argue that the Church cannot go into politics in the sense of being 'a revolutionary force in society', because it is itself a 'huge business institution'. However I do see a role for the Church, which is 'to make humanity aware of the suffering of our time'. I go on :

. . . I feel that if before the war the Church had attempted to share the suffering of the victims of fascism, there would have been a tremendous imaginative response from people. If fasts had been ordered in sympathy with people in concentration camps; if weeks, not days, of prayer had been devoted to this suffering, if preachers everywhere had preached the lesson of human misery, then that AWARENESS might have been created, the lack of which nearly cost us the war, and will now almost certainly lose us the peace.

When the Archbishop of Canterbury gave a talk to some firemen recently about religion, I asked him why it was that the Church had not before the war tried to make people aware of the suffering in Europe. He answered that the Press might have taken any such movement badly. One had to remember that the newspapers often misrepresent Churchmen etc.

In spite of your saying that the religious life cannot be carried on satisfactorily without the Church organization, I would say that such religion as we have had in the past hundred years has been conducted almost entirely outside the Church . . .

Consider the Church's attitude since the war. In the first place, the Church of England is hopelessly involved in supporting the war; instead of comforting the victims of war, instead of refusing to judge our enemies, instead of sternly insisting on the moral blindness of all sides, the injustice on all sides, which made the war possible . . . instead of preaching the justice and the mercy which alone will make peace tolerable, the Church supports the war almost without reserve, accepts everything that is supposed to be necessary for the war, prays for victories instead of praying for victims, and understands nowhere the deeper causes and consequences of our actions . . .

The rhetoric of this tends to incoherence but it brings to mind something which I had almost forgotten : the religious mood of the war. There was a feeling of incandescent faith which never quite took fire. It was present in Eliot's *Four Quartets*, Edith Sitwell's *Still Falls the Rain*, Dylan Thomas's *Refusal to Mourn the Death, by Fire, of a Child in London*, in John Piper's paintings of churches burning, in Henry Moore's drawings of people in air-raid shelters, and in the apocalyptic paintings of buildings on fire and of blast furnaces, by Graham Sutherland. Some of these I have mentioned above. The mood was compounded of seriousness through constant confrontation with death and destruction, of the sense of belonging to a community where all classes were drawn together in sympathy, of the phoenix-like rebirth of the English past from the ashes of burning cities, and of awe at the terror and grandeur of history endured. These attitudes meet in the idea of the sacred, that England itself was sacred. During the war-time forties there was indeed the sense of the sacred associated with certain nations, however far they had wandered from the path of institutional religion. England was holy, so was France, so were the Jewish people in the concentration camps, so even was Stalin's Russia. Together with this went the feeling that after the war a better world must come into existence : an England like Blake's Jerusalem.

Air raids, with the fire engines with their clanging bells, ambulances with tinkling electric bells that seemed to run quicksilver along the streets and the burning building which amid the crackle and roar of leonine flames held a core of silence, could seem ritualistic. The City of London acquired an extraordinary almost regal dignity at the centre of the flames. I tried to convey this in some lines of a poem called 'Epilogue to a Human Drama' :

London burned with unsentimental dignity
Of resigned kingship : those stores and churches
Which had glittered century-long in tarnished gold
Stood near the throne of domed St Paul's
Like courtiers round the royal sainted martyr.

In April 1941 I remarried. My wife and I lived in Mares-
field Gardens in Hampstead, a few yards from the house
of Anna Freud where she conducted a nursery for children
whose homes and families had been shattered as a result
of the war. The children sometimes had dreams which
have got into Anna Freud's case histories of the fireman
down the road – a reassuring figure, it appears. Natasha
and I occupied a garret on top of a house where we
lived. One night a bomb fell on a house just across the
road from us, destroying it completely. The noise of the
bomb was like that of a train emerging from a tunnel,
and one felt oneself to be tied to the rails. Most of the
ceiling of our sitting-room collapsed and we were rained
on by rubble but nothing much was broken. Natasha, who
is without fear, seemed scarcely affected by this. I felt
pulsingly alive and ran downstairs and out into the road
and walked for miles and miles through London. The
town seemed untouched, as though ours was the only
bomb that had fallen that night, and yet when it rushed
out of the tunnel of the darkness I had what I supposed
to be my last thoughts : 'This is something I have all my
life been waiting for,' and it seemed the end of the world.
(Later I told Auden of this and he commented, 'What an
old solipsist you are !')

Natasha was pregnant, and during air raids and buzz-
bombing, one was conscious of the angels of death outside,
riding the night skies, and the child in the womb, un-
conscious and as peace-enclosed as a mollusc in a shell.
The confidence this inspired and the contrast between
minuscule and weak life and machinery of killing out-
side was also a religious feeling like that of one candle
burning on an altar in a dark cathedral.

Later our son was born, and riding on top of a bus

which went from Swiss Cottage all the way to Hammer-
smith, where Natasha and Matthew – our son – were in
hospital, again I had the feeling of mystery as though the
dreary, almost trafficless, partly-wrecked streets were the
base of a Jacob's ladder which stretched into the sky, upon
which the born and the unborn children climbed from
heaven to earth and earth to heaven.

George Orwell, in a 'London Letter' contributed to
Partisan Review dated 3 January 1941, writes as though
England were a pendulum swinging between extremes of
what he calls 'a revolutionary situation' which occurred
in the summer of 1940 and a 'backwash' of reaction in
the following summer. These extremes he attributes to the
'people' who are the revolutionaries and 'the reaction-
aries which means roughly the people who read *The
Times*.' In a kind of No Man's Land between these op-
ponents there were the left-wing intellectual anti-fascists,
whom Orwell could not abide. He is rather uninformative
as to whom these are apart from being readers of the *News
Chronicle*, the *New Statesman* and the Left Book Club.
(Cyril Connolly and I might be thought to belong to this
group, but he ends his letter with the words 'Cyril Con-
nolly and Stephen Spender send their best' which seems
to let us off – though one cannot be sure about this.)
Orwell writes:

> During the Spanish Civil War the left-wing intellectuals
> felt that this was 'their' war and that they were in-
> fluencing events in it to some extent. In so far as they
> expected the war against Germany to happen they
> imagined that it would be a sort of enlarged version of
> the war in Spain, a left-wing war in which poets and
> novelists could be important figures. Of course, it is
> nothing of the kind. It is an all-in modern war fought
> by technical experts . . . At present there is no function
> in it for intellectuals. From the start the Government
> have more or less frankly gone on the principle of
> 'keeping the Reds out of it', and it was not till after the

disaster in France that they began to allow men known to have fought in Spain to join the army. Consequently the chief activity among left-wing writers is a rather petti-fogging criticism which turns into a kind of dismay when England wins a victory, because this always falsifies their predictions.

Both Orwell and I expected something more spectacular than Attlee's England of the Beveridge Plan and the Welfare State which followed on the sweeping Labour victory of 1945. As a material and spiritual phenomenon, this was aptly symbolized by the Festival of Britain on the South Bank of the Thames, with its look of cut-rate cheerfulness cast in concrete and beflagged.

Probably the soldiers who attended Army Education courses, and the Civil Defence workers who went to our discussion groups (I think that in *1984* somewhere Orwell refers to the 'solemn farce of a discussion group') were contented with this symbol. But Orwell wanted the symbolism of the Welfare State to be that of manifest revolution.

Late in 1949, a few weeks before his death, I visited him in his sick-room at University College Hospital. He complained that despite there being a Labour Government there were far too many visible signs of wealth in London. There were all these Rolls-Royces. I mentioned that I had been told by Hugh Gaitskell that a count was kept on the Rolls-Royces and their owners in London, that most of these belonged to foreigners, or to embassies, and that getting rid of them would not markedly improve the condition of the country. 'That may be so,' he said, 'but there shouldn't be visible signs of one class being much better off than another. It is bad for morale.' One wonders what Orwell would have said had he lived to see the fifties.

Late in 1944 I was moved from the Fire Service to an intelligence branch of the Foreign Office. There, at the end of the war, I volunteered for the Occupying Forces in the British Zone of Germany, and was asked to de-Nazify and then re-open public libraries. My job was neatly summed up for me by one lady librarian at a library I re-opened. 'I understand exactly what you want, Herr Spender. I must take all the books by Nazis off the shelves and put them in the cellars, and bring up from the cellars all the books by Jews and put them on the shelves.' In the course of doing this, I had to travel all over the British zone. I wrote a book describing these journeys which I called *European Witness*. This is out of print, so I have included four passages here.

September Journal

Horizon I, 2 (February 1940) & 3 (March 1940)

1939

3 September

I am going to keep a journal because I cannot accept the fact that I feel so shattered that I cannot write at all. Today I read in the paper a story by Seymour Hicks of a request he gave to Wilde after his imprisonment, to write a play. Wilde said : 'I will write a wonderful play with wonderful lines and wonderful dialogue.' As he said this, Hicks realized that Wilde would never write again.

I feel as if I could not write again. Words seem to break in my mind like sticks when I put them down on paper. I cannot see how to spell some of them. Sentences are covered with leaves, and I really cannot see the line of the branch that carries the green meaning.

I must put out my hands and grasp the handfuls of facts. How extraordinary they are! The aluminium balloons seem nailed into the sky like those bolts which hold together the radiating struts of a biplane between the wings. The streets become more and more deserted and the West End is full of shops to let. Sandbags are laid above the glass pavements over basements along the sidewalk. Last night during the blackout there was a tremendous thunderstorm. We stood at the bottom of Regent Street in the pouring rain, the pitch darkness broken intermittently by flashes of sheet lightning which lit up Piccadilly Circus like broad daylight.

4 September

Greenwood and Sinclair were on the wireless last night. They talked about gallant Poland, our liberties, democracy, etc., in a way which raised very grave doubts in my mind. Greenwood even talked about fighting the last war to end war. Personally, I prefer Chamberlain's line to all this sanctimoniousness, which is that he has done his best to give Hitler everything but now feels that he can give nothing more. I dislike all the talk about God defending the right.

There is no omnipotence on one's side. One doesn't have to choose between good and evil, right and wrong, but between various kinds of evil. It is not a conflict between God and the Devil, Christ and Judas, but between the systems represented by Hitler and Chamberlain.

With all humility, I am on the side of the Chamberlain system against fascism. The fundamental reason is that I hate the idea of being regimented and losing my personal freedom of action. I carry this feeling too far, in fact, I must admit I carry it to the point of hysteria – i.e. the point where I would really fight. I dread the idea of being ordered about and being made to do what I don't want to do in a cause I hate. This fear has even forced me into a certain isolation, in which I find that the personalities of my fellow beings often impose a restraint and unwelcome sense of obligation on me.

There you are, you analyse your hatred of fascism and it comes to a desire to be left alone. At school you allowed the other boys to take your possessions from you, but finally there was something which you fought for blindly – the possibility of being alone. When you felt that they were compelling you to be like them, and never to get away from their system and their standards, you bit and scratched. The same is true of all your relations with people. When you feel that another personality is obstructing the development of your own, you feel an embarrassment which is really the repression of rage.

Of course, there are other reasons, arising from this. As long as somewhere in society, in individuals, there are centres of isolation, there is also a possibility of development and change. Fascism is not even an aristocratic form of society in which the people at the top have windows in their minds, light within darkness, centres of air and space. They are just the levers which crush the lives below into a solid mass of weight and darkness. I am living all the time for the possibility of change. The life I love is now like a tepid current in a pond which threatens any moment to become one solid block of ice.

Well then, if war is madness and Hitler is mad, why reply to madness with madness? Why fight? Why not be a pacifist? The answers are (1) That I am not sufficiently a mystic to believe that if Hitler won we would not lose the values which I care about – the possibility of individual development, artistic creation and social change. (2) That in politics, the possibilities of acting effectively are always limited to certain very definite lines. They are not, as some people seem to imagine, extended to every possible idealistic and utopian attitude. Given a war like the present, a pacifist is simply a person who has put himself politically out of action, and who in doing so is probably helping the other side. Possibly helping the other side may sometimes further the cause of ultimate peace, but in this war I don't see how it can. Of course, there is a great deal to be got out of refusing to touch evil, in the way of saving one's own soul and being an example to future generations. But actually, personal salvation and getting myself into a morally correct position superior to my contemporaries don't appeal to me, perhaps because I don't believe in a system of rewards and punishments in an after-life. If I ran away it would be because I wanted to save my skin or get on with my work, not because I felt that even the world at war was unendurably wicked.

5 September

Oh, but books are crammed with all these arguments. If I started making speeches I would use them, and as I did so, I would feel a growing doubt in my own mind about their validity. I would be saying to myself, 'Yes, I do, really and truly, believe that, so why is this doubt growing like a fungus in my mind? Why do I imagine that someone over there in the corner is sniggering? That that man with hair too far back over his temples and wearing a brown tweed jacket knows the answer to everything I am saying? Gradually Conviction is seeping out of the hall, like water out of a tank, with every word I say.'

Doubtless my own contempt for my father's recruiting speeches during the last war undermines my faith in political arguments. When I start a train of argument it is like one of those trains on the Berlin underground which strut confidently above the street on their raised viaducts, surrounded below by the tenements which seem to ask whether after all everything is going quite so well as the passengers, flashing through the slums, seem to think.

I shall try to recollect Germany as it was 1929-32 when I lived there for several months of each year. The people I knew were not like the present rulers of Germany, not like the SS men, not like the army, though I think I understand the army. Germans have a greater capacity, I should say, than any other people, of evoking the idea of peace – Ruhe. To us and to the French, peace is a negative state when we are getting on with our business and private lives and are not at war. But to the Germans a state of peace is something positive and breathing and constructive, as opposed to a state of war. The positive idea of peace permeates a great deal of German romantic literature and music. Works like the slow movements of Beethoven's Second and Fourth Symphonies are hymns to peace. They summon up a vision of a landscape exhaling peace. Daemmerung is a peaceful word, and words like Heim, Heimat, Friede, Ruhe, are loaded with a greater weight of emotion than the corresponding words in other languages. Other peace-music is Schubert's songs, Beethoven's early piano and piano-and-violin sonatas.

Perhaps it is that the German landscape is particularly peaceful. I think of the Rhine at evening, the Harz mountains, the shores of the Alster at Hamburg with the heavy scent of lime blossom on a summer evening.

I have a German relative who is the wife of a U-Boat Commander. They live in Kiel, which has just been bombed. She plays the piano very well. Recently she came to London and she played an early Beethoven Sonata to us at my grandmother's flat. After she had played the slow movement her face was streaming with tears. 'Excuse me,' she said, 'but this music is so full of peace.' [I remember expressing to this same relative my doubts about the Nazis. She said, 'Oh, but I saw Goebbels address a meeting. He has the face of a saint – *ein Heiliger*.']

Ten years after the war, Germany was full of peace, it dripped with peace, we swam in peace, no one knew what to do with all the German peace. They built houses with flat roofs, they sunbathed, they walked with linked hands under the lime trees, they lay together in the pine forest, they talked about French art. Above all, everything was new, and everyone was young. They liked the English very much and they were sorry about the war. They talked about the terrible time they had during the inflation.

This was in Hamburg. I used to bathe, and I went to parties of young people. I had never enjoyed parties before and I never have since, but these were like living in the atmosphere of a Blue Period Picasso. Everyone was beautiful, and gentle, everyone was poor, no one was smart. On summer evenings they danced in the half light, and when they were tired of dancing they lay down in the forest, on the beach, on mattresses, on the bare floor. They laughed a great deal, smiling with their innocent eyes and showing well-shaped, but not very strong, teeth. Sometimes they let one down, sometimes the poorer ones stole, for example, but there was no Sin. I am not being ironic. There really was no sin, as there is in this kind of life in Paris or London.

Of course, it was all very superficial, it has been blown away now. I could not dance. I could not speak German. I stood rather outside it. I think now of the sad refugees who were the exquisite, confident students of the Weimar Republican days. Perhaps it was all fictitious, but now in letting the mirage fade from the mind, I got very near to the truth, because everything in Germany is inclined to be fictitious. The German tends to think of his life as an operatic cycle emerging from a series of myths.

There was the War, then there was the Inflation, then there was the period of Youth and the Weimar Republic, then there was the Crisis, then there was Hitler. Every German can readily explain him- or herself in terms of What We Have Been Through.

This passive attitude to life, the tendency to consider oneself a product of circumstances and environment beyond one's control, gives one the connection between the breakdown of external standards and the private standards of people. A young man fighting in the Spanish War wrote a poem to his beloved, beginning :

Heart of the heartless world.

He was either optimistic or very lucky. It would have been truer to write :

Heartless one of the heartless world.

I was twenty in those days, and I was caught up mostly with the idea of Friendship – *Freundschaft*, which was a very significant aspect of the life of the Weimar Republic. This, if it was frank, was also idealistic. It was not cynical, shame-faced, smart, snobbish or stodgy, as so often in England. It was more like Walt Whitman's idea of camaraderie. I admit that I do not feel at all easy about this now, but I set it down for what it was. Two friends, young men, faced the world together, they camped, they travelled, they were happy in each other's company. There was usually a certain unpossessiveness about these relationships, a certain casualness, a frank and promiscuous admiration of beauty. The Germans had a reputation at that time of being homosexual, but I think it would be truer to say that they were bisexual, though there were of course a few of those zealots and martyrs who really hate women, whom one finds everywhere. But what the young, free, handsome German looked for in the world was a reflection of his own qualities in either man or woman. It was part of the myth that he should 'travel light' and have no responsibilities.

A life in which people are exercising sexual freedom without, apparently, anyone suffering or paying for it in any way, is attractive. One wonders how it is done. In this case, I think it was done at the price of making everything exist on the same level. The new architecture, the Bauhaus at Dessau, the social equality, the most casual affair, marriage, an abortion, a party, were all just the same. They were a pack of cards all of equal value precariously built up, so that when one fell, the whole house came down.

Again and again I had experience of the German ignorance of Jews. Later, when Christopher Isherwood and I were staying on Insel Ruegen, and when the Nazis were doing exercises every evening in the woods and the 'movement' had become a serious menace, I got to know one or two of these young men. They were not gay, irresponsible, intelligent, like my Hamburg friends. They were heavy, stupid, but friendly and well-meaning. They seemed perfectly content to lounge round all day sunbathing, listening to the band, going to the dance hall in the evening and having their girls in the pine trees afterwards among the hungry mosquitoes. But actually their fun lacked lightheartedness. For instance, when they sunbathed, they would build little forts for themselves on the beach, set up a flagpost, hoist a Nazi flag on it and gaze upwards in reverence. Whilst they were lounging round listening to the music, they seemed always to be waiting for a patriotic air, and when one was played, they would stand stiffly to attention.

I was with two of them on some such occasion as this when suddenly I lost my temper and said 'Ich bin ein Jude!' They laughed incredulously: 'You a Jew? Impossible. Why, you're the perfect Nordic type,' said one of them. 'You're tall, you have blue eyes, fair hair, Scandinavian features,' said the other, 'that's why we like you.'

This astonished me. 'Then what do you think when you meet a Jew?' I asked. 'We want to kill and destroy the pest,' they said, 'we want to crush him and knock him down.' 'Then knock me down,' I said. 'Here I am, I'm a Jew, please knock me down.' They looked at me, dazed and injured by the deceptiveness of this wolf in Nordic clothing. I felt quite sorry for them. Then I got angry : 'I don't believe you have any idea what a Jew looks like,' I said. 'You imagine a monster when really you have to deal with a human being. I don't believe you know what you're talking about, and your heads are stuffed with stupid hatred and lies.' Probably I didn't know enough German to put it quite like that, but I worked myself up into a rage and rushed home to laugh with Christopher about it.

On another occasion someone made friends with me in a train specifically because I was of the Nordic type, and, indeed, now I know exactly the kind of warm response that a Nordic appearance arouses in some Germans. How can one understand the tremendous interest in appearance of a military race? A uniform face, in a uniform physique, dressed in uniform, and marching. In a way my Hamburg friends who wanted girls to be like boys and everyone to have a lovely face on a perfect body, had their craving for uniformity too.

Certainly, 1929 was the beginning of the slump and the end of the efflorescence of the Weimar Republic . . .

6 September

I want to go on about Germany, about my landlord in Berlin, about Curtius, but I feel too tired, I can't go on. The first thing about any war is that everyone is tired, countries at war are countries of tiredness, fatigue becomes a spiritual experience. It become an illumination, fetters of habit which make one wash and shave every day, which make one preface every contact with one's neighbour with embarrassment, fall away, and one enters into a more easy relationship with one's fellow beings, an exhausted simplified state of being oneself. The wrong words which come into one's mind, which the rigid discipline of wakefulness would reject, are suddenly the right ones, everything flows freely and nervously, one does not even resent the heavy weight on one's eyes, because one sees so much light.

There was an air raid warning last night. A—— seems so far away now, I imagine her in a red dressing gown and she looks pale and dazed. I don't imagine her happily. But I imagine her tenderly.

I remember again the water, the flowing line of the hills, the rich harvest quality of Germany. Immediately, of course, I suspect it of a certain falsity, a certain coarseness and thickness and monotony of texture, but still it is there, there like Wordsworth's poem about the peasant girl. E—— took me all over the place. He had a little car, and when he wasn't watching the road, his eyes were on me watching the effect of the storks on the roofs of North German villages, of monkeys playing at the Hagenbeck Zoo, of the Harz mountains. 'If you like music we shall have a great deal in common,' he said when we first met, and if ever I admitted for one moment that I appreciated anything, his eyes were ready to smile : 'Ah, we have a great deal in common.'

So we went to the Harz mountains stopping on our way at Brunswick where we saw in a very dusty and deserted gallery one of the finest Rembrandts I have ever seen. We visited some people called Harman who had a house in the Harz mountains. Like everyone else they had lost their money and all they had was the property itself and, I suppose, the salary of Professor Harman. The whole family, grandmother, son, daughter-in-law, a grandson, two daughters and a brother and sister who were fellow-students of Wolfgang, the son, at —— University, were there. Like nearly everyone I met in Germany at this time, they were obviously living from hand to mouth, they spent what they had, they laughed and talked a great deal, and yet they had an air of having lost everything.

Wolfgang had rather pinched, vague features which had a certain pallid, distracted beauty which attracted me at the time.

Several years later, after Hitler's rise to power, Wolfgang came to visit me in London. Earnest, and pale as ever, he had a mission : he wanted to convert me to Nazism. 'Of course, there are things I do not like about the Nazis,' he said. 'I do not agree with their views on literature and art. I do not sympathize with the persecution of the Jews. I do not accept their explanation of the Reichstag fire (though there is more in it than you would think). I do not like Goebbels's propaganda. In fact, I dislike everything nasty about them. But all the same, they have a Faith.' Here his fists clenched and his eyes burned with a dubious mystery. 'They have restored to us our belief in Germany and Life. Some of them are Idealists. There is a good deal of socialism in their economy.' I raged as I had done before. I told him that the most dangerous propagandists of Nazism were people like himself who pretended that they did not approve of its bad qualities and yet had accepted it. I told him he was a dupe, and that the Nazis wouldn't care a damn about his footling little qualifications to satisfy his own conscience, so long as they had got him where they had got him. I said : 'If I were a German, as I well might be, I would by now either be in a Concentration Camp or else deprived of every means of earning my living. You can't expect me to be fair. I don't care about your reasons.' And I am ashamed to say that I kicked him out of the house.

This was an unnecessary piece of self-righteousness on my part, because I heard later that he became disillusioned about the Nazis and was one of those unhappy, pained, gentle creatures who represent the heart of another Germany, and do not understand what is happening to them. I have touched a deeper chord than I knew here, for have I not met two or three of them, don't I know very well the peculiar whiteness and stillness of their eyes, which seem to have been drained of pigment? These poor ghosts are really beautiful in a sexless way, because, if one is a young man of another era, naturally one cannot expect to be virile. How closely I press now upon a secret! Why am I always attracted by these desolate spirits? There was one whom I met on the Hook of Holland boat once, shortly before Hitler's rise to power. He was the son of a general, and now that at least four names crowd on to me, I remember that they are all aristocrats and often close to the higher ranks of the army. I cannot remember the names exactly – oh yes, this boy was called Horst. He had a round face with very well-formed features, delicate lips, china blue eyes, a tender complexion and brown hair of an almost feathery lightness. He was quiet and polite, and he had some small out-of-the-way interest (just as Wolfgang had a card-index in which he 'collected' Shakespeare's imagery) – Horst's hobby was playing the flute or making musical instruments or something. There's really nothing much more to it than that. He had a Rhodes scholarship at Oxford and I used to call on him there and we went for walks. But he never became part of the life at Oxford. He was always just as gentle, just as isolated, and gradually one saw beyond the varnish of his interest in the musical instrument – or whatever – to a distress and restlessness of spirit that never ceased.

Another such was surely Jowo von Moltke who wandered about Europe looking at pictures. They all had some mild aesthetic interest which obviously was not their life, but which covered their refusal ever to speak about Germany. Perhaps, like Wolfgang, when the Nazis first came to power they flamed with a momentary hope which soon disappeared as they reverted to their former hobbies. Adam von Trott [hanged in 1944 after the July conspiracy against Hitler] was a more energetic variation on this type of German. When I first met him he was an ardent Social Democrat, in fact he was literally holding up in his rooms at Oxford a red banner which a Jewish girl with whom he lived had embroidered for a Peace Procession. When the Nazis came into power he took the complicated view that this after all was perhaps the socialism he had been fighting for. He was a law-student and he pretended to admire enormously the legal code which the Nazis introduced with their revolution. He forced, rather cruelly, the Jewish girl (who still used to visit Germany and camp with him in the woods) to admire this masterpiece. She told me that although she did not agree with the treatment of the Jews, etc., nevertheless, the documents in which the new laws were codified were marvellous. It was pathetic. I showed my lack of understanding again by fulminating.

But the most remarkable case was that of the young aristocrat I met at Isaiah Berlin's only a few months ago. He was a Prussian and his name was Jobst. He had the fine looks of all these well-bred Germans, though in his case something seemed to have gone wrong. There were the blond hair, the blue eyes, the well-defined bones and strong jaw, and yet in spite of its fine structure, his face seemed to have collapsed. Perhaps his mouth when in repose was almost too rich and well-formed, and when he moved it it seemed to become distorted and his lips to disappear inside his mouth. He was tall and strongly built, but his movements were so nervous, and the veins of his hands stood out so much and were yet so fine, that he seemed to be pulled the whole time by hundreds of thin threads. We talked about music, for which he had a passion. I remember that, for some reason, we discussed love in music. But the idea of Germany hung over us, because he was going back there the next morning. His mother who was travelling with him was waiting somewhere a few doors away.

We stayed up till three o'clock, Isaiah and Jobst talking without ceasing. I got very sleepy, so sleepy that I lay down on the sofa and attempted to doze off from time to time. But the spirits of Horst, of Adam von Trott, of Wolfgang Harman, of Jowo von Moltke, were pacing the room, and would not let me rest. He did not really attempt to apologize when he said 'Excuse me for keeping you up, but we shall never meet again.' 'Oh, nonsense,' said Isaiah. 'No, no. It's not nonsense. I know it. We shall never meet again. This is our last day of peace together.' He did not mention Germany. He only said : 'It is very sad to leave Oxford. I shall never see anything of this again.' Then he started once more on music, illustrating his conversation by singing, and conducting with his hands.

Next morning, he turned up again before breakfast. 'I have not slept,' he said, 'I went to bed at three, lay down for three hours, and got up at six.' 'Why did you get up so early?' 'Because it's my last morning and I shall never see Oxford again.' He held out his long, expressive, conductor's right hand. Other people called, but even when Jobst was silent it was impossible to escape from his drama. He did not rest. When he stopped pacing round the room he knelt down, with those speaking hands of his touching the carpet. The worst of it was that he was not an actor, he was by nature a quiet, scholarly person, with a rich inner life. Seeing him act was as unexpected and shocking as, say, seeing my father cry.

8 September
When I come to think of it, the trouble with all the nice people I knew in Germany is that they were either tired or weak. The young people in Hamburg were tired, the young Nationalist aristocrats were weak. How arc the people of good will today to avoid weakness and fatigue?

9 September
Yesterday morning while I was waiting for a bus, some soldiers passed down the road singing 'It's a long way to Tipperary'. An unshaved and very ragged old tramp wearing the ribbons of several medals so loosely attached to his coat that they were almost falling off, said to me : 'They're singing now, but they won't be singing when they come back. Hearing 'em sing reminds me of when I went out to fight in them trenches. We went out singing, but we didn't sing for long.'

In the afternoon I got a taxi to Waterloo before going into the country. We were stopped near Southampton Row by five Frenchmen carrying a flag and singing the 'Marseillaise'. The taximan said to me : 'They won't be doing that for long.'

Peter Watson travelled from Paris to Calais a few days ago in a troop train. The compartment was crowded with soldiers. They sat all the way in absolute silence, no one saying a word.

10 September

> The best lack all conviction, while the worst
> Are full of passionate intensity.

W. B. Yeats, who wrote these lines, himself became a fascist sympathizer. He was prepared to accept the worst. He wanted strength at any price.

Why were the gentle and kind people I knew in Germany, tired or weak?

The tiredness of our generation consists in exploring unimportant and superficial aspects of the idea of freedom, without trying to discover the strong basis on which any really free life must be built. Freedom, the young people in Hamburg said, is sexual freedom primarily, then freedom to enjoy yourself, to wander, not to make money, not to have the responsibility of a family, or the duties of a citizen, generally. Freedom is one long holiday. They were tired. What they wanted, in fact, was a holiday.

Beware of people who explain themselves in terms of the difficult childhood they have had, the economic conditions of their country since the war, and everything, in short, that they have been through. Beware of people who say : 'You don't understand me.'

After 1929, it became obvious that the world of these irresponsible Germans was threatened.

> New styles of architecture, a change of heart.

The architecture was mostly swimming baths built with money raised from American loans. The change of heart, sunbathing and sexual freedom, was almost as uneconomical an investment as the new architecture. That's to say, although it produced a charming little shoot, it didn't take root in the stony and barren soil of the difficult post-war years.

I feel uneasy about discussing these things in an airy, Left Book Club manner, suddenly identifying myself with the Workers, in order to sneer at the people with whom I spend my weekends, and dismissing my own promiscuous past as though I have renounced it finally. The fact is that I have just had a first class failure in my personal life, and I am so full of regret and bitterness that I cannot stay in the country because I dream of nothing else.

However, important as these things are, the first sign of the 'German tiredness' is to treat them as though nothing else were more important. My friends in Hamburg behaved as though nothing mattered in life except sex and personal relationships, and at the same time they kept these problems in a state of perpetual, unsolved, pleasurable suspense.

But if a human relationship becomes more important than anything else in two people's lives, it simply means that there is a lack of trust between these two people. A relationship is not a way of entering into a kind of dual subjectivity, a redoubled and reciprocal egotism, it is an alliance of two people, who form a united front to deal with the problems of the outside world, and who understand that their trust in each other will not be broken up by impertinent outsiders. The problem of married people is not to become absorbed in each other, but how not to become absorbed in each other, how, in a word, to trust one another, in order to enter into a strong and satisfactory relationship with the society in which they live.

A great cause of weakness today is people putting less important things before those that are more important, for example, personal relationships before work and an objective philosophy of life, sex before love. People who put personal relationships before their work become parasites on each other, form mutual admiration societies, agree to do nothing that may make one jealous of the success in the world of the other. People who put sex before love flee from one marital relationship to another, using love as their excuse; because, for them, sex has become a thing in itself dissociated from personal relationships. They have an image in their minds of one hundred per cent sexual satisfaction, and when they are in love, they are continually asking themselves, 'Am I satisfied?' and they are continually tormented by the thought that perhaps they are not. For them love, at first an opportunity, soon becomes a trap, forcing them to give something instead of taking all the time, and preventing them from grasping at the possibly greater delights they might get elsewhere.

Satisfactory personal relationships exist when the people who enjoy them have a satisfactory relation with society. They exist within society, they are not a conspiracy against society. In the same way, satisfactory sex exists within love and can be attained through love, which means patience and loyalty and understanding.

Another cause of weakness is not to admit, but to pursue our failures blindly. There is such a thing as real failure in personal relationships and in sex. How easily, then, that which symbolizes failure, the poor substitute improvised for love, becomes the most important thing in life! How people build it up and call the scars of failure their dazzling successes! Masturbation, homosexuality, following people in the streets, breaking up relationships because one has failed in one's own, all these compensatory activities form a circle of Hell in which people can never rest from proving that their failures are the same as love. Yet the lives of countless men and women show that the great compensation lies in accepting failures as failures, and recognizing substitutes as substitutes, and making the most of the rest of one's life. In fact the great artists and poets have almost without exception been failures in life. By this I mean that their relations with their fellow beings were really and truly at some point unsatisfactory, that most of them were fully conscious of this, and that their honesty in admitting a defect restored to their lives a sense of scale which hopelessly neurotic people lack. Baudelaire's relationship with a negress, the breakdown of Gauguin's marriage which led him to go to the South Seas, Van Gogh's fiascoes in love, Rilke's wanderings and sense of being *outside* love, to mention only a few examples which immediately come to mind, were all real failures in life and to 'the man of genius' the failure to be a complete man must always be a humiliation. The compensations of genius are so dazzling that it is difficult to realize that Beethoven and Balzac paid so great a price, when they yet had the infinite privilege of being Beethoven and Balzac. They suffered as men, they rejoiced as creators.

The creative artist realizes that art is not a complete life, otherwise he would be self-sufficient, he would isolate himself from the world of ordinary living, and there would be happy, unreal artists creating a truly pure art. Some people, who are not artists, or who are bad artists, think that art is like this, a world cut off from the world, where aesthetic experience is everything. These are the virtuosi of art and of appreciation : spirits which have flowed completely into an aesthetic medium, without the friction of living their lives.

Of all the arts, music provides the most self-sufficient alternative world removed from the real world. Painting is the most objective of the arts because visual imagery always has a direct reference to real objects, and in order to get away from the broad day, painters have deliberately to paint visual experiences remembered from sleep – dreams. But music is not a dream that imitates our sleep, it is a world of its own, of abstract aural patterns, which are not recognizably related to the noises we hear in everyday life. At the same time it attains tremendous conviction. The absolute ideas, which have such a wavering meaning in words and which it puzzles us to attach to human behaviour, have their fixed places in music. Schiller's *Ode to Liberty* is a work which conveys little more to us today than a sense of enthusiasm for ideas which meant a great deal to Schiller but which the time between him and us has cast a doubt if not a slur upon.

But in the music of the last movement of Beethoven's Ninth Symphony these ideas are fixed in a world of their own which one can enter without referring it back to the real world and the disillusion of the past hundred years.

Actually the value of the music lies in the fact that it does nevertheless refer back to the real world of experience. The triumph of art is not merely a triumph over technical difficulties, but the triumph of resolving the conflicts of life into a more enduring form of acceptance and contemplation. To regard these great acts of acceptance – the masterpieces of art – as acts of rejection and escape, is simply a way of losing grip, it is letting the engine run without the wheels turning. If one looks at the faces of people in a concert one can see the difference between those who use music as a form of living and those who use it as a form of dying. The virtuoso of listening is, like the virtuoso of performing, a wonderful child, one who has never grown up but melted himself on the furnace of great works of art where he continually flows away. The people who are not virtuosi have a certain sculptural rigidity – the face of Schnabel or Toscanini – because they are always discovering a unity between the experiences of life and art.

The young aristocratic sons of German militarists whom I call 'weak' were trying, without much conviction, it is true, to use the appreciation of art as a complete way of living, and as an escape from their despair about Germany. But this does not work. You go to the concert and music offers an interior life of sounds inside your head which is as complete as anything you have experienced. You read a play by Shakespeare, and you enter into a love and a courage of feeling completer because more explicit and final than anything that your own life may provide. 'This is where I live most intensely,' you think. 'This is real for me. Everything else can be put aside and forgotten.' But it can't. The felt life in the work of art is only intense, and often painful, because it actually becomes the life of deep and terrible experience. If this were not the case, art would simply express a frictionless movement towards a vacuous perfection. But in true art there is a real conflict of things, a real breaking up and melting down of intractable material, feelings and sensations which seem incapable of expression until they have been thus transformed. A work of art doesn't say, 'I am life, I offer you the opportunity of becoming me.' On the contrary, it says : 'This is what life is like. It is even realer, less to be evaded, than you thought. But I offer you an example of acceptance and understanding. Now, go back and live!'

12 September

Today I applied for a job as a translator at the War Office. Yesterday I received a printed slip from the Ministry of Information saying that my name was on a list of writers who may be used later. But I don't think I have a chance, as I'm told that they are very overcrowded with applicants. Nor do I think that the War Office will want me, as there must be many translators far better qualified. But as long as I can write and read a good deal each day, I am not really bothering. What I would like most is to complete three books, this journal, a novel and a book of poems, before I am called up.

I want to remember all I can about Ernst Robert Curtius.

For some reason, E—— became very excited at the idea of our meeting. He therefore arranged that I should go specially to Baden Baden in order to meet Ernst Robert. What I find difficult to explain is my own willingness to fall in with this proposal. It may have been that I had in any case later to meet my grandmother at Frankfurt, so that it was quite convenient; or it may have been due to a certain trustfulness and credulity in my nature which I still pay dearly for and which, in those days, led me to fall in with every suggestion that was made to me. I might have been less willing had I reflected that Curtius might not want to see me.

This thought did not trouble me. I simply got out of the train, booked a room in a hotel and, as soon as I had washed, walked straight to the house where Ernst Robert

was staying. I do not remember the details, I only re-
member the feeling of that first meeting. As far as I can
recall the house was outside the town and I had to walk
some way along a road past various hotels and then
along a path through the edge of woods before I came to
it. I think that I was shown into a room on the first floor,
and perhaps there was a cold meal with fruit and wine
laid on a table with a white cloth spread over it. There
were bay windows opening out on to a balcony, and a
pleasant freshness of the forest at evening filled the room.
Everything, I think, gave me an impression of coolness,
and for some reason I thought the host and hostess were
ill. The host, whose name I never knew, was dressed in a
white suit, and both he and his wife seemed pale.

I did not stay long enough to get to know them, for
Curtius immediately stepped forward, grasped my hand
firmly and told his friends that he would go to a Bierhalle
in Baden with me.

Railway journeys have a disconcerting effect on me.
They stimulate me so much that all my usual impressions
seem to flow much faster, with the train like a film that
is shown very quickly. I cannot check this. In spite of my-
self every sort of sensation pours through my mind during
a train journey, and when I was younger and played at
'thinking books', a project for some unwritten novel or
play would force all its images on to me during a journey.
This excess of stimulation leaves me afterwards in a state
of drugged tiredness in which I appear stupid to myself
and either am able to talk revealingly, or else get con-
fused in every word I say. I was in this mood that first
evening, and I talked very freely and indiscreetly to Ernst
Robert about my life at Hamburg.

He listened to me with an amusement which slightly yet
affectionately was laughing at as well as with me. It for-
gave a lot. In my deepest friendships, with Auden, with
Christopher Isherwood and with Curtius, I have been
conscious of being thus 'taken with a pinch of salt'. Some-
times it is disconcerting to be laughed at when one is
serious, but as long as it is done affectionately, one is

grateful to people who enable one to see oneself a little from the outside. From the first, Ernst Robert's atitude to me was one of gentle raillery; and I think that because he saw so far beyond me and at the same time loved me, I owe more to him than to any other older person.

Being anxious to impress him, I talked about literature, and especially about Dostoievsky, whom I was reading then. I was interested in madness, partly because at school and Oxford I had been taught to regard myself as mad, and because Auden, who, when he was an under-graduate, was anxious to maintain a certain superiority over his contemporaries, always treated me as a lunatic! Experiences like my cerebral excitement during train journeys, my excessive credulity, my lack of a complete understanding with even my best friends, so that I always felt they stood to some extent *outside* me – bore out the theory of madness. Above all, I was, like everyone, in search of that ecstasy which is so lacking in our civiliza-tion that even war and violence are to some people a secret consolation in a world of routine governed by material values; that ecstasy which justifies every kind of un-scrupulousness and adventurousness in private life. In Hamburg E——, with his collector's zeal had discovered an expressionist artist, a woman with a real talent for drawing, recently released from a lunatic asylum where she had done some really terrifying portraits of lunatics. In Hamburg, she had done a portrait of me making me look wild and mad. I was proud of this, and took Ernst Robert to my hotel bedroom to see it. But, so far from being impressed or interested, he would scarcely even look at it. He said that it was mad and that I did not need to be mad.

During the next few days I walked much with him in the Black Forest, we went swimming together, we drank beer every evening. He criticized Dostoievsky, he told me to read other books than the Russians, particularly the French. I showed him poems I had written, and, to my surprise, instead of reading them with the superiority which I might have expected from a scholar immersed in the world's greatest literature, he read them with evident delight, and made some translations of them, which were afterwards published in the *Neue Schweizer Rundschau*. He listened to my accounts of my life at Hamburg and scandalized me by treating this life, which I thought of so seriously, simply as pornography in which he was unashamedly interested. But to him it was pornography, it was not, as it then appeared to me, ecstasy.

15 September
I shall try to make this journal into a book with several levels of time, present and past, which I am able to move in as I choose. During these first days of the war I have tended to live in the past, partly because the present is so painful, partly because it is so fragmentary and undecided. We live in a kind of vacuum now in which the events on which we are waiting have not yet caught up on us, though our hour is very near. We have seen the whirlwind in China, in central Europe, in Spain, in Poland, and now we ourselves are the next on the list. If I let my mind drift on the present, I have terrible daydreams. Last night, walking the streets in the blackout I had one of an aggressive alliance between Germany and Russia which would not only destroy the whole of the rest of Europe, but divide it utterly on questions of principle. Another of my unpleasant daydreams is a growing fear that this is only the first of a series of wars. This springs from the following reflections. Supposing the Allies win the war, what sort of peace will they make? The answer is that they must either repeat the mistakes of the Treaty of Versailles, or else establish Germany as a strong power under a military dictatorship.

I think that this time they will probably plump for the military dictatorship. What they hope for, I suppose, is a military coup in Germany, whereby the generals will get rid of Hitler and sue for peace. A smashing victory for the Allies would mean complete internal collapse for Germany, followed perhaps by a communist revolution backed by Russia, and probably a war of reactionary intervention which would be boycotted by the workers here and in France. I am sure they do not want that. They are hoping that the military caste in Germany will be pacifist and reactionary. But I fear that they are wrong. Hitler has really transformed and stupefied Germany into a military camp, and we must choose between a socialist Germany and a more or less permanent state of war.

Supposing there were an aggressive alliance between Stalin and Hitler, on the understanding that Germany was socialized, there would then follow a revolution dictated to the rest of Europe by the combined air fleets of Russia and Germany, and including the most rigid tyranny and suppression of personal opinion. In the long run, it might be a good thing, because at any rate it would mean the breakdown of the tragic cycle of rival nationalisms. But it would mean the surrender of everything we call freedom in our lifetime. If such a combination occurred, I think I would become a pacifist, because nothing would then seem to me worth fighting for.

I do not think these speculations are of much value, it is better to go back to the little world I have some concrete understanding of, and the only point in giving rein to the nightmare is to preserve a sense of proportion: to show I am aware of the fact that the life of myself and mine is like Lear's hut on the moor, in the thunderstorm, and filled with madness from within and without.

My mind is terrible, but there are a dozen people worse off than I whom I know, so I should not complain. There is Fini, whose brother is a socialist made to fight in an Austrian division for Germany, there are one or two Germans I know here who are interned. The whole of Germany is filled with people violently separated from those they love, whose homes and children are torn from them, who search for their possessions in a heap of ashes. Compared with these brutal realities, my luxury relationship and luxury separation seem an extravagant game of people who are millionaires in the way they spend their feelings. I ought to be glad to be alone and away from all this nonsense. Perhaps in the next few years, it is only people who are alone who will be able to put their minds in order and realize what is going on around them.

18 September

When our existences are threatened, the most sensible thing is to start living as though one could see beyond the darkness of the tunnel to the light outside. However closely one becomes involved in the struggle from day to day, one must have a long-term view of the final issues for civilization, and also for reconstructing people's personal lives. Politics alter from day to day and therefore lack continuity : for this reason, private life and personal standards become important because they have a continuity which one mustn't allow to be interrupted by outside events.

19 September

With Curtius I was in contact with the Germany of Goethe, Hoelderlin and Schiller. That is an Apollonian Germany, a Germany of the sun, not the Dionysian Germany of Hitler who rouses himself from a torpid dullness into a frenzy of words and actions. After the war and the blockade, perhaps even the Germans who lay with no clothes on, crucified by the sun, expressed the need for a Germany of 'Light, more Light'.

It was not the madness of Hoelderlin that Curtius liked but the peaceful development of a poem such as 'Brot und Wein' in which the sun-steeped and vine-bearing German landscape is lifted at the end of the poem into a unity with the German conception of Greece. We read Hoelderlin together, and later on the poems of the Greek Anthology, particularly the erotic ones, because he had a taste for such poetry.

Curtius was an egotist, an egotist of the liberal, Goethe tradition. His life was organized with an enlightened selfishness : he did not take more than he could take, nor give more than he could give. He would not put himself out, even for his best friends, if he thought that his own resilience was going to be depressed by their needs. One could say, perhaps, that he was a fair-weather friend. Once,

when I was hard up, I wrote asking him if he could intro-
duce me to people in Berlin to whom I could give English
lessons. He wrote back about other things, ending his
letter with the curt, *'leider kann ich keiner Verbindungen
fur Ihnen im Berlin schaffen.'* I asked a friend of his
about this, and he told me how at a period of crisis and
confusion in his life, Ernst Robert had cut himself off
from him completely. I myself have a tendency in my
relationships with people never to refuse anything, and
often to promise far more than I can undertake. I know
how this leads to a feeling of resentment which affects one's
relationships with people, and to a fear of making new
acquaintances who may plunge one into new commit-
ments. Ernst Robert remained happy and broad and objec-
tive. He would not lose this by identifying himself with
others in their predicaments.

I do not mean that he was unsympathetic, but that he
was un-self-sacrificing because what he had was of too
great an objective value to himself and to others to
sacrifice. He did not enter into their lives because his
generosity lay in the freedom with which they could enter
into his.

If one accepted this, he gave a great deal.

Once, when I was staying at Bonn, I went into Cologne
for a night and got into an extremely nasty scrape. I liked
going to very squalid places and I went to a hotel near
the railway station, in the lowest part of the town. When
I got into bed I didn't notice 'that the lock of the door
was on the outside instead of the inside, so that the
guests in this hotel were like prisoners locked into their
rooms, instead of guests who could lock out intruders. In
the middle of the night the door was flung open and a
man came who put his hands to my throat and threatened
to throttle me unless I gave him my money. He was much
stronger than I, and I was undressed, so I asked him to
pass me my clothes. He did this, and I gave him my money.
It amounted to about 60 or 70 marks, which he did not
seem to think enough, so he said he would take my coat
as well. I protested, but it did not seem much use, so I

asked him to leave me a mark at least, to pay my fare back to Bonn. He flung a mark down on the marble-topped table beside my bed, and ran out of the room. I lay in bed staring into the darkness and listening to the noises from outside of whores talking and screaming, and a continuous sound like water running away into the darkness. I felt as though I had reached the goal of something horrible and mysterious in my life, as though it were unfolded from my own flesh and a part of myself. I did not resent the theft, because I thought of it as something I had let myself in for. I did not blame the thief at all, for what had happened seemed an automatic consequence of my choosing this way of life, and, in short, I felt passive, as though a whole process which I had called into being by my own actions were now happening to me, and I knew that I would never escape from this. Because I knew this, it was very difficult for me to resist, but at last I realized that I must do something, so I sat up in bed and shouted for the landlord. A few minutes later, he and two or three other men came into the room, switching on the light, and standing round my bed as though I were an invalid, seriously ill, and they were doctors or nurses whom I had summoned. 'Why are you making such a noise in my respectable hotel?' asked the landlord, in injured tones. 'Until you came here, I always had the highest reputation. I shall call the police.' 'For heaven's sake, do call them,' I answered, feeling that I was now prepared for any kind of disgrace, 'I would like to speak to them very much.' This seemed to make him hesitate, and he said quite kindly, 'Why, what do you want then?' 'Someone in your hotel has just stolen all my money,' I said. 'This is a disgrace,' said the landlord, 'I won't have things like this going on in my hotel. Why do you come here and bring this disgrace on me?' 'It isn't my fault,' I answered, 'I am very sorry. I don't mind my money being stolen, but I must have my coat and also an assurance that my trousers won't be stolen, else I won't be able to get home.' 'Nothing else will be stolen,' said the landlord honourably, 'I can assure you of that.' 'Well, might I at least have my coat back?' I asked. He nodded to one of the other men who left the room and returned a few seconds later with my coat on his arm. Then he said 'Good night,' reassuringly, and they left the room.

I felt that nothing else was likely to happen, but I could not sleep, and continued to lie with eyes open in a waking nightmare. At last it was dawn. Then for the first time it occurred to me that when I arrived on the previous night, I had been made to pay my bill before taking a room. Therefore there was not the slightest reason why I should stay any longer. It surprised me to realize that I was free and that nothing final had happened. I quickly put on my clothes and ran downstairs and out of the hotel, without anyone stopping me. I ran until I came to the river. Outside it was cold and raw. In the grey light the cathedral and the bridges and the modern Exhibition Building had a photographic quality. Suddenly I started laughing. I had a gay sensation of release.

After an hour or so of waiting, I went back to Bonn. When I had rested and changed, I called on Ernst Robert, partly to borrow some money from him. When he saw that I was upset he took me for a walk by the Rhine. Full of shame, I told him my story. But to my surprise, instead of being shocked, disappointed or upset, he started laughing, and, putting his arm round me, patted my shoulder.

While I have been writing this last page and a half, I have had the wireless on, broadcasting Hitler's latest speech. His voice varies from a cavernous rumbling to the peaks of an exalted hysteria from which he shrieks like a raucous beast of prey, until the whole chorus of his followers breaks into a stormy night's thunder of triumphant hatred. Undoubtedly there is something disintegrating about that voice, that applause, and everything they stand for. The cities of one's mind seem to be bombarded, as though a threat could make them fall to pieces. He speaks of a new, terrible, secret weapon, which, if the English oppose him, he will use. When he does this, I feel as though the world could be destroyed by pressing a button, and he were a madman who had access to this button and was about to press it.

I go to the gramophone and play 'Agnus Dei' and 'Et in Spiritum' from Bach's *Mass in B Minor*. During the week-end, in Sussex, I played records from Gluck's *Orpheus*. Reality and exaltation lie in those transparent harmonies, not in the violence and high-pitched shrieks of hysteria. One need not ever be afraid that death and destruction are the real world. They are the real world broken to bits. It is possible that I shall be broken and unable to understand Gluck's wonderfully formative and coherent music any longer. The part of my mind that composes itself into a dance or a crystal when I hear this music will be a cathedral that has been bombed. But that is no tragedy. It is only an accident. It would be a tragedy only if the destructive form of a life and a civilization which has met with decay were the final goal of man, instead of the frag-ments of an experiment which has been discarded.

29 September
The probability is that Germany will come more and more under Russian influence, as her militarized state and economy become further socialized. This process will prob-ably absorb all the Central European countries. Then our war will develop into a war of intervention against a revolu-tionary situation in central Europe. At the same time, the war in its early stages will provide the impetus for such a revolution.

The English communists have now twisted again and say that we should make peace on what they call 'the Russian terms'. I think that they are probably insincere in this. What they want is what Russia wants : i.e. to let the war go on, while dissociating themselves from it and using it as a means of getting their own ends. Unfortunately the continuance of the war not only suits the hidden com-munist aims, it is also essential to the British Empire. If we gave up, Germany and Russia would be able to dictate any terms they like in the east of Europe, France would become a minor power, the British would have lost all prestige, and the Dominions would adopt a policy of *suave qui peut*, which would lead to the break-up of the Empire. If the war leads to a revolution under the influence of Russia, involving the whole of central Europe, we shall at least have a breathing space, as the Red Armies will be occupied in regulating this vast new internal situation.

Then what are we fighting for? I think that we ought to be fighting a kind of defensive rearguard action against the development of absolutely chaotic and brutal conditions. In a way, I think the German-Soviet Pact holds out a hope for the future because (a) It may lead to a breakdown of the present system of warring nationalisms. (b) The larger the bloc becomes the less important becomes the Prussian element in it. If it extends from Moscow to Berlin, the rights of the Czechs will have to be considered. (c) Communism may, if it expands, recover something of its former liberating zeal. In short, the larger the movement becomes, the more likely it is to overthrow the tyrants who have started it. First Mussolini becomes a cypher, then Hitler, last perhaps Stalin.

In 1929-31, one saw for a short time clearly enough the direction things were taking. Then, for some people, the conditions they were accustomed to re-established themselves, there was 'recovery', and for ten years there was in England and France a precarious state of suspense. Now we see again the plot of our drama. But it may take a longer time than we expect to unfold itself.

The blackout time gets a few minutes earlier each evening, so one notices more than ever the drawing in of the autumn evenings. Actually, the weather has been particularly fine lately, the streets glitter a biscuit yellow all day, the crowd waiting at the bus stops for the few buses give the town an air of festivity, the sandbags on the sidewalks, the strips of paper on the windows, the balloons in the sky, are all sufficiently new in the bright sunlight to be interesting and almost gay.

I went for a few minutes to a party after lunch then, feeling tired and quite incapable of looking happy and keeping up a conversation, came home and lay down.

I am ashamed of these weak feelings. Weakness isn't going to help anyone today. It is only going to encourage a mood of self-pity which at once isolates people and drains away the energy around them. But after all I can't falsify things here. I am not writing down everything about myself as an example. Nor ought I to condemn myself. The important thing is to criticize and learn. I think that above all, people ought to be courageous and strong today. For example, I ought to work all day. There is no excuse for my failure in this respect. What holds me back is of course the fear of writing badly, the fear of not being able to express myself, lack of inspiration and the pain involved when one discovers the failures in oneself. But all that is subjective. What one wants is people who can create more strongly than bombing planes can destroy and burn more fiercely with life than incendiary bombs do with death. We want strength, lucidity, a clear line in writing, intellectual conviction, faith in life, a calm indifference to systematized political thought. I ought to be the saint of such a task.

When I drew the blinds I felt the autumn chill in my bones, and because of the decision I have taken which is simply a recognition of existing facts, I had a sense of the desolation of the world. Above all, the world should be home, it should be somewhere where everyone has his place, is surrounded by the simple machinery, the task, the house, the furniture, the companion, the river, the trees or streets which assure him that he is loved. Everything should be rooted. This is the simplest thing in life, it is the cocoon that surrounds childhood, it is the pure security of the flesh and the kiss and the fireplace and the setting sun which brings him home. The hands that destroy this homeliness, whether in children or grown-up people, are ripping the child in all of us that never leaves the womb away from the womb, and tearing the belly of the mother into ribbons. No one should want anything except to find his place in life, the centre of his potentiality to love and be loved.

Yet if love is the essential thing in life, loss of it is the will which enters certain bodies and tears the life around them into shreds. The depradations of the loveless and the homeless who seek power over their fellow beings can be seen everywhere today. The world suffers from the worst and least necessary of mental illnesses – homesickness. The papers are filled with photographs, and have been now for years, of those who have been driven out of their homes – the endless rustle of shuffling peasant feet through the dust all night along the road outside Malaga, the family with their possessions piled up on a cart outside a burning Polish farmhouse, the widow searching amongst the ruins of her house for a souvenir. They are driven from the little hole which surrounded and comforted them, into the elemental world of alien stones and light.

Most homeless of all, little shreds of matter from distant countries that have nothing to do with them are driven through their flesh. The whole universe of Outside enters their bodies – a fragment of a bomb, a bullet.

After that, in the world today there is the desolation of ideas. In times of war and revolution, the great comfort has always been that in place of home there is the home of the idea. Patriotism suddenly becomes the home. One goes out into the street and finds that everyone is friendly, everyone is a brother or sister of everyone else, because the family of the homeland is threatened. The home of the idea, patriotism, revolutionary fervour, can knit people together into a spasmodic unity which is even stronger than the happiest family life. But today, for hundreds of people, even that consolation is denied to them. The greatest desolation in the world is produced by the confusion of ideas. Many can no longer fight for their country with any conviction, which is to fight for the home of the Past. And the Home of the Future, Revolution, is so compromised that only the most ideological thinkers are able to want to fight for that, either. The world appears a desert. There is no woman, there are no children, there is no faith, there is no cause.

The moon shines above the London streets during the

blackouts like an island in the sky. The streets become rivers of light. The houses become feathery, soft, undefined, aspiring, so that any slum of this town might be the most beautiful city in the world, sleeping amongst silk and water. And the moon takes a farewell look at our civilization everywhere. I have seen it as an omen in Valencia, Barcelona, and Madrid, also. Only the houses were not plumed, feathery, soft, there : the moon was brighter, and they seemed made of fragmented bone.

Rhineland Journey

European Witness (1946)

COLOGNE

At Hagen I had seen a good deal of damage and again at Hamm where most of the centre of the town was destroyed. Also along the route from Oeynhausen there were bridges destroyed, detours, temporary wooden bridges touchingly named after some member of the Royal Engineers – M'Mahon's Bridge, Piper's Bridge, Smith's Bridge, etc. : but it was in Cologne that I realized what total destruction meant.

My first impression on passing through was of there being not a single house left. There are plenty of walls but these walls are a thin mask in front of the damp, hollow, stinking emptiness of gutted interiors. Whole streets with nothing but the walls left standing are worse than streets flattened. They are more sinister and oppressive.

Actually, there are a few habitable buildings left in Cologne; three hundred in all, I am told. One passes through street after street of houses whose windows look hollow and blackened – like the open mouth of a charred corpse; behind these windows there is nothing except floors, furniture, bits of rag, books, all dropped to the bottom of the building to form there a sodden mass. Through the streets of Cologne thousands of people trudge all day long. These are crowds who a few years ago were shop-gazing in their city, or waiting to go to the cinema or to the opera, or stopping taxis. They are the same people who once were the ordinary inhabitants of a great city when by an incredible, retroactive, magical feat of reconstruction in time, this putrescent corpse-city was the hub of the Rhineland, with a great shopping centre, acres of plate-glass, restaurants, a massive business street containing the head offices of many banks and firms, an excellent opera, theatres, cinemas, lights in the streets at night.

Now it requires a real effort of imagination to think back to that Cologne which I knew well ten years ago. Everything has gone. In this the destruction of Germany is quite different from even the worst that has happened in England (though not different from Poland and from parts of Russia). In England there are holes, gaps and wounds, but the surrounding life of the people themselves has filled them up, creating a scar which will heal. In towns such as Cologne and those of the Ruhr, something quite different has happened. The external destruction is so great that it cannot be healed and the surrounding life of the rest of the country cannot flow into and resuscitate the city which is not only battered but also dismembered and cut off from the rest of Germany and from Europe. The ruin of the city is reflected in the internal ruin of its inhabitants who, instead of being lives that can form a scar over the city's wounds, are parasites sucking at a dead carcase, digging among the ruins for hidden food, doing business at their black market near the cathedral – the commerce of destruction instead of production.

The people who live there seem quite dissociated from Cologne. They resemble rather a tribe of wanderers who have discovered a ruined city in a desert and who are camping there, living in the cellars and hunting amongst the ruins for the booty, relics of a dead civilization.

The great city looks like a corpse and stinks like one also, with all the garbage which has not been cleared away, all the bodies still buried under heaps of stone and iron. Although the streets have been partly cleared, they still have many holes in them and some of the side streets are impassable. The general impression is that very little has been cleared away. There are landscapes of untouched ruin still left.

The Rhine with the destroyed bridges over it had a frightening grandeur on the day when I crossed over the

Engineers' bridge. There were black clouds broken by
glass-clear fragments of sky. Gleams of light fell on the
cathedral which, being slightly damaged, looks like a worn
Gothic tapestry of itself with bare patches in the roof
through which one sees the canvas structure. But it is the
comparatively undamaged cathedral which gives Cologne
what it still retains of character. One sees that this is and
was a great city, it is uplifted by the spire of the cathedral
from being a mere heap of rubble and a collection of
walls, like the towns of the Ruhr. Large buildings round
the cathedral have been scratched and torn, and, form-
ing a kind of cliff beneath the spires, they have a certain
dignity like the cliffs and rocks under a church close to
the sea.

The girders of the Rhine bridges plunged diagonally
into the black waters of the Rhine frothing into swirling
white around them. They looked like speedboats swooping
into the river, their beautiful lines emphasizing the sense
of movement. Broken girders hang from piers in ribbons,
splinters and shreds, a dance of arrested movement. In
the destroyed German towns one often feels haunted by
the ghost of a tremendous noise. It is impossible not to
imagine the rocking explosions, the hammerings of the sky
upon the earth, which must have caused all this.

The effect of these corpse-towns is a grave discourage-
ment which influences everyone living and working in
Germany, the Occupying Forces as much as the Germans.
The destruction is *serious* in more senses than one. It
is a climax of deliberate effort, an achievement of our
civilization, the most striking result of collaboration be-
tween nations in the twentieth century. It is the shape
created by our century, as the Gothic cathedral is the
shape created by the Middle Ages. Everything has stopped
here, that fusion of the past within the present, integrated
into architecture, which forms the organic life of a city, a
life quite distinct from that of the inhabitants who are,
after all, only using the city as a waiting-room on their
journey through time : that continuity of the city has been
disrupted. The city is dead and the inhabitants only haunt

the cellars and basements. Without their city they are rats in the cellars, or bats wheeling around the towers of the cathedral. The citizens go on existing with a base, mechanical kind of life, like that of insects in the crannies of walls which are too creepy and ignoble to be destroyed when the wall is torn down. The destruction of the city itself, with all its past as well as its present, is like a reproach to the people who go on living there. The sermons in the stones of Germany preach nihilism.

POLISH DISPLACED PERSONS

Sitting on a bench under some trees, with behind them a large plain white modernist building, which has been taken over as a barracks, were six men, gazing dully out over the Rhine. They had pale blue or else brown eyes, the same salmon-pink skin like painted wood, and hair either rather weedy or else bristly.

At first I took them for members of the Reichswehr. The German soldiers now have the soulless ground-down expression of carved-wood faces of Slav peasants. Two of the men who were older than the others looked worn and tired. They sat leaning forward, and there was a network of fine lines of painful thought on their foreheads in addition to the weathered lines around the eyes and mouths.

There were a boy and a young man. These two younger ones in their patched blue uniforms, with their thin pinched faces, had the detached floating melancholy air of harlequins.

I asked them if they were German prisoners-of-war. They were annoyed at this, so they started talking, with the air of spitting at me, but with a friendliness in their resentment. They said : 'No we are not German swine. We are Poles.' They talked very bad German, expressing themselves with heavy gestures rather than with words.

'You English are much too kind to these Germans, much too kind,' one of them said. Another took up his meaning : 'Now they all go round, they all go round, every one of them, saying : "I was never a Nazi. Oh no, I was never a Nazi." ' A third went on : 'They take off their hats, they all bow. They can't be kind enough, they can't do enough for you. They fall over themselves trying to help you.'

As each spoke, he moved with angular gestures, crudely imitating the Germans. The effect was of a cubist picture : these peasants with their elbowing movements, their flat voices rising to an apex of momentary irony and then sinking back again into boredom.

After a burst of speech they were silent, as though at the end of a stanza of their chorus of commentary with which they wished to provide me, a stranger, coming from an island. Then they were inspired again :

'How do you think they treated us before?' the youngest but one asked. The chorus went on, passing from one to another. 'We were herded together like cattle.' 'We were made to work like slaves.' 'Nothing was bad enough for us.' 'When we arrived at a place, the children used to gather round us and shout "Dirty Polack!" "Filthy Polack!" ' There was something particularly distressing in the bitter way they said 'Polack', which in English has an affectionate ring.

'We never received a kind word from anyone, not one kind word, not a single kind word in five years.' 'No one ever helped us, no one ever smiled at us in a friendly way. No one.' 'And now they all lie to you. They say that they never liked the Nazis and that they were wanting you to come and rescue them.'

The silence into which they relapsed became like a shrug of contempt. I asked : 'Where did you come from?'

The oldest one, not answering my question directly, said : 'Thirty thousand people were murdered in the town which we came from. The town was burned down and many people we knew were hanged on trees. But my son here escaped with me.'

His son was the youngest of them and, being mentioned, he looked self-conscious in a very physical way, squaring out his elbows.

'I am with my father,' he said, 'but we know nothing

of my mother and my sister. All the others here have lost their relatives.'

They all assented to this, then there was another silence, pause at the end of a stanza.

'We were paid twenty marks a month for our work. But most of even that they took away.'

'Why was it taken away?' I asked.

They laughed. 'Look. Two of us were made to unload a truck of wood or coal. We were expected to do it in one morning, and at the same time we were not properly fed.' 'If we couldn't unload it, then we were fined a proportion of our wages.' 'In that way, by the end of the month, almost all our wages had been taken from us by fines.' 'So we were in every sense slaves.'

'But now, do you want to go back to Poland?'

'Yes. We want to go back. It is our own land.'

'What do you think about the Russians in your country?'

'We are not afraid of the Russians. The only people we hate are these Germans.'

'We would sooner work for twenty years under the British or the Americans than for one year under the Germans.'

'How would you treat the Germans?'

'We would treat them as they have treated us.' 'Make them work. You never make them work, as they understand how to make other people work. You're too kind to them.' 'You take trouble about feeding them, you calculate the rations they should have, as though they were being cared for in a hospital.' 'Do you think they measured out our rations?'

'Agreed that the Germans deserve whatever they get, however bad it is. But if Germany was treated as Poland has been, then the greater part of Europe would become a desert.'

'Yes, that is so,' they replied without interest, and they relapsed into the apathetic silence in which I had first found them.

Yet apathy is only a surface expression. Behind it there is something much more menacing, something which has happened and left its impression, the fires which burned the cities of Europe still smouldering in the minds of men. This is a state of mind which glows beyond despair, beyond the destruction of our civilization.

I have seen this expression in the faces of the desperate young men of the demobilized Reichswehr, also in those of the French repatriated prisoners and in those of other men and women labelled Displaced Persons.

CONCENTRATION CAMP INMATE

One afternoon while I was walking along the road which goes alongside the railway from Bonn to Godesberg, a young man came up to me and asked me if I would stop a car and request the driver to take him to Godesberg. While we were standing by the side of the road waiting for the car, I thought that perhaps I should see his papers, so I asked him to show me them. He showed me a paper, signed by the commanding officer of Bonn, to say that he was Rudolph Clarens who had spent six years in the concentration camp of Esterwegen. This paper asked the *Officer for Those who had Suffered Injuries through Fascist Oppression* to render him assistance in the form of money and clothing.

Clarens was unshaved and dressed in extremely dirty clothes with a shirt torn open and revealing his thin white chest. He had a square bony head covered with short dark brown hair, and eyes with a rather fixed gaze, each of a slightly different brown colour which made them appear to have different expressions. His face had a look of silence and suppressed eagerness, like the faces of some blind beggars and also like the faces of some of the unemployed during the great slump of 1931. He smiled timidly at me with a friendliness which, although it was not uncalculating, was different from the subservience of the officials I had met.

He said that he had been a student at Aachen. At the age of seventeen he had been arrested and sent to a concentration camp. He was now twenty-three. He wished as soon as possible to resume his studies, in order that he might become a journalist.

I asked him to call on me at the Transit Mess Hotel in Bonn the following afternoon, as I was interested to know what would be the result of his visit to the office at Godesberg.

The next day he arrived at four-thirty while I was having a large tea in the lounge. I could not offer him, a German civilian, tea, so I sent him up to my room while I finished off my excellent repast with far more butter and jam than one gets in England. I was aware of the contrast between my own standard of living and that of this concentration camp inmate, but although this worried me, on the whole it had the effect of making me eat perhaps a slightly larger tea than I would have done otherwise, because this worry was a form of anxiety and anxiety tends to make me greedy.

When I went up to my room I found Clarens looking better dressed than before. He said that he had borrowed a suit from people with whom he had been staying. I noticed that both his wrists were bound round with straps. He said that this was to strengthen them because they had been weakened by digging the moor at Esterwegen. He said that the *Wohlfahrtsamt für Beschädigte* had not given him clothes but had given him thirty marks. I said that I would like to inquire into this and I left the room, announcing my intention of telephoning the *Beschädigung-samt*. I could not get on to the number, however. He did not look perturbed at my saying this; he just sat in his chair with his usual air of patiently waiting, with his hands resting on his thighs, fists slightly clenched. He looked as if he were made of light and springy wood.

By the time I came back, another visitor, Dr L——, the University librarian, had arrived. Dr L——, a pink-complexioned mild-mannered man of about fifty-five, with rather protruding pale blue eyes, was looking with pink and blue astonishment at Clarens, who, although he appeared poor and out of place, yet looked at ease to the extent that he would have looked at ease anywhere. Before, at the age of seventeen, he went to the concentration camp, he had been (as I got him now to explain, excusing myself to Dr L——) in Holland. So whatever he may have done to be sent to a concentration camp (and he may have committed some quite ordinary crime) he had not shared the everyday experiences of every other German civilian during the past six years of the Nazi regime.

I asked Clarens what he proposed to do now. He said hitch-hike to Freiburg, where his mother lived. There he would rest for a time, after which he would write a book. What would his book be about? 'My experiences in a concentration camp.' 'What will it be called?' '*Human Beasts.*' 'Please give me an outline of some of the incidents which are to be in it, because your experiences interest me.'

At this he leaned forward in his chair, clasped his hands together, half-closed his eyes and began to recite in a low voice. What he recited began with some such phrases as : 'How is it possible that human beings can behave to other human beings with an inhumanity far greater than that ever shown by the animals . . .' By heart, he developed this thought rhetorically for some minutes. Dr L—— opened his china-blue eyes in his pink face ever wider and wider. Clarens then began speaking about the godlessness of humanity, and I realized that if ever he wrote his book, all of it would be like this and that it would contain nothing sharp, fierce, concrete or interesting.

But I was reminded by this recitation of a scene in Spain when on to the stage of a theatre where a meeting was being held, a German hero of the International Brigade was wheeled in a chair, and with the same half-closed eyes, the same swooning dead-pale expression, he spoke about the crimes of fascism. I had then been over-whelmed and at the same time horrified, feeling that while the young German commanded all my sympathy, some-where a serpent lurked in the heart of his rhetoric.

When Clarens had finished reciting I questioned him about some of his actual experiences. He said that when he was fifteen he had left Germany and wandered about Holland. Then he had been taken up by a 'countess aged forty-five who was still a beautiful woman.' Here he looked confidentially at Dr L—— who merely looked down primly at his fine hands with their well-trimmed nails, folded neatly as kid gloves on his neat grey flannel trousers. The countess was a socialist countess, apparently, and she had instructed Clarens in the falsity of the Nazi ideas which had been imbued in him by the Hitler Youth organization. He had returned to Germany and taken part in anti-Nazi activities. He was probably one of those youths who have been used by political parties, often by both sides, in the great underground struggle of left versus right during the past decade.

He told me some curious details of his experiences when he was arrested and examined by the Gestapo. They made him walk along a corridor which was traversed by another corridor. When he reached the place where the corridors crossed, shots were fired across his path. They put him in a cellar like a showerbath. This was constantly filled up with water which he had to pump out with a handle in order to save himself from being drowned. The strangest of his stories was that when he had been beaten and thrown into a cell, one of the SS men who, as he said, 'seemed more human than the others', came into the cell with a large ball made of wood and played a game of football with him.

When Clarens was gone I said to Dr L—— : 'What did you think of that young man? Did you believe what he was saying?'

'I don't know what to think,' said L——. 'He didn't seem to me altogether very honourable, but there were things which it is difficult not to believe. For example, I can hardly imagine he invented the story about the wooden ball.'

THE STUDENT AULACH

From a long time before I spoke to him, I had noticed Aulach and wondered who he was. Dressed always in civilian clothes, he never spoke to the officers and never dined in our mess, choosing to sit alone at a table in the privates' mess. He was tall and thin, with sculptural bones which seemed to carve their shapes through his flesh. He was extremely pale. His face had a white transparency which gave it refinement, especially as the features went very well with such a marble pallor.

He had a proud, remote, yet not hostile or unfriendly expression. He used often to look at me and for a long time I half wished to talk to him, but my sense that he was a complex and difficult person inhibited me, as I felt that if I became involved in any way in his affairs I would have no easy escape from him since he lived at the Transit Mess.

So it was not until a few days before leaving for England that I spoke to him. He at once told me an involved story about his situation. He had lived all his life in Germany, but his parents were anti-fascist refugees, both of whom had acquired foreign nationality. He was now almost twenty-one and in the position of being able to choose his nationality. He had chosen not to be a German. He was now waiting 'at the Transit Mess while long negotiations were going on to enable him to join his father abroad. This is enough of his story to explain how it was that he, though born and living all his life in Germany, was at the British officers' Transit Mess.

Aulach said he hated all the Germans. He did not wish to remain in Germany and he felt himself to be a foreigner there. His mother was an aristocrat of the family of von H——, which Aulach for some reason said 'was the most famous anti-Nazi family' in Germany. His father, of Jewish origin, was an artist now living in Paris.

Aulach was at present occupied in interpreting for the

British officers controlling forestry. He claimed therefore that he knew what the ordinary Germans were really saying, since he worked with them and they accepted him as a German. He said that the Nazis were getting quite cheeky and were satisfied with the behaviour of the British authorities towards them which was favourable beyond their expectations. In fact they had very little with which to be dissatisfied, since most of them, as middle-men, were still in powerful controlling positions. At present they looked forward with confidence to a war between the Western powers and Russia, which they regarded as inevitable, when the democracies would look to them for aid. He said that amongst themselves the Germans scarcely discussed any political topic except the next war. The elaborate political parties with democratic liberties attached to them, promoted by the Allies, were regarded as a debating society for backward children, and these backward children, the Germans, were living in conditions which made them interest themselves either in much closer or else in much remoter topics.

During the war Aulach had been employed (he said) in the German branch of a Swiss firm which made batteries for U-boats. He said that this firm, by faking results of experiments, managed to delay the invention of batteries which would enable U-boats to remain under water for periods of up to three months on end. He said that the inspectors whom the Nazis sent round to factories were idiots, and nothing was easier than to impose upon them.

I said to Aulach that everything I saw in Germany went to convince me that we must do all that we possibly could do, to prevent another war.

'So. You have come to Germany because you believe that it is possible to prevent wars by taking some kind of action, improving conditions, removing the causes of war, planning a new world, founding a society of nations,' said Aulach. 'You are quite wrong, you'll never succeed.'

'My idea of whether I'm right or wrong isn't based on

my certainty of success,' I said. 'I simply don't want all this
to spread. I don't want the whole world to be transformed
into the ruins of Germany, and I think it's right for me to
do my best to prevent this happening.'

'You are wasting your time,' Aulach said. 'Nothing will
stop it happening. The world is doomed. You can't obstruct
the development of history.'

'We are history. Human consciousness is history. Anyone
who puts an idea into the heads of his contemporaries to
persuade them to take an effective social action has in-
fluenced the course of history.'

'That's where you're completely wrong. History has
nothing to do with the conscious will of people living at a
given time, for the simple reason that there is no such
conscious will which can affect the whole course of events.
History is the development of the unconscious mind and
life of humanity, which is a stream flowing from the past
and leading into the future. The wills of men and women
living at a particular time are not a decisive bend in the
stream of life, they are just straws afloat and carried along
by the stream, which consists of the unconscious life of
the sum of the whole past and future humanity. At the
moment the human stream is falling over a precipice and
we are being carried over the precipice by it. There is
nothing that we can do.'

'If there is nothing that we can do, there is still nothing
to be said against our doing our best,' I said. 'I am not
interested in the idea of history outside our wills. If there
were such a kind of history, I would be against it. I do not
object to being historically unfashionable. I am interested
in doing my best according to my lights.'

'That is quite wrong also,' said Aulach. 'In a time such
as the present the only way in which to be strong and real,
to exist in the fullest sense, is to realize within oneself
the dynamism of the forces which are bearing the whole
of our civilization to destruction. Your point of view is
completely superficial because it is only concerned with
your conscious will.'

❋

The night before I left Bonn I asked Aulach to accompany me on a walk to Professor E——'s house, as I had to return some books to the professor. It was a very stormy evening. Before we had gone a hundred yards heavy rain began to fall, so we took refuge in a tunnel under a bridge of the railway for half an hour. At the end of this time, though it no longer rained so hard, the storm was not over and flashes of lightning lit up the town which, a moment later, was plunged into darkness. These dramatic white flashes made the ruined walls look flat like grey cardboard. The wind rattled through the hollow buildings with a noise of flapping rags and rattling tins. The roofless half of Bonn absorbed with a purring sound the rain, which flooded rooms and soaked through putrescent rubble as through a sponge. A damp, heavy, oversweet sickening smell began to rise from all the ancient rubbish heaps along the roadside.

This dramatic setting was an admirable background to Aulach who talked about himself without stopping, and louder than the thunder. He explained to me that he was half Jewish, half pure Nordic, so that he incarnated in himself the ideological struggles of the Third Reich. His Nordic personality hated his Jewish personality, his Jewish personality was continually trying to sabotage his Nordic. His Nordic side was creative, bold, bad, generous, ruthless; his Jewish side was analytic and self-destructive. His Jewish side prevented his Nordic side from being as ruthless as it would have liked to have been. Evidently there was also a super-ego in his make-up, a kind of third Aulach who was a detached observer standing above both these contestants which heartily took the side of the Nordic Aulach against the Jewish Aulach. What he hated most about his Jewish self was its habit of questioning the activities of his noble, fearless, mystical, creative, intellectual, Nordic self.

Aulach said that the Jews were not only uncreative but also incapable of arriving at any conclusions even as a result of their analytic researches. I suggested that Einstein had perhaps arrived at some conclusion. He replied that

Einstein was the most destructive spirit of the age who had attempted to build up a system of Jewish ideology to undermine all the crystallizations of the creative Nordic spirit, by making any fixed point of truth untenable.

Meanwhile it had started pouring with rain again. I was afraid all the time of being late for the professor, so we pushed on through this storm. When we arrived at the professor's it was dark and no one replied at first when I rang the door bell. At last he appeared, wearing a dressing gown. I thought that at least he would be amused at or appreciate my being soaked through but he looked disgruntled, particularly as Aulach was with me, and he did not ask us in. He took the books and said, 'Good night.' I realized that he was a man who liked every moment of life to be lived with art, and it was painful to him that our last meeting before my departure from Germany should be in these circumstances.

On the way back through the storm, Aulach went on talking. He told me that at Heidelberg he had belonged to a group of students who discussed philosophy all night long. He had been chosen to make a speech at some annual function and he had given an address which had offended the Nazis. When he was a boy he had injured his back and had to wear a steel support, but he had nevertheless won a race. Aulach went on and on like this. He was not stupid, he was not boring though rather tiring. Why did I feel that he appealed for sympathy and that yet I could never be able to help him although I did care and sympathize?

I went to Paris for a month and then returned to Bonn. One morning I met the student Aulach again, and went for a walk with him. He was still negotiating to go abroad and cease to be a German. He was well informed about the Germans, since he works with them all the time as one of them, and they say things to him which they would say to no foreigner.

Aulach said that he would take me to his favourite hideout in Bonn which is a deserted landing-stage on the

Rhine. While we were walking there – through all the dust and ruins of the deserted area of the town near the river – he said that he hated these ruins of Germany. 'I have no connection with them. They are not *my* ruins which have been taken away from me personally, nor am I in the slightest degree interested in reconstructing them.'

We got to the landing-stage, which was very pleasant. Here you can lie down on a little peninsula formed by the float of the landing-stage projecting into the Rhine, blown over by fresh breezes and surrounded by running waters which wash away the humid stinging scent of Bonn. Aulach said that he comes here often. Sometimes he lies here alone at night until two or three in the morning. What thoughts must be chasing through his handsome, bony, solitary, defiant, intelligent, rather mad head!

Aulach is significant, not because he is in any way 'typical', but because he is one spirit thinking and brooding in this post-war Germany, just as after the last war there were the Nazis thinking their nihilistic thoughts. The Germans are very cerebral, but today most of their stupefied brains resemble a confused mass seething with apathetic sullen ideas. Aulach is in a state of ferment, highly infectious to the German passively celebrating mass, filled with its dull sense of injury, self-pity, cruelty, bitterness and potential fury.

I told him that I had just read Ernst Jünger's *Feuer und Blut* and Goebbels's novel, *Michael*. Aulach said that Jünger wasn't merely a nationalist writer, he was also regarded with some favour by the communists, because he expressed a ferocious radicalism which, being essentially anti-bourgeois, was a meeting-place of the nationalist and communist ideas. I said that Jünger was diabolic and that *Feuer und Blut* was a masterpiece written from the depths of an experience of hell. Aulach said: 'I cannot disapprove of that. Jünger is a devil. And I have so much understanding of devils that I do not condemn diabolic books at all.'

When he said this I felt a strange and exciting sympathy for him. 'What do you mean by a devil?' I asked.

'A devil is a person who is aware of himself as a unique part of existence. To him, the fact that he exists and that he is a part of the human condition of existing is more important than society and than the whole world. Most people consider themselves part of their social environment, their job, their class, etc. They do not think much about the fact that they exist. Therefore a devil is quite *outside* his environment. A devil despises in his heart the whole social and political structure of our time. He realizes that democracy is just as bad as fascism, for example: or that if there is any difference, that perhaps it is just one per cent better, and this is so little that it is not worth arguing about. Anyway, the whole conflict as it is presented to us in the form of a struggle between external political systems is unreal to him. If anything about it is real, it is the fact of the struggle itself — the violence, the hatred, the destruction, the chaos which it involves.'

Aulach said that he despised the Nazis because they were not honest devils. He said that there was a diabolic side of Hitler which he admired because Hitler really saw through the sham of bourgeois society. But at the same time Hitler was not honest with himself, nor was he true to his friends. 'A true devil recognizes in the world a few other devils, people who despise all the fixed forms of society. They are willing to destroy all the outward political forms in order to intensify the sensation in themselves of their own state of being. They will put towns and even whole countries to the sword, but they remain true to themselves and loyal to each other. A true devil regards the majority of human beings as just outward external institutions to be no more respected than a city company or a society for the protection of animals. But the test of the true devil is that he is loyal to other devils. The Nazis failed by this test.'

I said that I was ten years older than he and that although I certainly shared the experience of a sensation

which he was talking about, I did not believe that the whole
of society should be sacrificed to the contempt of a few
people who, justifiably or unjustifiably, believe themselves
to be more authentic than other people. Suffering was also
real – even the suffering of dishonest people and of people
lacking in the genius to be honest with themselves – and
it was the duty of people who realize the vanity of most
human aims and institutions, nevertheless to mitigate hor-
ror and suffering.

Aulach had no sympathy with this point of view. He
said : 'I have noticed in your poems, which you showed
me, that you sometimes write simply of the experience of
being alive and of your own intimate experience of
yourself as an individual isolated within the universe.
When you write in this way you are filled with social des-
pair, and you have no religious or political beliefs what-
ever. Directly, out of a sense of conscience, you try to
introduce a constructive idea into your writing, you
fail.'

'All the same,' I said, 'one must look for a constructive
idea. If one has the sense of despair and of evil, then one
must look for the sense of hope and of good with which
to confront despair and evil.'

'There are no such alternatives as good and evil. There
is only truth and untruth. Truth is diabolic and energetic
and destructive. What is called good is only a façade of
untruths. All social aims of democracy, and progress and
reconstruction and re-education, which you talk about,
seek to establish a kind of routine, on the false assumption
that there is something concrete and enduring in nations,
parties, businesses and machinery which can absorb
people's lives and make them think of themselves as parts
of a structure which has nothing to do with the inner-
most reality of their existence. All talk of right and wrong
is an attempt to make one loyal to something outside the
truth about oneself – which is that one is alive and is going
to die and that one has no loyalty to anyone except one-
self.'

After this I had to go back to the Transit Mess. Aulach

walked back with me. En route, he said: 'Recently I have written an essay on the significance of the atom bomb.'

'What is significant about it?' I asked.

'It is very significant that ninety per cent of the scientists who invented it were Jews. We are not grateful to the Jews enough. The atom bomb is the final culmination of the Jewish analytic and destructive genius which can create nothing but only destroy. It will result in the Third World War which will complete the unfinished task of this war.'

'What is that?'

'Destroy the whole of this unnatural, decadent civilization of great cities and false values. After that, among the ruins of our civilization, a new civilization of people who will renounce our materialism for ever, will grow.'

We talked also a bit about psychoanalysis. Aulach said that psychoanalysts were 'devils on a very low stratum of intelligence'. It was characteristic, he added, that most of them were Jews. They realized that the innermost being of the individual was more important than the social structure, but they interpreted this being entirely on the sexual level, which was of slight importance. What was important was the whole condition of existence of which sex was only a small part.

PART THREE

The Fifties

Background to the Fifties

Since the war, I think, no decade has left an impression as distinct and separate as did the twenties, thirties or the first half of the forties. The fifties remain in my mind as a blur of many things without obvious features in common apart from the fact that all were symptoms of or reactions to post-war recovery. This was the decade of Suez. Churchill's senescence, Eden's valetudinarian government, Soviet invasion of Hungary, Stalin's death, Malenkov, Kruschev, de-Stalinization, Eisenhower's Presidency, McCarthyism. There were Nuclear Disarmers, Cold Warriors, Angry Young Men, Kitchen Sink painters, Teddy Boys, U and Non-U. It was the decade of expense accounts, and quick fortunes being made by dubious means. These continued into the sixties.

If one were to attempt to characterize the fifties by a catch-word, I think it would be 'Anti'. It was a time of negation and reaction in which whatever was in part positive was, to a larger extent, negative – against something-or-other.

It was asked at the time what the Angry Young Men were angry against. Insofar as there were writers who really fitted that description, the answer is that they were angry against the existing set-up for which a journalist coined the name 'establishment'. They sympathized with whatever appeared to be against what they were against – for example, early in the decade, the Labour Party. But having made a success of being anti-establishment, they later turned against socialism which appeared to be frustrating to them. Kingsley Amis, who in the early days had written a pamphlet explaining why he supported Labour, became extremely conservative. John Osborne, who in the early days was against people who complained about having to pay supertax, at the time of the invasion of Czechoslovakia by Russian tanks in 1968 wrote to *The Times* that although he considered the 'British tax man' worse

155

than 'the Russian tank man', still these goings-on abroad made him grateful that he was English.

One of the Angries wrote an article in which he said he did not wish to have social relations with anyone who was brought up in a house with an indoor lavatory, but only with people with outside ones. Obviously, success made this social qualification difficult to maintain. The Kitchen Sink painters stopped painting kitchen sink scenes, and one of them became a Royal Academician. The fifties was a decade when a good many talented young people, very conscious of the social class which they had risen above, paraded evidences of their lower-classishness. But since they had little visible attachment to their origins other than these signs of social inferiority, when they ceased to be poor these tended to evaporate. Since John Osborne's whole style of rhetoric was vested in being angry and against things, it was unfortunate for him that commercial success deprived him of opportunities to complain about being poor and neglected. He ended up by being angry with his critics.

One reason for the negativism of the fifties may have been that it was a time when the English became conscious of the consequences of the decline of Empire. This had the result of driving them back upon England, making them in an almost literal sense, 'little Englanders'. Poetry is always a barometer of this kind of change, and the best poets of the fifties – Philip Larkin, Donald Davie and Kingsley Amis – were extremely conscious of their Englishness in their work, hostile to the whole idea of 'abroad'. They were anti-foreign. They explored the limitations of English greatness, the destruction or disappearance of the industrialized countryside, the tenuous connection of the modern England with past tradition, in poetry which aimed to be clear as translucent prose.

The fifties was certainly a negative period in my own life. It was largely taken up with anti-communism. The fact that I was anti-communist does not, I think, require apology. Like many, though not all, who worked with communists in the thirties, my reason for becoming a communist was fundamentally the same as that which made me anti-communist later. This was that early in the Spanish Civil War I saw the communists as the defenders of freedom against the fascists. As the war went on, I began to realize that the unification of all the anti-fascist parties in Spain, which communists advocated, was really preparatory to unification under Communist Party dictatorship.

What I really cared about was the freedom of the individual and I could never accept the communist attitude towards this. This was that individual freedom was a bourgeois illusion. The party, we were told, applied in an objective, scientific way theoretic Marxist analysis to day-to-day political situations. In doing this, the party represented the interests of the proletariat, so there was no question but that the procedure was extremely democratic. Moreover, the party leaders, in the course of making their decisions, had different attitudes and argued democratically among themselves. But when they had arrived at their interpretation of events, this was the correct one and not to be disputed. The individual who thought he was exercising freedom in having his own subjective reservations about the party line was merely defending the position of the class enemy. This is how communists such as Harry Pollitt, the secretary of the English Communist Party, and the commissars of the International Brigade talked.

My position was that while I could accept that much of this criticism did apply to myself, yet in the last analysis I did not accept it at all. The communist argument injected into my mind self-criticism. This became an essential part of my thinking, an introduced objective consciousness criticizing my subjective self. I had to admit to myself that I did care about my standard of living and my privileged position as a bourgeois writer, and that although I was completely sincere and undeviating in my hatred of fascism, when it came to supporting fascism's ideological opponent, the communists, I secretly feared the Revolution. I could not suppose that I would cut any sort of figure after the revolution under communism. I had none of that confidence which French intellectuals who were communists seemed to have – that after the revolution the workers would be so appreciative of them and their talents that they would be in a position even more privileged than that which they enjoyed in a bourgeois society – provided, of course, that they remained good communists. I think I imagined that if the workers ever came into power I would have to scrub floors.

If a sense of my own guilt, in which I was strong, had been the deciding factor, I would have been a convinced, albeit unsatisfactory, communist. But I saw, with inescapable clarity, that even though one might be with nine-tenths of one's consciousness a bourgeois representing one's own class interests, with the remaining one-tenth of it one was a unique individual and an independently judging consciousness. It was indeed with this uniqueness of judgement that one had chosen to support the communist anti-fascists, against one's own interests. Much more important than this, I saw that if one made oneself the thinking, behaving and acting object of an ideology, one had surrendered all responsibilty for the actions of the party to which one belonged. One simply was a mental and physical function directed by the party line imposed by top functionaries.

This way of thinking may seem naïve but it is central to the history of my generation of so-called intellectuals. One can illustrate concretely what I mean by the intellectuals' surrender of individual responsibility. Many intellectuals were to discover that in permitting themselves to become creatures of the party line in circumstances when they had been free not to do so, they had contributed to establishing a dictatorship which withdrew their freedom of criticism once and for all when it came into power. And then they became dumbly assenting witnesses of terrible events : innocent people sent to prison, deceptive and lying propaganda, against which they had deprived themselves of the power to protest.

I came to realize that what we call the freedom of the individual is not just the luxury of one intellectual to write what he likes to write, but his being a voice which can speak for those who are silent. And if he permits his freedom of expression to be abolished, then he has abolished their freedom to find in his voice a voice for their wrongs.

In the essay I wrote for the famous collection of essays by ex-communists, *The God that Failed* edited by R. H. S. Crossman, I described meeting the liberal President Benes in 1947 in Prague. I do not mention there one part of my interview with him in which I asked whether he was not apprehensive of the communists in Czechoslovakia making a coup, and of his then pointing to a telephone on his desk and saying, 'If ever I have trouble with the communists in my country, I pick up that telephone and get on to my friend Stalin.' The fate of the Czechoslovakia of Benes surely demonstrated the danger of putting one's trust in Stalin.

The other writers who contributed to *The God that Failed* were Arthur Koestler, André Gide, Ignazio Silone, Louis Fischer and Richard Wright. There was also an introduction by Crossman himself, explaining that he had never been taken in by anyone or anything. When Crossman asked me to contribute, I pointed out that I could scarcely be described as having been a communist with a genuine communist experience. The essays by Koestler and Silone, both of whom had been convinced party members and important communist functionaries, bear this out. However there seemed, at that time, to be no other English writer who had belonged to the party and then left it and become an anti-communist, so I decided to write the essay. I was fascinated by the problem of the totally convinced communist who might be an intelligent and good person but who yet had succeeded in suspending in himself all power of criticizing the party. It mystifies me that anyone who had once destroyed in himself the power of independent judgement and whose thoughts were all in conformity with the party line could cease to be a communist. The context of ideology, action and identification with the party seemed to me so powerful in the lives of communists that I found it difficult to believe that someone who stopped being a communist had ever really been one. I continued to find it so until the time of the de-Stalinization when Kruschev de-mythified the whole Stalinist era.

As a matter of fact, if one reads the essays of Koestler and Silone in *The God that Failed*, one finds that, in the absolute sense, they probably never were communists. They were incorrigibly individualistic and they had been merely pretending to themselves and others that they had no doubts about the party line. There is not an essay in Crossman's collection which could not be sub-titled, 'Why I was never a communist though I thought I was one'. The ideal essay for *The God that Failed* would have to be by Karl Marx or Lenin.

My anti-communism in the fifties was based on the view that communism was something right which had gone wrong. I could not agree with Orwell's view, which he put forward whenever attacking the 'pansy left', that Stalinism was just as bad as fascism. Fascism seemed to me perverse, destructive, wicked, with its racialism and anti-intellectualism. Still less could I have believed what some Soviet dissidents in exile appear now to believe – that Russian communism is worse than fascism ever was.

My feeling that in being anti-communist I was opposing a system which in its beginnings, however far it had deviated from these, was purer than the capitalist system, made me resent being called a 'Cold Warrior', though I suppose it is what I was. Anti-anti-communist was high up in the list of anti-labels of the fifties, like the strongest anti of all – anti-American. The two were indeed connected because anti-communism was notoriously supported and subsidized by Americans. The anti-anti-communists were anti-American and included, of course, many Americans.

In 1947 I first went to America, to teach for a year at Sarah Lawrence College. Since then I have spent much time in the United States, probably as much as four months in most years. Ever since the thirties, three of my closest friends had been Americans and, perhaps for this reason, I acquired rather quickly an American point of view and was in Europe, during the most anti-American decade, a pro-American. By 'the American point of view' I mean, I suppose, that I became unconsciously American. To anti-American Europeans, the name America seems to convey not so much the idea of a country as of a conspiracy and this was especially true during the Cold War. The purpose of this conspiracy was firstly to undermine European values, secondly to involve Europeans in American capitalist policies. There is, of course, a side of America which lends force to this image. In the fifties, McCarthyism at home and the endeavour abroad to draw all nations into an anti-communist crusade were the most obvious aspects of this.

But to me America did not mean American policy. It meant Americans I met, most of whom were strongly opposed to McCarthyism. America was a perpetual transformation. Whatever else was true of it, one could not imagine it ever getting stuck. For this reason, however alarmed people were about Senator McCarthy, it seemed extremely unlikely that there would be a McCarthyite dictatorship, because it is the characteristic of totalitarian dictatorships to get stuck.

I was therefore happy at the idea of co-editing an American and English magazine. The idea of this was first mooted by the directors of the Congress for Cultural Freedom. I insisted, though, that it should not be a magazine that was international in the sense of appearing to be published in mid-Atlantic. It should be published in London and reflect primarily the interests of London. It should have

an American and an English editor. The names of the
sponsors should be printed on the title page of each num-
ber. In the editorial of the first number of *Encounter*,
written by my American co-editor Irving Kristol and
approved by me, we made the following statement about
the Congress, which I do not think untrue[1] :

> The Congress for Cultural Freedom, which sponsors this
> magazine, is made up of individuals of the most diverse
> views, as can be gathered from a mere listing of the
> names of its founding honorary chairmen : Benedetto
> Croce, John Dewey, Karl Jaspers, Salvador de
> Madariaga, Jacques Maritain and Bertrand Russell.
> What caused them to come together? Two things : a love
> of liberty and a respect for that part of human endeavour
> that goes by the name of culture.

The Congress for Cultural Freedom had its headquarters
in Paris. The remarkably intelligent members of the
secretariat were anti-communists. They meant by the de-
fence of freedom, primarily, the defence of American and
European democratic freedom against Russian communism.
This was the time of the taking over of Eastern Europe
by the communists, the Berlin airlift, brutally crushed re-
volts in East Germany and Czechoslovakia, and the de-
feated Hungarian rising. However ardent their political
anti-communism, the Congressists had great achievements
in the field of culture. Under the directorship of Nicolas
Nabokov, the composer, the Congress organized concerts,
exhibitions, conferences, on a scale which would have been
remarkable even from such an organization as Unesco : a
Festival in Paris at which Stravinsky conducted his own
compositions; a meeting of economists from all over the
world (among the British were R. H. S. Crossman, Hugh
Gaitskell and Anthony Crosland) in Milan in 1958. It
subsidized several magazines of which the most notable
were *Encounter* in London, *Preuves* in Paris and *Tempo
Presente* (edited by Ignazio Silone and Nicola Chiaromonte)
in Italy.

It would be untrue to write that the Congress never tried to influence the editorial policy of *Encounter*, although the influence it attempted to exercise was by no means always political : simply, the people in Paris had bright ideas about the kind of articles we should put in. They also, in the early stages, wanted us to be an organ for Congress activities, with a column devoted to them. Irving Kristol and I resisted this pressure and *Encounter* became an independent magazine, partly of literature and the arts, partly of politics. The political articles were the domain of the American editors.

The Congress was enterprising and imaginative and staffed by people I was glad to consider friends, particularly Nicolas Nabokov and the head of the organization, Michael Josselsen, a man of wide interest, real culture, imagination and humanity.

The Congress was, to all appearances, funded by about forty different American Foundations. There was a published list of these. The head of one of them, Julian Fleischmann, a Cincinnati millionaire who had his own Foundation, the Farfield, told me, on a voyage in the Aegean on his yacht, that it was he who paid for *Encounter*. He asked me to write occasional letters to him about *Encounter*. Later, at a time when there were rumours that the Farfield Foundation was a channel for funds from the CIA, I wrote a letter to him, and another to his Foundation's New York director asking whether there was any truth in this allegation. Fleischmann wrote back, several months later, denying it. His director, B——, wrote me an abusive letter stating that I could accuse him of a great many things, but not of deceiving me about the sources of the subsidy for *Encounter*.

Finally, in 1966, the magazine *Ramparts* revealed the fact that many of the Foundations funding the Congress were in fact channelling funds from the CIA. One of these was the Farfield. Frank Kermode, who had taken my place as co-editor of *Encounter*, and I, who was then acting as a corresponding editor, resigned.

Public reaction to these events was sharply divided. On

the one hand there were those who were delighted to think that all those contributors and editors who were indirectly and without their knowledge subsidized by the CIA were indelibly branded; on the other hand those who asked : 'Since you were free to publish whatever you liked in an excellent magazine which contained no material you disapproved of, what does it matter?' The answer to this question is that it does matter. In the English Parliament there is a convention that any Member speaking on a subject in which he himself has a business interest should name that interest. What would one think of the position of a Member of Parliament who was a director of a firm which deceived him about the sources of its capital and income? He would be put in a position in which deception practised on him resulted in his deceiving others.

As I implied above, there was a great preoccupation with questions of class in England in the fifties. The lower- or lower-middle-class young who benefited from the educational opportunities offered by the Welfare State tried to define themselves socially, and often their way of doing this was so attractive that their upper-class contemporaries imitated them. Etonians spoke with working-class accents. Brilliant young playwrights like John Osborne and Harold Pinter seemed to be writing texts for young actors to speak in those accents.

At the same time the emerging new élite of often very rich pop singers and business operators was frustratedly aware that the old upper class still remained as a ceiling above them.

In September 1953, we published in *Encounter* an article by Nancy Mitford entitled 'The English Aristocracy'. When Nancy Mitford first sent in the article that we had commissioned, it was a thousand words short of the length I had asked for. I pointed this out, and she good-naturedly replied that she could easily fill out the space with quotations from a paper written by Professor Alan Ross of Birmingham University, printed in Helsinki in 1954, on

'Upper Class English Usage'. Nancy Mitford quoted from this pamphlet examples of 'U and Non-U Usage', for instance :

> *Dinner* : U-speakers eat *luncheon* in the middle of the day and *dinner* in the evening. Non-U speakers (also U-children and U-dogs) have their *dinner* in the middle of the day.

With the publication of Nancy Mitford's article, and the ensuing correspondence in our pages, *Encounter*'s success was assured. Circulation rose by several thousand. U and Non-U became in the mid-fifties a craze, a centre for that debate about old and new classes, accents, life-styles which was such a preoccupation of the fifties and sixties.

The best thing I wrote in *Encounter* were journal entries, and I kept a journal intermittently during the fifties. Here is a note dated December 1953 :

> 'Dylan Thomas died in New York.' Having written these words I went to bed and had a dream about him. It was in a large and beautiful chapel or church. The choir sang a requiem. The music was modern and yet like Monteverdi, though it was not pastiche. Dylan was lying on the floor beside the place where I was standing, rather pale, but still transparently alive.
>
> I woke up thinking there was something I now realized : death was a sham, invented by the living, a pretence that the dead were not here, whereas in reality they are alive and omnipresent. As I felt, waking, that the sensation of Dylan's physical presence was fading, I was still hammered, as it were from inside my skull, with this knocking awareness of how *living* the dead are. I felt wearied of their forcing themselves upon us with that insistence and persuasiveness which the living lack.
>
> Matthew, our son, aged 8, who was sleeping in my room, had woken me, as he always does, with dawn. We heard a drumming of hooves in the road outside. It was

the cavalry exercising horses from the barracks stables nearby. M slipped out of bed, drew back the curtains of the window, and kneeled on the floor. 'Look! Their heels are on fire,' he said. I replied, 'They always do that.' I realized that was the first time he had seen so much iron strike sparks from stone. Kneeling beside him, I saw the hooves agitate through the haze against the surface of the road and burst into white flowers of sparks, and the shadowy horses move through the milky dawn, as though with M's eyes, seeing them for the first time. The sensation of first-timeness also made me think how Dylan would see them and describe them, entering into the realness of the scene and singing from core and centre of its being. At the same time, I realized that I myself saw things clearly but from the outside, at a distance, through the instrument of what I am – saw them small and clear and looking-glass and upside-down, as on an old-fashioned camera's ground-glass screen.

1 Except that, as correctly noted on page 3 of that issue of *Encounter*, Reinhold Niebuhr, and not John Dewey was among the honorary chairmen.

Journal

London Magazine, new series 16, 2 (June/July 1976)

Recently I turned out a great many boxes contained in a basement room which we call The Bottomless Pit. In a large cardboard box I found fragmentary diaries, written over the past thirty years. In the pages of journal that follow I shall print extracts from them, with explanatory comments.

1950

In 1950, I was asked by the *New York Times Magazine* to write an article about the attitudes of European intellectuals – particularly those with a communist past – to politics. The article was commissioned by way of the then London representative of the magazine who was an extremely nice and very scared-looking man by the name of Bailey. He was scared because he lived a terrifying life poised between the Scylla of his editor in New York who was called Markel and the Charybdis of the British intellectuals from whom he was expected to obtain articles. Markel was one of those editors who believe that editing means one of two things : either rewriting the material sent in by authors or making them rewrite it. Markel must have held a record, even in America, for changing, or making authors change articles. Poor Bailey had the, to him, terrifying task of writing to Bertrand Russell and others and telling them that the articles they had been commissioned to write required changes. The entry with which I concluded the journal of my interviews with these European intellectuals throughout April, 1950, ends on 1 May :

Returned to London. Took my piece to the *New York Times* London office. Bailey read it through once and then said, with a sad expression on his face : 'What strikes me about this piece is that it gives too much of their, not enough of your, views.' Then he went on to say it was not sufficiently focused, did not analyse the attitudes of those interviewed adequately, did not draw conclusions, did not proclaim some Great Faith pronounced by Malraux, Silone and Koestler which would provide American readers with a Lead. He broke off suddenly, gazed at me with an expression of deepest melancholy and said : 'I know I'm being very stupid.' He looked like Laurel of Laurel and Hardy. I felt as miserable as he did.

In my journal, I noted down the views of Ignazio Silone and Elio Vittorini in Italy, André Malraux and Arthur Koestler in France. I also noted occasions which had nothing to do with my interviews :

25 March, Florence
Luncheon at I Tatti, with Bernard Berenson. Raymond Mortimer was there, also B.B.'s companion Nikki Mariano and a woman whom I had met once before in New York. Impossible to talk to B.B. at luncheon – too far away from him, and no general conversation. After the meal he drew me aside and talked very amiably. In his extreme old age he has something of the spirituality of certain El Greco portraits, together with a shell-frail delicacy of the texture of his skin. Every line of his face seems drawn separately, with precision of a steel engraving. He said he was sorry I had never stayed with him and asked me to do so if I was able while he 'was still here to receive me'.

Later Eudora Welty came to dinner with B.B. : when I was there. B.B. remarked on her great charm. Of her novels, he said they were clearly talented, but 'like all those Americans, having found one thing she could do

she went on doing just that, and nothing else . . . It's like
Walt Disney and all their other discoveries.' I liked
Eudora Welty very much. Tall and dark-eyed, rather
craggy yet soft-looking, a slight rolling of eyes which went
well with her Southern accent. She was accompanied by a
young man called R——, solid but mysterious and sub-
ject of much speculation. Eudora Welty talked about a
mutual friend of ours a once young writer, called Sam . . . :
said she was greatly impressed when Sam sent her his
first long story, but liked less what he sent afterwards. So
she wrote to him and criticized the other stories. Six
months later she received a letter from him, saying that he
had just recovered from the shock of receiving her letter.
'Now,' she said, 'it struck me that a person who receives
criticism in that way cares more for himself than for his
writing. Perhaps he regards his writing simply as an ex-
tension of himself.'

28 March
The famous poet Eugenio Montale, now literary editor of
the *Corriere della Sera*, was at dinner with the Elio
Vittorinis. I was struck by his extremely ironic manner.
He told me that as a poet he could not receive as good pay
as the other journalists on the *Corriere*. Being the most
famous poet in Italy was a grave disadvantage which he
had long had to struggle against.

14 April, Paris : Arthur Koestler's row with J. P. Sartre.
Koestler told me that when he last said goodbye to Sartre
and Simone de Beauvoir outside the Hotel Pont Royal, he
remarked : 'Let's have luncheon together soon.' There was
a pause at the end of which Simone said : 'Koestler, you
know that we disagree. There no longer seems any point
in our meeting.' She crossed her arms and said : 'We are
croisés comme ça about everything.' Koestler said : 'Yes,
but surely we can remain friends just the same. Let's meet
soon.' She said : 'As a philosopher, you must realize that
each of us when he looks at a *morceau de sucre* sees an

entirely different object. Our *morceaux de sucre* are now so different that there's no point in our meeting any longer.'

Since Koestler has made no political pronouncements for many years, his remarks of 1950 are interesting, and remain largely true of today when the English Labour Party still appears to be less internationalist than the Conservatives.

Koestler said that the most important fact to grasp about the present situation was that the labels 'left' and 'right' have lost their meaning. Labour had fallen down on internationalism, and the England of the day with its Labour Government was the main obstacle to European union . . . Orwell had rightly said that the Left had never faced the contradiction that if you want internationalism you have to sacrifice a national standard of living which has been gained at the expense of the rest of the world. Koestler was thinking at this time of European union as the answer to Russian communism. He said : 'There are 215 million Western Europeans and under 200 million Russians. Yet we are helpless because there is no unity. European unity must be achieved. It will lead to European upheaval but this will be less than that caused by war. A main objection to American foreign policy is that it does not tell Europe, "Unite, or perish!" '

At a party given by Nancy Mitford, I met the famous aide of de Gaulle, Gaston Palevsky, who remarked of André Malraux that he was a romantic who wished always for some adventure in life which would lead to final truth. Gaullism had put him in contact with a heroic crusade personified in the figure of de Gaulle. This was amusing because Koestler had told me that Malraux's true passion was art. His politics were his thyroid gland. And Malraux said of Koestler that he was a person perpetually in search of a country. He had sought it in communism but failed to find it. Then he thought he would return to the Jews in Israel, but they did not care for him.

※

Malraux has a beautiful house in the Avenue Victor Hugo, Boulogne-sur-Seine. The main room is a large drawing-dining-study-music room. It has a show-case running along one side, and a kind of alcove. The walls are white. There are paintings by Picasso, Dubuffet, etc. Also colour reproductions of the same size as the original paintings. (Malraux has a theory that the relation of colour to colour only works in a reproduction if it is of the same size as the original. He is surely right about this.)

I thought he looked well and less nervous than usual. Also I myself felt more at ease than often when with him. It was impossible to write down what he said, partly because of the rapidity of his speech, partly because the conversation was conducted largely over the dinner table, so it was difficult to take notes.

His way of talking is special. Conversation for him is a succession of formulations of topics, each of which he proceeds to deal with separately and decisively. If the subject remains the same the conversation becomes like a brilliant set of variations on a theme, each variation complete in itself.

Malraux dealt first of all with the theme of European union. He said that this was always put before us as a nineteenth-century parliamentarian view of Europe. But the idea of the parliament at Strasbourg was quite inadequate to present circumstances. England, he went on, had interests which put her quite outside the project of a United Europe, if we thought of this in nationalistic European terms. We should therefore look for a basis for European Union wider than that of Europe itself – a new enterprise, an area of exploitation into which Europe could enter and reach beyond itself. This was undoubtedly the exploitation of the African continent. Of course, mention of Africa at once raised the objection that it would be colonization. However, this problem would not be as serious as a hundred years ago, because Africa would be exploited not with human bodies but with bulldozers and tractors. At this time, the idea of the exploitation of Africa appealed greatly to the Gaullists . . . Malraux evidently had a Gaullist vision of Russia and America suddenly waking up one morning to discover themselves confronted by an enormous new continent, the most powerful in the world, called EurAfrica.

He now passed on to Russia : the important thing to realize was that Russia was no longer an ethical symbol for the rest of the world. It had become two things : firstly, an economic structure of communism; secondly, the police state . . . Apart from all arguments about the economic structure, we reject Russia because we reject the police state. This brings us to America, for the US is above all the country which rejects Russia. We are told that we are as different from America as from Russia and that we have to choose between American and Russian cultures, each of them equally alien to us. But although the Russia of Tolstoi, Dostoievsky and Turgenev turned towards Europe, the Russia of Stalin has definitely turned away from our culture and is in fact completely alien to it. What is America, though, but Europe? America is the extension of the European culture within American conditions. America has done nothing to shut us out : on the contrary, it is overwhelmed with our productions in every art gallery, every concert hall, every library. It is flooded with exactly those manifestations of Europe which Russia does everything possible to exclude.

We are told that many American phenomena are stupid and dangerous. But when people say that, they concentrate on the American phenomenon which we understand very well because they are in fact also European. Their radio is stupid and dangerous – well, so is ours. Who would want Europe judged just by the radio or the newspapers or the movies – or, indeed, by any of those things which we choose to label American, though they derive from us?

Russia is analogous not to Europe but to Japan at the time when Japan was rejecting everything European. The museum of Europe becomes more and more open and is included within America, that of Moscow is more and more closed.

After dinner we moved to another part of the room where we had coffee and cognac. Malraux showed me the proofs of the third volume of his *Psychologie de l'art*. Later we returned to our conversation about Europe and he said : 'Of course, there is a great difference between the American and the European concept of individualism. A good deal of misunderstanding is precisely due to this. Americans make individual values too dependent on the possession of personal belongings. Now although it is nice to enjoy things and possess them, we know very well that we are not dependent on them for being ourselves. During the Spanish Civil War, you and I were just as much individualists as we are now, though we had nothing then. There are two fundamentals of European individualism. Firstly, the feeling of the individual that, by virtue of his naked existing, he is both separated from and the same as others, e.g., Rousseau; secondly, the sense of being great as an objective reality – the sense, that is, of knowing one is a great man. The great man recognizes himself : is recognized by others as such because he is a meeting place of their aspirations and dreams . . .'

Malraux gave me a very beautiful reproduction of a painting by Paul Klee, made by a new process.

Previous to this, on 11 January 1950, we went to see George Orwell in University College Hospital. He told me he had lost over two stone. He looked very thin and worn out. He said I was wrong to attempt to reply to the communists : 'There are certain people like vegetarians and communists whom one cannot answer. You just have to go on saying your say regardless of them, and then the extraordinary thing is that they may start listening.'

1953

30 January, London
Yesterday Herbert Read lunched with me at the Savile. We began talking about filing cabinets. He said that he

wanted one and I told him how sorry I was that I had not started one, ten or fifteen years ago, and how having one now enabled me to keep a journal, which I had never succeeded in doing.

We then went on to talk about money. He told me that now he is 59, he has no prospect of being able to retire, because he has to go on supporting his family for the rest of his life. He said that living in the country was not really much of an economy. People come and stay every weekend, and there is a good deal of local life among the gentry, and still more among neighbouring seminarists. The monks, he said, love eating and drinking a great deal, because this is their substitute for sex. In the country they have to have a gardener, and the idea that one saves by consuming one's own produce is an illusion : eggs laid by one's own hens cost more than eggs in shops, etc.

H.R. is a man of great sensibility and beauty of personality, real fineness, who has been unable to coarsen himself, but who has been forced to produce a far too large quantity of generalizations, very carefully reasoned, about art, literature, education, etc., etc., in order to live. The creative side of his talent has gradually been submerged, and the more this has happened the more depressed he feels about the arts in general. He has a line which is to support nearly everything that is experimental and he therefore gives his readers the impression of being in the vanguard, and someone in the vanguard is supposed of course to have burning faith and vitality : qualities which, in reality, H.R. lacks.

He told me that the new paintings by a Paris group which are now on show at the ICA are by painters who feel that their art has come to a near-vanishing point where the only thing that can be expressed on canvas is something like a single bare gesture, a signature, a line drawn, a few blotches. This is also the dead-end of the modernist movement which Herbert himself nevertheless feels bound to support.

He is depressed by an overwhelming sense of decay, and by loss of faith in the social ideas – and perhaps the aesthetic theories – which have kept him going all his life. He described the rot of the houses in the Yorkshire village where he lives, which have not been repaired for many years, because the families which own them are crippled by having to pay death duties. He said that he thought that death duties were a pernicious tax responsible for the decay of England. I said that I thought income tax was really little better and that we were living through a transitional time in which we combined the evils of capitalism with those of collective bureaucracy. I said the state ought really to own a few great industries and make its own money and not live on taxation. Herbert cheered up a bit at this and talked happily for a few minutes about the single tax theories of Henry George.

We talked about Eliot. He said that one day he must write something about his relationship with Eliot. The great reputation of Eliot had overshadowed him all his life. He said he thought Eliot did not want to see anyone, was curiously lacking in affection for 'perhaps everyone', and that all Eliot wanted to do now was to 'slink away into some corner and die'.

'Everything is dead,' he said at some point in the conversation, and I think really this is what he thinks now.

Two evenings ago I walked through the streets near Maida Vale, in the damp, misty darkness and had a strong feeling of the complete rotting away of England which Herbert had spoken of. This district where I lived fifteen years ago is now simply falling to bits. The stucco in places is like decaying teeth with huge holes of blackness and filth in it, and the streets give off a decaying smell like that of bombed houses . . . In this damp cold weather, after the fog, a lot of London had this horrible sweetish sour odour.

1956

The European Cultural Association had arranged to hold in Venice a small meeting of the following persons : J. P. Sartre, Merleau Ponty, Vercors, from France; J. D. Bernal, Alan Pryce-Jones and myself, from England; Fedin, Mikhail Alpatov, V. Volodine and Boris Polevoi, all from Russia; Ivaskievitch, from Poland; Ignazio Silone, Carlo Levi, Piovene and Compagnolo (the head of the Association), from Italy; and Mario Ristic from Jugoslavia. I wrote for myself a journal about this meeting.

26 March, Venice
The idea of Literature *Engagée*. The whole afternoon was devoted to this, as a result of Compagnolo's insistence that any meeting between writers from East and West must discuss the Writer and Society. Sartre and Merleau Ponty put forward the idea of the writer being *engagé*. I maintained that the only writer who had to be *engagé* was the one whose social conscience could be realized in the results of his imagination. A writer who wrote poems about bees did not have to be told to write them about factories.

The reaction to this example shows the degree of subtlety or crudeness of the idea of 'engagement'. With Merleau Ponty the idea is subtle : by 'engagement' he means that everything one writes reflects a social choice. One's way of describing the bees, the metre one chooses, all reflect one's attitude to society, one's environment. However, this (with which I would agree) means that there is no difference between engaged and disengaged literature. One is always, consciously or unconsciously, 'engaged'. Sartre makes a difference by insisting on the importance of

176

consciousness. One should be fully aware of which side
one is on and consciously direct one's writing towards it.
An example he gave seemed a bit crude but had the
advantage of being very concrete. When he was in China,
Chinese writers were called upon to write children's
stories. Should they or shouldn't they do so? He emphasized
that there were very few writers in China and a great
many children. What he didn't seem to take into account
(nor did anyone else) was that the stories would have to
please not only the Chinese government. Merleau Ponty
said he would be glad to write a children's story. I said
that if I were a Chinese child I was not sure that I would
be delighted by the story of a Chinese Merleau Ponty.

J. D. Bernal brought up the subject discussed by Shelley
in *A Defence of Poetry* (not that he mentioned Shelley)
that 'we should imagine that which we know.' He said
that we were on the threshold of a future of enormous
scientific development and control of resources, which
would transform life. For the first time, he said, we lived
in a history in which immense changes benefiting every-
one could be achieved simply through knowledge and
without a revolution. (Will the communists perhaps be-
come Godwinians?) He reproached writers for not writing
works that revealed any awareness of this future. He said
there had never been such a gap – not even in the 1890s –
between the littleness of literature and the greatness of
man's powers and knowledge.

I must say I am Shelleyan enough to feel the force of
Bernal's reproach. All the same, he was discussing in terms
of knowledge what would only be real if discussed in
terms of imagination. I pointed this out and after the
meeting he said, 'You have me there.' But nonetheless, he
said, there were non-literary writers despised by critics,
who did try to grapple with this future.

Vercors put the case for *engagé* writing in what seemed
to me the most journalistic way : he said, 'If I am con-
fronted by a great injustice, I feel called upon to set
aside my own preoccupations and interests and write
about that.'

The Russians, who had brought their interpreters, were so badly served by these that they obviously could not understand what was being said. However, they improvised for the time being, and said that tomorrow – when they had studied the translated material – they would speak. Meanwhile, Fedin said that he thought the first demand on a writer was to be sincere with himself, the second to be responsible towards society. It was out of the tension between these two sometimes opposed loyalties that literature was made. Boris Polevoi whenever he speaks says the same thing: 'Let's not talk about politics, dear colleagues, because if we do that we'll find we disagree. Let's just stick to culture.' To illustrate this line, on which he is evidently very determined, he told me that when he accompanied Molotov in America and there was much political discussion it was impossible to come to any understanding with anyone. But as soon as he travelled around alone, disembarrassed of Molotov, he found himself getting on excellently with 'ordinary Americans'. 'Ordinary Americans', he discovered, loved Russians, and wanted peace.

The Polish delegate, Ivaskievitch, whilst explaining that he was not a Marxist, adopted very much the social realist line.

Compagnolo insists on dominating the discussion and is very opinionated. The thesis he wants to thrust on us all is that the writer must not only be *engagé* but must enter completely into politics. All he omits to say is *what* and *whose* politics. At the same time, in an effort to avoid disagreement, he is capable of saying things like: 'No one here is a Marxist or anti-Marxist, communist or anti-communist. We are all completely objective.'

28 March
Last night at La Columba, sat with Boris Polevoi, who looks like Malenkov, and the mysterious official (whom Silone calls the Fourth Man), who supervises the Russians. Polevoi was friendly, inviting me to stay with him in Russia. The Fourth Man, who always overdoes

things rather, told me that when I was in Russia they
would be glad to hear my criticisms because although they
were proud of their achievements in some ways, they were
always grateful for criticism.

The previous evening I had sat next to Carlo Levi. He
is cheerful-looking with a curly head of hair and a profile
in which the forehead forms a continuous curve from the
base of the hair to the tip of the nose, and the neck
starts off just below the chin. He looks very like a stoutish
tortoise. Disregarding the menu fixed for us all, he had
made friends with the waiter and ordered on his own
an hors d'oeuvre of calamoretti and scampi, which he
followed up with a course of razor-shell fish, that looked
like long white worms in their knife-blade shells. He told
me that you could attract these animals by sprinkling salt
over the small holes they leave in the wet sand. Sensing
the salt, they think the tide has come in and come out
of their holes. He talked with charming vanity about the
immense popularity of his own work, answering a question
of mine, whether it was true, as I'd heard, that Italians
don't read many books. He said that where he lived there
were peasants who knew pages of his works by heart, and
that it was the custom there for someone who could read
to read a page a day of Carlo Levi to the other villagers.
Thus – allowing for harvest and holiday – they read 300
pages of Carlo Levi per year.

I have seriously offended J. D. Bernal. Answering Silone,
in his role of objective scientist weighing the facts very
scrupulously, he said 'there was something in' the accusa-
tions of germ warfare conducted by the Americans in
Korea. He would not say whether there had or had not
been microbes – it was not quite established – but he would
say there was a *prima facie* case for saying so. I said that
I thought in meetings of this kind the issue became very
confused if delegates from the West, without declaring
themselves to be so, were communists. Everyone knew
that the East had one point of view and contained no
delegates opposed to it – Compagnolo, violently annoyed,

interrupted to say that no one was a delegate 'representing anything'. Everyone here was here simply as a member of ECA. I said that in this case it would be nice to invite a few people from countries behind the Iron Curtain who were anti-Communists.

Bernal did not reply but covered his face with his hands.

30 March

We went to see the film of a story by Pasolini called, I think, *Poveri amanti*. It counter-pointed the lives of Florentines living in a rabbit warren of workers' flats with the brutal events of the rise of fascism. Anti-fascists spent their time being shot up by fascists. I thought it must be curious for the Soviet guests – fresh from revelations about Beria, Stalin, etc., etc., – to observe the stone-age methods of repression of the fascists; and that it was still more curious to offer this film to our mostly leftist conference as a tribute to our Russian friends' hatred of oppression. Thinking these thoughts, I was curious to see how Bernal sitting on my left was reacting. So while an anti-fascist, who had been shot several times in the back, was being thrown by the fascists into the flames of his motorcycle, which they had set alight by firing a few shots through the petrol tank, I stole a few glances at my colleague. His mouth hung open, he was breathing heavily and perspiring. From time to time he passed his hand over his forehead, at moments he shut his eyes unable to bear the sight of the pain on the screen. This, I thought, from a man who is so intent on the vision of socialist construction that he considers the deaths of thousands of people, slave labour, etc., as irrelevant.

When we left the movie I bought a newspaper, *Il Gazzettino*, which was reeling with news of the rehabilitation of Rayk. After a committee meeting which went on till 1 a.m. I couldn't resist trying Bernal out about this. As we walked back across the piazza to our hotel, I said : 'Don't you think it amazing that Rakosi, who is still in power and who knew very well when Rayk was executed

Journal

that he was innocent, should now rehabilitate him? How can Rakosi do this and remain in power?' Bernal just walked on in silence as though he had not heard this question. Not answering is, in fact, part of Bernal's repertoire. It does not contribute to any impression of frankness he might possibly give. On the whole he simply ignores all 'subjective' questions, only answering 'objective' ones about things such as the world's population, education and science and the like. This morning, meeting him at the porter's desk when I came down to breakfast, I saw he was in a coat, so I said, 'Do you take breakfast outside the hotel?' He ignored the question and went out of the hotel. However, he is quite willing to give one a lecture on any of his subjects.

30 March

After this meeting to discuss the text of the communiqué and programme for the congress, I got hold of Sartre alone and asked him : 'What would you say if in certain circumstances you were imprisoned in a city where there was a communist government, and I, knowing you were innocent, started a campaign against the communists on your account?' 'Ah,' said Sartre, 'that is an extremely difficult question. It all depends. But it is just possible that I in my prison, though innocent, and even hating my oppressors, might nevertheless think it better that I should be condemned than that my case should be made the occasion for an accusation against the cause which in the long run is that of the proletariat.' I said : 'It seems to me that the only good cause has always been that of one person unjustly imprisoned – whether this has resulted in *habeas corpus* or a furious campaign conducted by Voltaire in pamphlets.' Sartre : 'That's the whole drama. That perhaps we live in a situation in which the injustice against one person no longer seems to apply.'

On the way to Torcello, in the motor-boat, one of the lady interpreters asked : 'How is it that Mr Bernal, who is so logical in every way, so objective, and who also has a sense of humour, can be so completely illogical and un-objective whenever the discussion comes round to communism?'

At Torcello I was asked to sit next to Karl Barth, the Swiss theologian. Beyond him was Bernal. Somehow, I managed the conversation so that I could make Bernal himself answer the interpreter's question. I asked him again what he thought about Stalin, and he said: 'We seem to have made some very serious mistakes. I don't know how it happened, but it is bad.' I asked him whether he did not think such mistakes were inevitable with a communist system. He said: 'There is not just one system in the world. There are two to choose from. And, of the two, I prefer the communist.' 'What makes you prefer it?' 'You have to think of the utter unnecessary misery and waste and lack of opportunity that exists in the world as it is at present. What people fail to realize is that things don't have to be as they are.' 'Then what prevents them being better?' 'Well, for one thing people themselves. Human beings are the trouble. One person who is greedy and dishonest who gets into a strong position can undo the good done by hundreds.'

I told Barth and Bernal about the question I had put to Sartre. 'Ah,' said Barth, 'But you assume Sartre to have been innocent. How can you invent a hypothesis of such a society in which people who are political prisoners are innocent?' 'Well, for one thing, they might not have committed the acts for which they are condemned.' 'Still, in the circumstances of that kind of society, they might have been out of step. It might be enough for them to be guilty in the minds of the rulers.' I said: 'All the same, the people who were condemned by Stalin are now rehabilitated.' 'It may be a matter of time. In 1956 they may be innocent. In 1937 they may have been guilty.' I looked astonished, and he said: 'All the same, I don't approve of such a society.'

There is a kind of *Schadenfreude* among theologians who are delighted to prove that without their absolute values, all justice is completely relative.

28 July

A week ago I lunched with the painter, Matthew Smith, at a Spanish restaurant in Kensington, and afterwards went to his studio. Matthew Smith is now about 70, has an almost retiring air of great timidity, looks out on the world myopically through his glasses. He is extremely mild and gentle yet uncompromising and acute, reminding me a little of E. M. Forster. Over luncheon he talked gently about many things, including painting and France and girls. He said that Morandi must be an interesting man, but he did not really altogether care for his painting, which he found affected. He said he liked some of the paintings of Jack Yeats but he found the large canvases which were exhibited at the Tate Gallery some years ago rather empty. He thought that Yeats should have been advised not to show them. He was very reserved also about Wyndham Lewis. Obviously, despite his gentle manner, he is not easy to please.

He showed surprising energy in his studio, dragging out dozens of canvases for me to look at. First of all there were two canvases of flowers. He said : 'Nowadays I don't seem able to paint flowers. When I was younger I could do so. I used to get so tremendously excited by flowers I saw that I wanted to take them home at once and start working on them.' His recent paintings have an astonishing violence of colour and freedom of line. I asked him if I might buy a painting, and he just murmured : 'That would be very difficult.' At the end of the afternoon, he suddenly pulled a water colour out of a corner of the room and said : 'Would you like this as a souvenir?' He apologized for the fact that actually there were two water colours, one on each side of the paper. He said : 'I believe this may detract from the value. There was a painting by Gauguin which had another painting on the reverse of the canvas, and it was supposed to be worth less than the others.' We took the water colour to the framers, and there Matthew Smith looked at an easel with a sketching box attached to it. I pressed him to allow me to buy this for him, but he told me he did not at all wish to have it as he could get the same kind of thing much more cheaply in France. Two days later I learned from Vera Barry that he was quite distressed about this whole incident. He was not certain I would like the water colour, and he was afraid I would be offended by his having refused the easel. I asked Vera Barry whether it would be possible still to buy an oil painting from him. She said that for some reason he will not show his recent work, which she thinks his best, and only exhibits rather inferior things. Nor will he sell any of his recent work. She did not understand why, as he has no one to leave either things or money to, his wife being almost the same age as himself.

Today I had lunch with a very different painter, Augustus John. He makes an extraordinary impression, like a character part, a knight, in Shakespeare, with his Frans Hals beard, and his general air of belonging to an era before Puritanism had been thought of. We spoke as usual about the past. He told me how fond he had been of Ottoline Morrell. As we walked Charlotte Street to the restaurant, he said : 'I used to know this street very well. Of course it was much nicer then. You could stroll down it and maybe you would meet Jimmy Whistler looking for the restaurant where he ate every day. He had an excellent meal for 1s. 6d.' He made one quite strange remark. For some reason today London is full of Salvation Army men and women. Augustus John cocked his eye at these, and said : 'I had two aunts who were members of the Salvation Army. They went to America and did a great deal of preaching there. Ha! The Salvation Army! Those were the heroic times.'

15 August
I had dinner on 27 July with I.A. and Dorothy Richards, at a restaurant in Heath Street. I rather dreaded this occasion, and felt inclined even to put it off. I. A Richards had told me he wanted to discuss my essay 'Inside the Cage', and I feared the evening might turn into a tutorial. Actually I enjoyed it very much. He said that he had

altered his point of view since he wrote *Science and Poetry*. However, he thought the nature of poetry was such that what the poet believed inside his poetry, need have no – indeed must have no – authoritatively rational connection dictated by outside belief. 'The curious thing about poetry is that anything can happen inside its peculiar world without commitment to what goes on outside.'

Dorothy tried to switch the conversation to Colonel Nasser, etc. Richards said : 'Don't let's talk about things that don't matter. This question of belief in poetry is much more important.' He was so extraordinarily alive in his interests, so considerate, so humble, so appreciative, so ready to discuss matters he was greatly learned in on absolutely equal terms – he was not at all my idea of the Cambridge critic. He illustrated some of his remarks by quoting whole poems – Hardy's 'After a Journey', de la Mare's poem about buzzing bees – conversationally, and yet with a wonderful perfection. We went back after the meal to their flat for a short time and I showed him the water colour Matthew Smith gave me. I saw him look at it with a kind of concentration peculiar to him, as though he were employing that technique for concentrating on a work of art which he describes in – I think – *Practical Criticism*.

Notes on Revolutionaries and Reactionaries

Partisan Review XXXIV, 3 (Summer 1967)

REVOLUTIONARIES

In England, the circumstances in which poets intervene in politics are special. In their study of Julian Bell's and John Cornford's tragically broken-off lives, *Journey to the Frontier*, Peter Stansky and William Abrahams inevitably devoted much space to explaining the family background and the personal psychological and intellectual problems which led these young men to anti-fascism and their deaths in Spain.

If they had been French biographers writing about the young Malraux, Aragon or Eluard, there would have been no need of such explanation. For in France the 1930s was only the most recent episode in the long involvement of the French intellectuals with politics since before the French Revolution. Writers like Romain Rolland, Henri Barbusse, Georges Duhamel and André Gide publicly discussed their attitudes to the Russian Revolution, the League of Nations, war, and disarmament, after 1918.

French intellectuals of both right and left had centres, organizations, reviews, newspapers, platforms. In taking sides, the intellectual exploited the legend that, *qua* intellectual, he represented detached intelligence. The 'clerc' descended from the clouds of objectivity to make disinterested pronouncements – *Et tu, Julian Benda*.

It is true of course that sometimes a Romain Rolland or a Henri Barbusse looked across the Channel and appealed to a Shaw or a Wells as '*cher collègue*' and asked him to attend some international conference or sign some declaration of human rights. But if and when they responded, these English *maîtres* did not descend as radiant messengers from the realms of pure imagination and impartial intellect. They were already publicists and not quite artists. Wells, although priding himself on being a social prophet, cultivated the manner of a travelling salesman for the scientific culture. Like Shaw, Bennett and Galsworthy, he thought of his public personality as anti-aesthetic, low-brow. He was forever explaining that he was a journalist who breathed a different air from that of characters in the novels of Henry James.

Eliot, Virginia Woolf, D. H. Lawrence saw to it that Wells and Bennett should never be allowed to forget their vulgar public streak – what Lawrence called the 'societal'. When during the thirties E.M. Forster appeared on *front populaire* platforms he did so because the time demanded that he should assume a role in which he had no confidence and for which he felt little enthusiasm. His presence at Congresses of the Intellectuals during the anti-fascist period, and that of young English poets, was an exceptional action produced by exceptional times – like lions walking the streets of Rome on the night preceding the Ides of March. The artist had become denatured by apocalyptic events.

Until the thirties, the younger generation of Oxford and Cambridge remained influenced by the anti-politics of their parents' generation. Stansky and Abrahams mention that the famous society of Cambridge intellectual undergraduates – the Apostles – which had such a close connection with literary Bloomsbury, agreed in the twenties that 'practical politics were beneath discussion'. In the early thirties, the Apostles ceased for some years to exist, as the result of the pressure of 'too many conflicting political beliefs' among their members. Yet so different was the atmosphere by then that to Julian Bell, no longer then an undergraduate, and to John Cornford, who was one, this must have seemed like saying that having at last something to discuss, the Apostles had decided to discuss nothing.

To the Cambridge and Bloomsbury generation of their

parents, Bell and Cornford seemed changelings, hatched by hens out of ducks' eggs, swimming out on those dirty political waters. Not that Clive and Vanessa Bell and the Cornford parents disagreed with the younger generation's anti-fascist politics. They sympathized with them. Yet more than this, they regarded politicians as philistines and the artist in politics as betraying the pure cause of art. Leftish political sympathies were almost a part of the ethos of literary Bloomsbury, but art had no connection with political action, nor with the good life of personal relations and refined sensations which could only be enjoyed by the individual in separation from society. J. M. Keynes and Leonard Woolf were, it is true, in their different ways, politically involved and influential : but Keynes loved the painter Duncan Grant and Leonard Woolf was married to Virginia. To both, 'Bloomsbury' stood for the values of living.

These attitudes are reflected in Forster's novels, in which the good characters have liberal values but subordinate them to 'personal relations'. Business, power, government for Forster belong to the world of 'telegrams and anger'. That Margaret or Helen Schegel should carry their socialism further than sitting on a few committees, and those difficult relations with Henry Wilcox and Leonard Bast which test their principles, seems unthinkable. And although Fielding, Aziz and the other characters who fight on the side of the angels are opposed to the British Raj, it is difficult to think of them taking any effective political action. They attempt to resolve their problems through personal relations between British and Indians. Their chief grievance against the Raj is that it makes personal relations impossible.

Forster's anti-politics, anti-power, anti-business attitude is implicit also in the novels of D. H. Lawrence, Virginia Woolf and Aldous Huxley, which have so little else in common. The separation of the world of private values imagined in art from the public values of business, science, politics was an essential part of the victory of the generation for whom 'the world changed in 1910' against their elders, Shaw, Wells, Bennett and Galsworthy. The accusation levelled against the 'Georgian' novelists was that they depicted characters who were conditioned by the social circumstances in which they lived. The aim of D. H. Lawrence and Virginia Woolf was to create in their novels isolated creatures of unique awareness with sensibility transcending their material circumstances.

Of course I do not mean that Lawrence had no political sympathies : still less that he had views in common with the liberal ones of Virginia Woolf and E. M. Forster. In his novels those characters like Birkin and Aaron, who are representative of the politically searching Lawrence, shop around in the contemporary world of action looking for lords of life who are passionate, violent and anti-democratic. Bertrand Russell, after some dealings with Lawrence during a few months towards the end of the First World War – when Lawrence toyed with the idea of founding some kind of brain (Bertrand Russell)-and-blood (D. H. Lawrence) political movement – came to the conclusion (stated thirty years afterward) that Lawrence's blood-and-soil view of life was later realized in the horrors of Nazism. What I do mean is that, apart from this one disastrous attempt to get together with Russell and the Cambridge intelligentsia, and apart from his general sympathy with what might be termed bloody-bodiedness (in Germany, Italy or Mexico), Lawrence found the world of public affairs, business and any kind of social co-operation, utterly antipathetic. He wrote a letter to Forster (in September 1922) charging him with 'a nearly deadly mistake in glorifying those *business* people in *Howards End*'. and adding that 'business is no good' – a conclusion with which he might have found his correspondent concurred, had he bothered to read Forster's novel.

Different as E. M. Forster, Virginia Woolf and D. H. Lawrence were, they all agreed that the novel should be concerned with awareness of life deeper than the conscious mind of the 'old novelistic character' and the computable human social unit. Lawrence in his essay on Galsworthy, and Virginia Woolf in her discussion of Arnold Bennett in her famous lecture 'Mr Bennett and Mrs Brown' attack Galsworthy and Bennett on similar grounds : that the characters in their books are 'social units'.

Although the Bloomsbury generation (I call them this to make them immediately distinguishable) sympathized with the anti-fascism of Auden, as also of Julian Bell and John Cornford, they were also horrified at the idea of poetry being compromised by politics. Virgina Woolf's *Letter to a Young Poet* (1935) is a subdued but troubled protest at the spectacle of sensitive and talented young Oxford and Cambridge poets echoing public matters with a public voice and not writing out of a Wordsworthian isolation, solitary among the solitary reapers. And E. M. Forster, with politeness and forbearance, indicated the underlying grief of Cambridge friends when he wrote that the future probably lay with communism but that he did not want to belong to it.

John Cornford was seven years younger than Julian Bell, who was almost contemporaneous with Auden, Day Lewis, MacNeice and myself. In our speeded-up century, those few years marked a 'generation gap'. Our earlier Oxford generation, with that which we valued most in ourselves – the poetic imagination – secretly identified with the generation of Forster and Virginia Woolf. And Julian Bell had begun by doing this but later – being born into Bloomsbury – had rebelled against the parents and aunt and, in effect, joined Cornford's Cambridge generation.

For John Cornford's generation of anti-fascist undergraduate agitators at Cambridge, and of the Oxford October Club, did not cherish our generation's sense of the supreme importance of maintaining the distinction between public and private worlds. This difference of generations is also reflected in the seven years' difference between Julian Bell and John Cornford. Cornford became completely politicized, but for Bell, to have to choose between personal loyalties and the public cause was always agonizing. By upbringing anti-political, his choice would have been always for personal values, had he not come to think of anti-fascism as a human loyalty beyond other public politics. But even so, he remained conscious of entering a new era where private loyalties had to be sacrificed to revolutionary politics. The private ones of poetry and of love for his family had to submit to the public ones of anti-fascism. Yet when he went to Spain, in joining an ambulance unit rather than the International Brigade, he sacrificed his interest in war and strategy to his parents' pacifism. He chose not to break his mother's heart : and he did not do so until he got to Spain and was killed there.

For Cornford, Julian Bell's junior by seven years, however, there was no question but that personal values had to be sacrificed to the public cause. All that mattered was to defeat fascism. For him, and for his already 'new generation', choices had to be decided by the Marxist interpretation of history. Subjective motives did not count.

In the jargon of the new communistic generation, all our seven-years-previous-generation's scruples about personal relations and subjective feelings could be consigned to the dustbin of liberal inhibitions. Cornford's conviction of the superiority of Marxist 'scientific objectivity' over personal squeamishness is the dominating theme of his poetry. Leaving the girl who is mother to his child, the communist reason becomes the image of the surgeon's knife cutting away the soft rot of compassion :

Though parting's as cruel as the surgeon's knife,
It's better than the ingrown canker, the rotten leaf.
All that I know is I have got to leave.
There's new life fighting in me to get at the air,
And I can't stop its mouth with the rags of old love.
Clean wounds are easiest to bear.

The assurance with which he asserts the superiority of the ideological 'new life' struggling in him over the real new life – a child – seen oddly as an 'ingrown canker' – struggling in her, tells a lot about young human nature dominated by an ideology.

To say that Julian Bell could not, except through changing his nature, have discovered such impersonal grounds for apparent callousness is not to say that he did not behave egotistically towards his mistresses (whom Stansky and Abrahams list as A, B, C, D, etc., far down the alphabet). The difference is that Bell would have found a subjective personal reason for justifying conduct which Cornford justified by an 'objective' one.

To most literary-minded readers, Bell will seem more interesting than Cornford because he is the more self-searching and literary character. Certainly his personality and his relations with his relations make fascinating reading. It is part of the excellence of their book that the authors, having put the reader in possession of some of the facts, often leave him wondering. For instance, when Bell wrote that dissertation *The Good and All That* which, it was hoped, would get him a fellowship at King's, there were plenty of psychological reasons why he should make a hash of it. On the one hand he wished to please his Cambridge mentors by writing an essay on good and evil in the manner of the discussions of the Apostles, but on the other hand, 'more perhaps than he himself realized, Julian was in full revolt against his Bloomsbury philosophical friends and relations, and their static conception of "states of mind" as values in themselves, or consequences that might ensue from them.' The confusedness was perhaps in part the result of a naïve desire not to shock Roger Fry, to whom the dissertation was sent for a report. This was of course a model of tolerance and fairmindedness. How *liberal*!

Anna Russell, in her famous burlesque skits on plots of Wagner's operas, points out (wrongly) that Siegfried had the misfortune never to have met a lady who was not his aunt. There was something of such a burlesque Siegfried about the burly young Julian Bell, who gives one the impression of always encountering very understanding Bloomsbury aunts. He certainly developed something of an anti-aunt complex. But, as with the other Siegfried, we are also left with a further question on our minds – wasn't this young hero after all a bit obtuse?

John Cornford was priggish but not at all obtuse, and it is this which in the end makes him more interesting than Bell. He was a Greek hero rather than a confused Wagnerian one, his speciality being the cutting through of Gordian knots. He dealt with family, school, Cambridge, love affairs, the problems dividing the poet from the man of action, all in the same way – cut right through them with the surgical knife of objective action. As between poetry and fighting in Spain, he decidedly chose the latter, after he left Cambridge :

> Poetry had become a marginal activity, and a private one. He never discussed his work with his friends in the party; most of them did not even know until after his death that he had been a poet . . . In the rare moments when he was free to do so, he wrote both personal and political poems. The latter represent a conscious effort to 'objectify' his ideas and attitudes as a revolutionary participator, and to transform them into revolutionary poetry.

Instead of being, like Julian Bell, a poet stifled by his need to take action, John Cornford put poetry aside and took part in the Spanish Civil War, but from this, and out of the ideology with which he tempered his will and determination, a hard clear new poetry of the objective will began to emerge. Sketchy, a bit turgid, yet effective, his poetry is dominated by the communist idea of transforming the dialectic into history – hammered out of his mind and body deliberately situated on the side of the proletariat :

> The past, a glacier, gripped the mountain wall,
> And time was inches, dark was all.
> But here it scales the end of the range,
> The dialectic's point of change,
> Crashes in light and minutes to its fall.
>
> Time present is a cataract whose force
> Breaks down the banks even at its source
> And history forming in our hand's
> Not plasticine but roaring sands,
> Yet we must swing it to its final course.

The attempt here is to write a secular communist poetry corresponding to religious metaphysical poetry. It is blurred because Marxism, in common with other analytic and scientific systems cannot be taken outside its method and terms, and interpreted imagistically, or converted into a mystique, without in the process losing its mechanical or scientific precision. The precision of science cannot be translated into the precision of poetry. Here the Marxist poet is encountering the difficulty of other modern poets who try to invent a mythology for their poetry in a secular world. Nevertheless, it is clear that Cornford was attempting to write ideological poetry. The ideology – the vision – is materialist. I cannot agree with Stansky and Abrahams that 'the abstractions and metaphors proliferate, taking us still further from reality and deeper into the visionary world of the seer.' From the Marxist standpoint, what is wrong with such a diagnosis is the idea that 'abstractions' (if they are 'correct') inevitably lead away from reality instead of penetrating deeper into it. Cornford might, then, perhaps have become a Marxist visionary or seer. And but for Stalin and the Marxists, this would perhaps not be a contradiction in terms.

In the thirties, anti-fascism was predominantly a reaction

of middle-class young men brought up in a liberal atmosphere, against the old men in power, of their own class, who, while talking about freedom and democracy, were not prepared to denounce Hitler or support the Spanish Republic. This older generation feared that the price of supporting the democratically elected Spanish and Republican Government would be that of giving aid and comfort to the communists, whom they detested considerably more than they did the fascists. That the old who professed liberal principles did not see the threat of fascism to democracy, or that, seeing it, they did not take action against the dictators, seemed to the young a betrayal of basic liberal principles by liberals. In the thirties, 'liberal' became a term of contempt. Cornford and Bell were not just young Oedipuses subconsciously wishing to destroy their father's image. They had conscious reasons for attacking it : their father Laius was a liberal.

REACTIONARIES

During the decade of the Popular Front the English anti-fascist writers became, as it were, honorary French intellectuals. This was due to the international tradition of the leftist intelligentsia. But fascism and the movements of the European right, were not internationalist in the same way. They differed in each country. Thus Yeats, Eliot and Pound seemed to be making a leap in the dark when they attempted to connect their own kind of conservative traditionalism, even when it was called 'royalism' and 'catholicism', with the politics of a Mussolini or a Hitler.

The political attitudes of Yeats, Eliot, Pound, Wyndham Lewis, D. H. Lawrence, consisted largely of gestures towards some movement, idea or leader that seemed to stand for the writer's deeply held sense of tradition. Such gestures were largely rhetorical. The politics of these writers were projections of their hatred of fragmented modern civilization and the idea of 'progress'. They were sometimes deeply meditated, sometimes irresponsible, attempts to translate traditionalist attitudes into programmes of action. But there was never an international 'traditionalist conservative front' corresponding to the 'popular front'. There were no meetings of the reactionaries in literature. Doubtless Mussolini, Hitler or Franco, if they ever learned that they were supported by W. B. Yeats, T. S. Eliot, Ezra Pound, and Wyndham Lewis would have taken credit for having such distinguished admirers. But they would never have thought of these great figures as part of a single international traditionalist movement with a single conservative ideology.

Whereas the leftist anti-fascist writers – believing that the overthrow of fascism was the most important task of their generation – discussed whether their writing should not perhaps be the instrument of a cause which they identified with that of the 'people', the reactionaries thought merely that they should perhaps support those leaders and political thinkers who seemed to be occupied in defending the past European tradition. However, they never thought that they should put their talents at the service of the ideas of these politicians and ideologists, or of their parties. On the contrary, they looked to the fascists as supporters of the traditions which they, the poets and writers, represented. Wyndham Lewis, for instance, never supposed that he should become the mouthpiece of Hitler and the ideas put forward in *Mein Kampf*. He had in fact a rather supercilious attitude towards Hitler whom he patted (metaphorically) on the back for having expressed rather crudely certain ideas already in the mind of Wyndham Lewis. Eliot was even more patronizing towards the fascists in regard to their ideas, even when he applauded some of their political actions. He regarded the fascists, Nazis and English blackshirts as rather inferior exponents of the ideas put forward earlier in the century by Charles Maurras. As an admirer of Maurras, he criticized British fascism, together with communism for its lack of intellectual content. On the one occasion when he met Mussolini, Pound was favourably impressed, because he thought that Mussolini, having read a few lines of the *Cantos* and pronounced them *'amusante'*, was superior to grudging literary critics, in recognizing the genius of Ezra Pound.

There is then this immense difference between the politics of the reactionary writers and that of the leftists. The reactionaries never thought that they should put their art at the service of the authoritarian fascist leaders, in the way that many leftists thought that they should put theirs at the service of Marxism and of the political bureaux which laid down the Communist Party lines. The reactionary writers never thought that they should 'go over' to the most aristocratic and conservative interests in the society, identifying their whole behaviour with the pattern of their lives, in the way that leftist writers (and most of all George Orwell) thought that they should 'go over' to the proletariat in order, in all their thinking and being and creating, to identify themselves completely with the working-class interest.

On the contrary, the reactionaries tended to think of the fascist parties as potential mercenaries who might perhaps be the armies defending the past civilization of which they, the great artists (those whom Wyndham Lewis called 'the party of genius'), were the intellectual leaders. If Hitler and Mussolini had cast themselves in the role of Defenders of the European Past, maybe they should be encouraged. That was Wyndham Lewis's attitude and when Yeats, for a short time, wrote songs for General O'Duffy's Blue Shirts, it was because he too thought that the soldiers of the right might be the mercenaries of past civilization with its artist-princes.

The reactionaries had a shared vision of the greatness of the European past which implied hatred and contempt for the present. It might be said that all their most important work was an attempt to relate their writing to this central vision. On the secondary level of their attempts to carry forward the vision into politics, there is a good deal of peripheral mess, resulting from their search for politics corresponding to their love of past religion, art, discipline and order. Their politics showed that they cared less for politics than for art.

Mr John Harrison, in his book *The Reactionaries*, takes some remarks of Orwell as his text which he sets out to illustrate with examples drawn from his authors. This text is worth examining :

> The relationship between fascism and the literary intelligentsia badly needs investigating, and Yeats might well be the starting point. He is best studied by someone like Mr Menon who knows that a writer's politics and religious beliefs are not excrescences to be laughed away, but something that will leave their mark even on the smallest detail of his work.

This sounds plausible enough, though it is perhaps too off-hand to bear the weight of Mr Harrison's thesis. But objections arise. If it were true that a writer's politics and religious beliefs extend from a centre outward into every smallest detail of his work, then the converse would also be true : that one could deduce his party loyalties from an analysis of any smallest detail of his work, regardless of whether the writer thought that he supported these politics.

What is questionable is Orwell's loose bracketing of religious and political beliefs, and his assumption that it is comparatively easy to discover what a writer believes politically. But it is not simple, for a writer of genius writes out of his unique vision of life, and not to demonstrate shared attitudes. Orwell appears to think that Yeats's symbolism, mythology, imagery – his poetry, in a word – are projections on to the plane of the imagination of his political and religious beliefs. It is really the other way round. Yeats's religion and politics are attempts to relate his intuitive poetic vision to beliefs and political action. Yeats's fascism, not his poetry, *was* an excrescence. It grew rather approximately and grossly from the centre of his poetic imagination which was neither approximate nor gross. To anyone who reads *A Vision* or his journals and prose, it must be quite clear that his opinions are attempts to rationalize the intuitions of his imagination. They are perhaps irresponsible attempts to be politically responsible.

Add to this that even when they are stated as prose, one cannot discuss Yeats's beliefs without making many qualifications. Outside of believing in art and in some universe of the spirit in which the imaginings of poets become literal truth, Yeats himself was uncertain as to what he believed. He cultivated beliefs and attitudes in himself for the purpose of propping up the symbolism of his poetry. He also had a sharp picture of a materialist world which undermined his world of the poetic imagination : this was Bernard Shaw's Fabian philosophy and belief in material progress. That which to Shaw was superstition and reaction recommended itself as belief and action to Yeats.

Dr Conor Cruise O'Brien, in *Writers and Politics*, has drawn up a formidable list in Yeats's pro-fascist statements, including one or two sympathetic to Hitler. But to the reader who thinks that Yeats's poems, and not his opinions, matter, it will seem, I think, that he used the political stage properties of the thirties in the same way that he used the assertions of his esoteric system set out in *A Vision* – as a scenario stocked with symbols and metaphors. To Yeats writing the tragic-gay poetry of his old age, Hitler had the seductive charm of an apocalyptic cat.

What is disturbing about the reactionaries is not that they were occasionally betrayed by intoxication with their own ideas and fantasies into supporting dictators who would, given the opportunity, certainly have disposed very quickly of them, but that in the excess of their hatred of the present and their love of the past, they developed a certain cult of inhumanity. One has to ask, though : was not their renaissance vision enormously valuable to us, and could it have been stated without dramatizing the statuesque figures of a visionary past against the twittering ghosts of the disintegrated present?

Eliot's political views, like those of Yeats, are a system hastily thrown out with the intention of defending a spiritual world deriving strength from the past, against modern materialism. One suspects that Eliot was convinced intellectually, as a critic, and not with his imagination, as a poet, of the necessity of defending traditional values by political actions. Without the example of T. E. Hulme and without some cheer-leading from Ezra Pound and some satiric pushing from Wyndham Lewis, Eliot would scarcely have made those remarks about liberalism and progress, which seem casual asides, and which yet set him up as authoritarian, defender of the monarchy and the faith. In his role of political commentator in the *Criterion* he must have baffled readers who did not realize that his mind was moving along lines laid down by Charles Maurras. There is something cloak-and-dagger about the anti-Semitic passages in the Sweeney poems which Mr Harrison inevitably relies on to demonstrate his thesis:

> The smoky candle end of time
>
> Declines. On the Rialto once.
> The rats are underneath the piles.
> The jew is underneath the lot.
> Money in furs.

Of course this is distasteful caricature, more so today than when it was written. But the Jew who is 'underneath the lot' is the symbol of a conspiratorial capitalism.

That Eliot, Yeats, Pound and Lawrence were all 'exiles' (and Wyndham Lewis a self-declared outsider – 'the Enemy') has a bearing on their politics. The exile is particularly apt to dramatize his mind or soul moving through a world of metaphors. Pound and Eliot left what they regarded as barbarous America to come to civilized Europe, where they found, in the First World War :

> There died a myriad,
> And of the best, among them,
> For an old bitch gone in the teeth,
> For a botched civilization.

Their poetry exalted the past which they had sought among the Georgian poets and found only embalmed in museums, and it derided the present, the decay of standards. They were, politically, Don Quixotes of the new world armed to rescue the Dulcinea of the old – whom they quickly discovered to be an old hag with rotten teeth. The aim of their polemical criticism was to re-invent the past, and convert it into a modern weapon against the arsenals of the dead men stuffed with straw.

They were attracted to those politics whose programme presented social and economic conditions as metaphors describing and dealing with the state of civilization. The appeal of politics in the guise of metaphor is curiously shown in the great attraction of Social Credit theories for a number of writers, including not only Eliot and Pound but also Edwin Muir – during the late twenties and the thirties. Social Credit is easy to visualize. One visualizes property, capital and manufactured products listed on one side of a column and on the other side money – credit – being printed equal to the wealth created. Since Schacht and Mussolini actually made adjustments to the German and Italian economies along Social Credit lines, Social Credit seemed to be an element which could be abstracted from fascism and applied to other systems. For reactionaries who could not swallow violence, it was a kind of fascism without tears.

Students of Ezra Pound's *Cantos* will observe how metaphors, drawn from a reading of economics, visualized and then applied to describe the moral situation, are used sometimes to justify inhuman attitudes. A famous example is the passage about usury in which Pound explains that the introduction of usury into the economic system falsifies the line drawn by the painter, causes his hand to err.

The left also of course had their metaphors, which by making history appear a poetic act tended to regard human beings as words to be acted upon, deleted if necessary, so that the poem might come right. The word 'liquidate' applied to killing all the members of some social class is, after all, a poetiç metaphor.

On a level of false rhetoric, so far from there being a separation of politics from poetry, there is a dangerous convergence. Marxism, because it regards history as malleable material to be manipulated by the creative will of the Marxist, is rich in raw material of poetry. Marx concretized the language of economics.

The temptation for the poet is to take over the rhetoric of political will and action and translate it into the rhetoric of poetry. If there is a sin common to Auden's *Spain*, the anti-Semitic passages in Eliot's Sweeney poems, the fascistic passages in Pound's *Cantos*, Wyndham Lewis's adulation of what he calls 'the party of genius' (meaning Michelangelo and Wyndham Lewis), Lawrence's worship of the dynamic will of nature's aristocrats (in *The Plumed Serpent*), it is that the poet has allowed his scrupulous poet's rhetoric of the study of 'minute particulars' to be overwhelmed by his secret yearning for a heroic public rhetoric of historic action. Sensibility has surrendered to will, the Keatsian concept of poetic personality to the dominating mode of political character.

In a period when poets seemed imprisoned in their private worlds, their occasional acts of surrender to the excitement of a public world of action in the service of what they could pretend to themselves was a civilizing cause is understandable. But the reactionariness of the 'reactionaries' is the weakness, not the strength, of their work. William Empson writes in his odd, sympathetic preface to

Mr Harrison's book that he doubts whether the political issues of 'their weakness for fascism' was 'the central one'. He adds :

> Now that everything is so dismal we should look back with reverence on the great age of poets and fundamental thinkers, who were so ready to consider heroic remedies. Perhaps their gloomy prophecies have simply come true.

We (and here by 'we' I mean the thirties writers) not only look back on Yeats, Eliot, Pound and Lawrence with reverence, but we also revered them at the time. It is important to understand that we thought of them as a greater generation of artists more dedicated and more gifted than ourselves. They made us reflect that we were a generation less single-minded in our art, but which had perhaps found a new subject – the social situation. We did not think this could lead to better work than theirs; we saw that young poets could not go on writing esoteric poetry about the end of civilization. In their end-games were our game-beginnings. Our generation reacted against the same conventions of Georgian poetry and the novel as did the generation of T. S. Eliot, Virginia Woolf, D. H. Lawrence and E. M. Forster. They were indeed our heroes.

Pound, Wyndham Lewis and Roy Campbell were the only reactionaries whose public attitudes we sometimes attacked : with the mental reservation that we thought them zanies anyway. As for Eliot, Yeats and Lawrence, if we minimized their statements about politics, there was much in their deepest political insights with which we agreed.

> Things fall apart; the centre cannot hold;
> Mere anarchy is loosed upon the world . . .

This describes our situation. By comparison the fact that Yeats went out and supported General O'Duffy seemed scarcely relevant. He was being just 'silly, like us'. No poem could show better than 'The Second Coming' how wrong Orwell was to approach Yeats's poetry as a symptom of his fascism. To us, his fascism seemed a misconception, but nevertheless it rose from deep political (and here the word seems quite inadequate) insight.

It is a pity that Mr Harrison, instead of accepting at their face value labels like 'left' and 'reactionary', did not compare at a deeper level than that of political parties the social vision of the poets of the thirties and the older generation. He might have found then that the two generations often agreed in their diagnoses : they came to opposite conclusions with regard to remedies. He might also have found that the younger generation, in coming to their revolutionary conclusions, owed their view that we were living in a revolutionary situation to the insights of the reactionaries.

Stansky and Abrahams point out that John Cornford, while he was still a schoolboy, was led to communism by reading *The Waste Land*. 'He believed it to be a great poem, read it not as a religious allegory . . . but as an anatomy of capitalist society in decay; it shaped his style, but more important, it was a preface to his politics.'

To the imagination, poetry does not preach Party programmes. It penetrates into the depths of an external situation and shows what is strange and terrible. Eliot drew conclusions from his own poetic insight with his intellect. Cornford disagreed not with the poetic insight but with the secondary political conclusions when he wrote :

The Waste Land . . . is of great importance not for the pleasure it gives, but for its perfect picture of the disintegration of a civilization . . . But something more than description, some analysis of the situation is needed. And it is here that Eliot breaks down. He refuses to answer the question he has so perfectly formulated. He retreats into the familiar triangle – Classicism, Royalism,

Anglo-Catholicism. He has not found an answer to the question in resignation. Rather he has resigned himself to finding no answer.

Eliot's imagination which can give the 'perfect picture of disintegration' is seen by Cornford as posing the question to which his intellect gives the answer – the wrong answer according to Cornford (just as Yeats gave the wrong answers to his insights), but even he, the convinced communist undergraduate about to go to Spain, cared more that the question should have been posed than that the answer should be 'correct', for the question suggests what was to him the 'correct' answer – which the subsequent history of Stalinist Russia also showed to have been wrong.

What was common to modern poets between 1910 and 1930 was their condemnation of a society which they saw as the disintegration of civilization. Given this agreed-on line, it was possible to be on the reactionary or the revolutionary side of it. The reactionaries, on their side, asked : 'How can there be new life?' The awesome achievement of the earlier generation was to have created for their contemporaries a vision of the whole past tradition which had a poignant immediacy : giving shattered contemporary civilization consciousness of its own past greatness, like the legendary glimpse of every act of his past life in the eyes of a man drowning. Without the awareness of drowning, of the end of the long game, the apprehended moment could not have been so vivid. Thus the gloomy prophecies of the future, and the consequent weakness for reactionary politics, were the dark side of an intensely burning vision.

The liberals, the progressives, the anti-fascists, could not invest their writing with a vision of the values of future civilization as great as the reactionaries' vision of past values. Perhaps, though, they secretly agreed with the reactionaries that the genius of our civilization which had flickered on since the Renaissance was soon to be extinguished. E. M. Forster, whose work stands midway between the idea of past and present, sees the greatness of England and Europe as over. The past commands his love, though the causes which should ultimately make people better off – freedom of the peoples of the world from the old imperialisms, greater social justice, etc., – command his loyalty. But his loyalty inspires him with no new love, and he has no enthusiasm for the liberated, materially better world which he feels morally bound to support.

The anti-fascists in the end accepted or were influenced by the idea that the struggle for the future meant abandoning nostalgia for a past civilization. They had now to emphasize 'new life', a new culture not obsessed with the past. Julian Bell and John Cornford came to feel that in putting the cause before everything they must be prepared even to jettison their own poetry. And they found themselves relieved to do so. In 1932, when he started becoming interested in politics, John Cornford wrote to his mother : 'I have found it a great relief to stop pretending to be an artist,' and in the same letter he told her that he had bought *'Kapital* and a good deal of commentary, which I hope to find time to tackle this term. Also *The Communist Manifesto.'* In renouncing being an artist he is also turning his back on the world of his mother, Frances Cornford, the Georgian poet. Julian Bell experienced an immense sense of relief when he decided to abandon literature and go to Spain. In doing so he is turning his back on his mother, Vanessa Bell, the painter. If Auden and Isherwood had written a play on the theme of Cornford and Bell, one can well imagine that the deaths of these heroes on the battlefield would have been seen as the finale of a dialogue with a chorus of artistic mothers and Bloomsbury aunts.

Feelings and motives involved here are complex. Uncertainty about their vocations, rebellion against their mothers and against the values of the literary world of Cambridge, Oxford and London, a suppressed anti-intellectualism and an expression of the tendency of the young in that decade to interpret all current issues as a conflict between principles of 'life' and 'death', the 'real' and the 'unreal', enter in. The reader of Stansky and Abrahams cannot help noting that in a decade when people were always being reproached for 'escapism' the immersion into the life of action and political choice filled Bell and Cornford with an elation remarkably like that of escape – escape from having to be poets. Escape is wrong if it means escape from high standards to lower or more relaxed ones. In their renunciation of those standards of their parents which were, perhaps, too aesthetic, Cornford and Bell shared a tendency to escape into accepting means which were perilously close to those of their fascist enemies. Thus Julian Bell writes :

> The disgraceful part of the German business is not that the Nazis kill and torture their enemies; it is that socialists and communists let themselves be made prisoners instead of first killing as many Nazis as they can.

And Bell states still more strongly the objection to the liberals. His reaction is all the more striking because it is so much a renunciation of that pacifism which was one of his deepest ties with his parents :

> Most of my friends are unutterably squeamish about means; they feel that it would be terrible to use force or fraud against anyone . . . Even most communists seem to me to have only a hysterical and quite unrealistic notion about violent methods . . . I can't imagine anyone of the *New Statesman* doing anything 'unfair' to an opponent . . . Whereas for my own part . . . I can't feel the slightest qualms about the notion of doing anything effective, however ungentlemanly and unchristian, nor about admitting to myself that certain actions would be very unfair indeed . . .

and he ends the same letter with a sentence that is surely very revealing :

I don't feel, myself, as if I could ever be satisfied to do nothing but produce works of art, or even really nothing but leading a private life and producing works in the intervals.

I do not quote these passages because I think them characteristic of Cornford or Bell (in fact they are out of character) but because of the light which – paradoxically – they throw on the relationship of the thirties generation with an older one. This balances the violence of the reactionaries supporting fascism in the name of art, against the violence of the leftists prepared to sacrifice art to the cause of anti-fascism.

The reactionaries cared passionately for past values. Their nostalgia misled them into sympathizing with whatever jack-booted corporal or demagogue set himself up in defence of order. As the history of Ezra Pound shows, the results of this could be tragic. But in their own lives, their own behaviour and activity, their work, they did put literature before politics, and their first concern was to preserve the civilization without which, as they thought, neither past nor future literature could survive. They did not, as the anti-fascist writers did, abandon or postpone their literary tasks. For the anti-fascists allowed themselves, rightly or wrongly, to be persuaded that civilization could only be saved by action : the logical consequence of this attitude was to put writing at the service of necessity as dictated by political leaders.

There was, then, the paradox that the reactionaries who were on the side of the past, the dead, lived, in spite of everything, for the sake of literature, whereas circumstances drove the most sincere anti-fascists – men like Cornford, Bell, Fox and Caudwell – to death for the sake of a public cause which they had made absolute. The reactionaries wrote out of their tragic sense of modern life. The Cornfords and Bells lived and died the tragedy.

PART FOUR

The Sixties and Seventies

Background to the Sixties

Apart from the selections from a journal which I kept when, in 1965, I was Poetry Consultant at the Library of Congress in Washington D.C., this book is scarcely concerned with the sixties and seventies. The concluding essays in it, being memoirs, are largely retrospective. The sixties was an interval of boom and the Beatles in England. It was above all the decade of American agony; of the assassination of President Kennedy followed by the anguished presidency of L. B. Johnson.

It was the first decade, surely, in which American events seemed to cast a shadow across the world. The assassination of Kennedy was received in London and Paris with awestruck horror almost as great as that felt in Washington and New York. This was partly because it was an occasion – like the missile crisis over Cuba – in which something that happened in America suddenly seemed to involve the fate of the West, if not the whole world. But it was also surely because many Europeans had received an impression of the chiselled features, the vibrant, forced intensity of speech, the look of suppressed pain and passion, of Kennedy, as both strikingly American and yet evocative of the Roman Empire. Features for chiselling on an intaglio or stamping on a medal, like those of a young, fatally struck-down emperor. One half of America seemed to be playing Roman imperial politics all through the sixties, while an impassioned minority provided a chorus of rage and contempt which ultimately pulled down the imperialists.

The Kennedy tragedy also shocked Europeans as having a peculiarly American kind of pathos : that of a private tragedy on which a world-wide public one was superimposed. It awoke echoes of the Lindbergh tragedy of the late twenties : the very American young man, the epitome of physical courage and dramatic flair, struck at by some hand which rises out of an abyss of the obscure forces of American violence.

No one could be more different from Kennedy than Lyndon B. Johnson, a man whose great sensitivity was concealed under a rhinoceros-hide exterior, the accents of Texas and a shower of obscenities and expletives. But his image does not in the eyes of non-Americans contradict the Roman imperial theme. There were Roman emperors like this brought in from the provinces and made to carry out the compulsive projects of the army. One can see Lyndon B. Johnson looking Roman in marble, with the deeply furrowed lines and folds of skin reflected by those of the toga.

For Europeans who had lived through the events of the thirties – the war and the post-war era of the loss of European empires – America in the sixties might have been seen playing over very rapidly the reel of their disasters. America, traditionally anti-imperialist – at least as far as other nations' empires are concerned – had watched the dismantling of the British, French and Dutch empires with a sense of righteous glee. Unfortunately the surge of anti-communism in America which arose in the fifties did not accord with that of anti-European-imperialism. The abandonment of the European empires produced power vacuums, or, even worse, whirlpools of leftism which sucked in communism, to take the place of the British, the French and the Dutch imperialists. Anti-communist America suddenly found itself in the position of facing the prospect of communist empires in Asia instead of capitalist ones. On a global scale, America became conscious of the predicament which in the past obsessed the British. That of a nation surrounded by seas (in a world of shrinking distances, America is an island) confronted by a continental landmass controlled by no single nation – but which might at some time unify and confront the island with its overwhelming population, its autocratic unifying government, its resources and its armies.

Although the American opponents of the war in Vietnam had the sympathy of those Europeans who had always been anti-imperialist in their own countries, I think that the general reaction of Europeans (including leftists) to the war in Vietnam was spectatorial : Europeans were horrified frozen onlookers, seeing America fall into elephant-traps in which they had lost so many lives, so much armaments themselves. And in America, on the campuses, thousands of young people made those protests against a colonial war which some British had made during the Boer War and with regard to India and during the period of anti-fascism, which was also anti-imperialist. In America, however, protests achieved an intensity of violence and frenzy which, if paralleled in Europe, took a peculiarly American form. One of the mysterious phenomena of the present century is American anti-Americanism. This seemed to dominate intellectual life in America in the twenties; but in the sixties it was much more violent and, although it quietened down after the end of the war in Vietnam, it is perhaps a force in American life to be reckoned with. In the twenties it took the form of many young Americans going to Europe and adopting a European lifestyle. This meant that when, after the abolition of prohibition, the disgruntled exiles returned to their own country, they could easily drop their European manners. But in the sixties, anti-American Americans adopted their own lifestyle which became a counter-culture within the existing one.

In 1968, the hysteria of the decade attained its climax and spread like a fire across the campuses of America and the world. Looking back on the sixties, one notes a tendency of Americans, as individuals, as groups – even as institutions – not merely to commit themselves to some cause which is obviously temporary, if not ephemeral, but to do so sometimes with almost suicidal intensity, like those American poets of this generation, who, in living out the intensity of the emotions expressed in their poetry, have either taken their own lives, or come to willed violent ends.

Teachers at the Sorbonne in Paris in 1968 got excited about the student rising there, but they did not regard it as the end of everything. It brought to mind ferocious actions by students of the University of Paris in medieval times, and reminded them that traditionally the university was a kind of city of youth within the greater adult city. The tearing up of paving stones and erecting of barricades had an element of play-acting of scenes from the French Revolution, accompanied by oratory and ritualistic acts of destruction – the setting alight of motor cars – symbolic consumer goods. There was something hypnotic about the Paris 'événements'. The students by sheer display, by uttering of maledictions, and by black magic, almost blew the immensely powerful near-dictator, General de Gaulle, out of office. At one time he was reduced to touring the scattered bases of the French army by helicopter to re-assure himself as to its loyalty. It was the failure of the workers to support the students – whose pranks repelled the workers' sense of stolid bourgeois virtue – which put paid to the student revolution.

But at Columbia University, many members of the faculty regarded the student violence and occupation of buildings as tearing the university apart, and saw the resultant damage as irreparable. This was partly, no doubt, because these academics identified with their institution to a far greater extent than did the French professors. Men like Lionel Trilling saw their whole lives being destroyed with the university and, as liberals, suffered terribly from the epithets hurled at them by the students.

I happened to be in New York at the time of the uprising at Columbia and other American universities. I visited the Columbia campus, became interested, and decided to write a book about the students of 1968 in Europe and America. This later appeared as *The Year of the Young Rebels*. Perhaps what excited me about the Columbia students was the way in which they seemed to be re-playing the actions of the Republican Army during the Spanish Civil War. This was my impression of the office of the president of the university (President Kirk) when it was occupied by the student rebels :

After the brilliant light outside it seemed dark, with bulky furniture, a very long table or desk, shadowy figures, girls and boys, both with long hair, jackets, open-neck shirts, belts, jeans, some medallions hanging from necks. A few of the students held carton cups in their hands from which they sipped soft drinks. 'Have one of the president's cigars,' someone said, and I declined, a sign that I was not taking their side. The door of the office was open and led to a corridor in which there were other groups of students standing, talking. Beyond this a door opened into a further room where there was a meeting going on. Someone explained : 'We are democratically deciding whether (a) to leave the building free of access; (b) to barricade ourselves in; and (c) whether or not to put up resistance if we are attacked.'

This use of the word 'democratic' by groups employing violent methods exactly reproduces the parlance employed by communists during the Spanish Civil War, in the International Brigade. The argument implicit is that any meeting of persons who take any kind of action is democratic, so long as decisions are arrived at by a majority vote of members of that group.

They considered each of these propositions in turn, making speeches for and against, and taking votes. A few minutes later the meeting ended and they drifted along the corridor and into the president's office, the decision having been made to barricade. Someone across the room asked me if this was like Spain. The question took me back to another scene : the University of Madrid over thirty years ago. Several of the students who in attire and hirsuteness were demonstrably followers of Castro added to the hispanic effect. What I remembered from Madrid was a large lecture theatre with lines of seats tiered down to the semi-circle of a professor's rostrum. High up in the room there were men in the slack uniforms of the Spanish militia. Some of them were reading books. Unlike the students here, they were using the university as a university, while making their revolution. On the speaker's platform there was a putrefying corpse. It could not be moved, because through a window above the platform it was in the line of fire of the window of a building just across the way, occupied by the Falangists.

This was very different from the street theatricals of the French students :

The street battles which took place near the Sorbonne in mid-May between students and police were ritualistic. In the late afternoon, while it was still daylight, the students started building their barricades. Those they built on 24 May were particularly elaborate. First they tore up paving stones and piled them up as though they were rebuilding memories of 1789, 1848, 1870. Then, in a mood of dedicated desecration, they axed down, so that they fell lengthwise across the street, a few of the sappy plane trees, spring-leafed, just awake from winter. Then they scattered over the paving stones and among the leaves, boxes, wood, trash from the uncollected garbage on the sidewalks. Lastly, as the night closed in, they tugged, pulled with much rumbling, neighbouring parked cars, with brakes of course on, but dragged along the streets just the same, and placed them on their sides, like trophies of smashed automobiles by the sculptor César, on top of the paving stones, among the branches. In an arrangement of this kind on the Boulevard Saint-Germain, they had extended the contour of a burned-out car by adding to it the quarter section of one of those wrought-iron grilles that surround the bases of trees on the boulevards, to protect the roots. After the night's fighting, this chassis had acquired a beautiful coral tint. On its pediment of bluish stones it looked like an enshrined totemistic museum object. It was left there for two or three days and much photographed by tourists who came to witness the student revolution.

✳

Background to the Sixties

That was the mood of 1968 in the West. In Eastern Europe, where the bright flame of Dubček's Prague spring still burned, it took a very different form. Instead of being against the government the students were for it, instead of burning consumer goods such as automobiles they petitioned to be allowed more of them. They did not base a revolution on the idea that they could remain all their lives twenty-one-years old, and hate the old as though they were members of an enemy nation.

While the students were staging their revolt, representatives of my own generation, and of that earlier one which we admired so much, were beginning to die. This book ends with the deaths of Eliot, Auden, MacNeice, Day Lewis and Cyril Connolly.

Journal

Art and Literature 9 (Summer 1966)

1965

26 September, New York

Dined with the Stravinskys and Robert Craft. Stravinsky seemed in very good form, talking a great deal – much about the Soviet edition of the works of Chekhov. He said how stupidly this was edited : e.g., in a stage direction, it says that a character wears *pince nez*. A note explains : '*Pince nez*, a French expression.' I.S. pointed out anyone could tell it was French. If a note were required it should be to explain what a *pince nez* is – such spectacles being unknown in the Soviet Union. He said that the Soviets had a very selected and edited conception of Chekhov.

Before dinner I had several martinis at the M——s. These were followed by more vodkas with the Stravinskys, and with wine at dinner (I.S. seemed very content, going to and fro among his guests, offering them caviare sandwiches).

At dinner we got drunk – I, most of all – and I can remember little of it except that towards the end of dinner I.S. appeared to be talking about (I think) Poles and Russians, and I was suddenly seized with a sense of the transcendent importance of Stravinsky writing a message of encouragement and faith to the young musicians and artists of that part of the world. I repeated this a good many times, sometimes appealing to Vera Stravinsky. Each time I did so, she shook her head and said in her tolerant, smiling way: 'But you know, my husband hardly ever writes letters.' . . . Anyway, we did not stay too long, getting back to our hotel about 10.30.

✳

Journal

On Friday, we took the Isaiah Berlins, Robert Lowell and Bob Silvers out to dinner at the Coffee Club. Lowell made several interesting pronouncements : that Ezra Pound is the greatest translator of the twentieth century; that the poems of Wordsworth's last ten years have – some of them – rhythmic qualities as good as *The Prelude*. He must have meant 'as the best of *The Prelude*' since it would be easy to be as good as the worst. Lowell is very taken up with translating, and asked me : 'Would you rather have an exact rendering of a masterpiece, or a poem which was equally with the original, a masterpiece in English?' – which seems a loaded way of putting the alternatives. He talked a bit about Catholicism (discussing it as though it were a thing of the past for him),[1] and said how difficult it was to think what Christ's attitude would be today were he living. Isaiah agreed, saying it was difficult to think of Christ in a world in which even the most important leaders have to say things like : 'The U.S. (or the communists) have a case, but on the other hand we have to take into account,' etc. . . .

Various dicta of Lowell keep coming back to mind : e.g., that Eliot's criticism is to the twentieth century what Arnold's was to the nineteenth, but that Arnold's is greater, wider, more generous, without the paranoid quality of some of Eliot's criticism; that he thought what made Housman a great poet was guilt about his homosexuality.

29 September, Washington
Went to the White House for the signing by President Johnson of the Arts and Humanities Bill. Arrived 9.30, waited for quarter-hour at the North West Gate where all invitations were scrupulously examined. Then went into a lobby where there were many official-looking people in dark suits. Among them the painter Morris Graves, tall, thin, bearded, like an El Greco saint, seemed outstanding. We moved from one waiting room to another, then along a corridor into a courtyard with a colonnade at the end, and chairs outdoors, where we sat down. After a time the President appeared, at first unnoticed among several

people standing on a platform in front of the colonnade. Then he moved over to a rostrum which had in front of it the enlarged insignia of the seal of the President of the U.S., and he made a speech. His face looked lined and corrugated to a point which made only two expressions possible : one, with the lines in waves, smiling; one with the lines flattened out, despondent. The President signed the document, using a battery of pens in front of him to do so. He seemed to write one part of one letter only with each pen. Then we filed past him and were each given in a box a pen with his autograph stamped on it. We shook hands. His hand seemed like the hoof of an elephant.

16 October

I telephoned Robert Lowell in N.Y. He was upset at the death of Randall Jarrell. R. J. had been ill – nervously ill – for several months, seemed to be better, went home, started teaching again, had returned to the hospital for further treatment. He walked out of the hospital and threw himself against a passing car.[2]

Randall had been Poetry Consultant at the Libary of Congress, and everyone from the reference division (to which the Poetry Consultant is attached) seemed upset. They asked me downstairs into an office where we stood round listening to the chief librarian's remarks about Randall, which were broadcast.

The thought that Jarrell had perhaps become disenchanted with poetry occurred to me. It was reinforced by the chance that a marine brought me his poems to read at the L. of C. They are interesting. He said he had stopped writing six months ago because he had become disillusioned with poetry. I asked why, and he said because he had decided that all poetry was rhetoric and he didn't see how rhetoric could cope with – or help one to live in – the modern world. He is being sent to Vietnam. He has decided to cultivate a detachment towards life and to regard fighting in the jungle simply as 'experience'.

All this relates to a fatality of American poets which is different from any English attitude that I can think of. Theodore Roethke died a few months ago, after several mental breakdowns. Lowell makes his own breakdowns the subject of some of his poetry, so that he evidently regards them as an inseparable part of his poetic persona,[3] Berryman has breakdowns, and so on. One of the things that puzzled me about Jarrell was his bitter complaint that the modern poet has no audience. I once heard him give a lecture, at Harvard, to at least a thousand people going on about this, which struck me as rather absurd, but in the light of what happened it now seems tragic. I think that American poets, far more than English ones, cling to the idea that the poet is 'unacknowledged legislator'. (I was surprised to find in Pound's letters a remark to the effect that Shelley was right about this.) They have a public concept of the efficacy of poetry : and usually they accept bitterly that the poet is quite inefficacious. The fact that they have readers, and audiences who listen to them reading their poems, does not at all console them. Indeed, the more readers and listeners they have, the more it is demonstrable that the values of American life are not affected by poetic values.

One great difference between English and American poets, ever since the early part of the century when Pound and Eliot came to England, is that the American poet feels himself to be conducting a war, through the values which he creates in his poetry, against the debased values of modern society. And this, of course, is a tragic conflict. English poets do not, like their American colleagues, reflect bitterly that all they are doing is writing poetry for other poets. Often it is exactly this they want to do.

In the evening we dined with Henry Moore and Harry Fischer the art dealer. After attending the unveiling of his large bronze at the Lincoln Center, and having a rackety two days of TV appearances, etc., in N.Y., they had gone to Chicago which they had liked better than N.Y. They were impressed by some collections they had seen in Chicago, notably those of Mary Block and Joel Starels.

After dinner, when we were having nightcaps at the bar, the talk got round to values in art. This began by my saying that I found I was less interested today in the work of Paul Klee than I had been when I was 25. Moore said he felt the same way, and it was because Klee was not really a major artist. This annoyed Fischer who said that Klee was just as good, in his own way, as Picasso. Moore said that nevertheless Picasso was a much greater painter and this was what mattered. He insisted on the importance of making comparative value judgements, on the importance of saying, for example – if one felt it to be so – that Goya was greater than Picasso, even though it might be impossible in our time for a painter like Picasso to have as central a position as Goya had in his time. Fischer bristled and said that this line of argument showed that Moore had no sense of history. Moore said that had nothing to do with it. History should not be used as an excuse for avoiding comparisons, for saying, for example, that Watteau was as good as Rembrandt, or that you were not entitled to compare them.

What stood out in all this was Moore's individualistic Renaissance idea of a hierarchy of greater and less great individual artists. He sees a line of dominating figures in his pantheon – Masaccio, Michelangelo, Rembrandt, Cézanne – who matter, and compared with them, Vermeer, Chardin, Watteau, etc., who are, as it were, minor. He likes the great figures who produce the great works.

22 *October*

Spent two days at the University of N——, Illinois. In the aeroplane on the way there, I was thinking compulsively of other things, so much so that I got into a slight panic, wondering whether I would be able to pay any attention to N—— University. Sometimes on these flying visits there is a feeling of complete unreality, as though an old movie is being run through for the thousandth time. One gets out of the plane, and walks into the airport lobby. There is a wild feeling that perhaps no one will be there to meet the plane. I am still free, perhaps I will take a taxi to the hotel, lie down on the bed, read a book, write a poem, look at TV (occasionally this has happened and I've been left alone for hours). But no, a pallid young instructor, or the head of the department, or two or three embarrassed giggling students, appearing out of nowhere, say : 'Are you Mr S?' 'We weren't sure we'd recognize you,' and I am led off to the car. If it is the young instructor, then there is nearly always evidence in the car of the young Planned Family – a baby's basket in the back seat, a miniature child's toy driving wheel parallel with that of the driver in the front seat. During the drive to the 'school', which can take anything up to four hours, frantic efforts are made to 'communicate'. Plans for the day are broken to one : the coffee hour with the students; lunch in the cafeteria, then a question hour, then an hour or so to 'rest up'; then a select dinner at 'the only moderately decent restaurant downtown', with a few of the faculty then – very sorry for you at this point – after the lecture, a party for graduate students and faculty. At this point I am struck by their extraordinary generosity, their real kindness and considerateness. We treat each other as though we are friends, with a sad feeling underneath that we will forget one another as soon as the occasion is over. They are frightfully apologetic for every inconvenience or unbargained-for demands, as though they have no idea that one is being paid as much for a few hours' appearance as they are for several days of drudgery. There is, in the end, a kind of magic of mutual appreciation and interest which works.

At N—— during question hour, a girl with a fringe and pale eyes and a voice like a mosquito said, holding out a book of my *Collected Poems* in front of her : 'Please will you read this poem and explain what it means?' Then there are the other questions : 'Why do you write?' 'How do you think of an idea for a poem?' 'When did you start writing?' Some of these questions are probably the result simply of the situation in which it is necessary to think up questions, but others come out of a real curiosity as to why anyone should do anything so apparently superfluous as write poetry : an activity which is on the whole envi-able perhaps because it results in all sorts of fillips and by-products, such as free trips to places, sinecures, lecturing and readings.

Owing to the fact that I had endless time at N——, some of these questions began to get rather near the bone, and verge on : 'Why are you here with us and not sitting at home writing poetry?' Then one has to explain that 'the poet' is not paid for writing poetry, but for talking about writing (or not writing) it. So generous are they that one becomes a kind of multiple object of sympathy . . . for being here at all and for being paid by them to be here away from one's 'real work' and not to stay home and get on with it.

As I was leaving, the little girl with the mosquito voice got into the back seat of the car in which I was being driven away, and opening my *Collected Poems* again, said : 'But you didn't quite explain this line?'

Reading one's own poems in front of an audience can be very strange. I begin with a big resolution to *concentrate* on what I am reading by paying close attention to the visual line (the life-line of any performance). The poem is called 'The Express'. 'After the first powerful plain manifesto', I begin, feeling hopeful. I'm really going to get through the ride this time without getting off that express, till it explodes into a branch of honeysuckle with the last line. It is like a film, a late 1920s film – Russian – called *TurkSib*, celebrating the opening of the trans-Siberian railway. But already I am thinking these thoughts and I am not yet at the third line which is 'But gliding like a queen, she leaves the station.' This line always embarrasses me a bit, and I begin visualizing not the express at all but an Oxford queen called M—— gliding down the High when I was an undergraduate. I was rather willowy myself and am still outsize. I wonder whether anyone has the acuteness to think it absurd – a six-foot-three poet with a limey accent and sibilant voice saying 'gliding like a queen, she leaves the station.' However, now we are off, and the verses are readable, I think, although onomatopoeic in effect :

She passes the houses which humbly crowd outside,
The gasworks, and at last the heavy page
Of death, printed by gravestones in the cemetery.

I succeed in seeing the gasworks and the heavy page of death. But, of course, I reflect, the lines 'further than Edinburgh or Rome . . .' have nothing to do with the trans-Siberian railway. And the gasworks seen as the train leaves the station are the Oxford gasworks, by the railway. And that is what I am in fact seeing now – visualizing hard – the gasworks at first shutting out everything, then as the window of the compartment slides past them – revealing tombstones like white sugar loaves, and beyond them the vertical spires. Often there are grey and white clouds in the sky, their turrets and scallop-shell curves echoing the rhythms of the grey and white domes and towers below. When I was an undergraduate there was a famous Oxford poets' walk along the side of the canal by the gasworks, what Auden called 'the most beautiful walk in Oxford'.

If there is question time and someone asks me about 'The Express' – where it came from . . . where it went to . . . what are its influences . . . I shall be able to bring some of this in, I think (like a double exposure on a negative a wide-angle shot of the first four rows begins to show beyond that of the 'dreaming spires'). Karl Shapiro wrote an essay somewhere saying that 'The Express' is about a communist revolution, and I have quite forgotten whether I thought this at the time. Quite recently a girl with a mosquito voice got up and asked whether it was about a girl losing her virginity.

It is now she begins to sing – at first quite low
Then loud, and at last with a jazzy madness –
The song of her whistle screaming at curves . . .

Now the printed page under my eyes seems torn with a
large hole, and the print that I am reading is at the edges.
In the centre there is quite other writing which I can
already envisage, in fact I must forget nothing that I am
now writing, so as to put it in my journal, about this
strange experience of thinking about writing about reading
'The Express'.

27 October
Dined with Jack Thatcher at his house near Dumbarton
Oaks. We were alone. After dinner he took me to see the
Byzantine exhibition which he is arranging and which is
to be opened on Sunday. It seems amazingly unready as
yet. Then he showed me Philip Johnson's museum for
the pre-Columbian collection. This is an absolutely stun-
ning display, a series of rooms, brilliantly illuminated
glass domes, around a central room, an enclosed patio
with a fountain : exhibits mounted on pedestals and in
cases or settings of plastic glass. The use of plastic is
revolutionary and the settings have extraordinary light-
ness and elegance. I had never before thought of plastic
glass as a medium which can produce brilliant effect.

After this we went to see what J.T. called the 'factory',
a series of connected workshops in another house where
half a dozen skilled blacks work eighteen hours a day
(sometimes literally all night) in a race against time to com-
plete the mounts in time for the Sunday opening. The best
of these coloured artisans, M——, came from the Smith-
sonian Institute, J.T. told me. M—— has very mobile,
quicksilver, intelligent features, and the scene of him and
the other blacks working made me imagine how blacks
assisting artists with mosaics at the Duomo of Venice must
have looked. M—— is the kind of *figure* one might see in
the background of a Veronese, or in a Guardi drawing.

Jack told me that M—— is a wonderfully confident technician who, on being asked whether he could do mounts far more elaborate than any of those in the Smithsonian, replied at once, 'Of course.' He also has much humour, and Jack asked him one day : 'Are all blacks as funny as you? Where do you get your sense of humour?' To which he replied : 'Maybe it is from my Irish grandmother.' J.T. told me these workers are very good at the job but liable to stop suddenly and completely. They need much supervision.

30 October

There were various writers on the faculty of H—— University whom I met. One had a theory about the connection of *Ulysses* with Dante, which he thinks much more important than that with Homer. He said he had approached Richard Ellmann about this and that Ellmann had said : 'I hope you aren't right,' dreading even more than I do, I suppose, that he might be, and that huge mines of research into the Dantesque parallels with *Ulysses* are going to be excavated under the galleries and corridors of the Homeric earthworks. A poet on the faculty who had listened in to these conversations took me aside and remarked : 'It must be trying for you having people tell you about their work; for that reason I'm not going to bother you with my poems,' which, an hour later, when I was giving him a drink at the motel, he discovered he did have on him, to the extent of about a hundred. They showed that he was serious, talented and Catholic. He confessed to some uneasiness because a colleague to whom he had shown two of the poems had remarked that their themes were homosexual. He was too cagey to say whether they really were, and some of the poems in which words like cunt were freely used could be said to compensate so fully for any phallic imagery that the responsibility for interpreting the poetry or the poet as normal or abnormal was, so to speak, cast back on the reader, who might be said to see in them his own psychology reflected as in a

Rorschach test. There were also Catholic poems. Also a long poem which was an elaborate transposition into a modern situation (that of characters met in an inn in Germany) of Chaucer's *Prologue*. All this was serious but baffling. It disturbed me a bit because it struck at my perhaps neurotically-held view that poems are not wares made to attract a consumer, or to persuade a critic to offer favourable judgement, or to perplex an editor into thinking he ought to publish them. As a matter of fact these poems may not have been written with any of these intentions. They made me reflect though that today there are so many standards of 'technique', wit, self-consciousness, sophistication, floating around, some of which are formulated into principles taught at writing schools, that the young writer is under considerable pressure to conform to these. So I am making no judgement on the poet and his poems when I say merely that they made me think of things which worry me a good deal. I know that young poets do have to be published, have to get into anthologies, have to interest critics, and that not to do any of these things – have them done to one – is like not losing one's virginity. So, up to a point, one has to regard the aggressiveness on their own behalf of young American writers as a sign of virility.

Very few writers manage to survive not losing their literary virginity, and even if they do go through life unpublished, there seems something nunnish or monkish about their work (e.g., Emily Dickinson, Gerard Manley Hopkins). So Mr —— was quite right to put his poems under my nose. All the same, the question still arises whether an intellectual supply-and-demand consciousness enters into the poems themselves : whether they are made up according to a prescription to fulfil the unconsciously imposed demands of the market. This is very difficult to answer because so much skilful stuff is done today in which the writer exploits even that which is most authentic in himself in order to produce a public commodity. I am puzzled. All I do know is that young Americans are more pressingly ambitious than the young English. A poet like —— may be ambitious even while he is in the act of writing his poem. He is all the time asking himself : 'Where does this fit in? How is it going to please?' This doesn't mean of course that he is not writing out of experiences, events, ideas independent of ambition. It means that they may enter into the work at the moment of writing, though in his particular case I have no reason to say this. It is merely that he makes me think of other cases.

Got home, tired. Thought I would go to a movie. Decided I waste too much time. In fact almost everything I do seems distraction from something better I ought to be doing . . . which relates to the preoccupations above about ambition. I ought to be writing poetry, but there is no *ought* about this. Writing poetry is the ought which has no ought. The thought, the wrong-headed sense of obligation separates into other strands of awareness. I think that being a poet is the most *intrinsic* occupation or vocation. It is the only one I know of in which the wholeness, the quality, the *virtù*, of what one is, becomes identical with the function which one performs. Vocation is profession, a poet is *quelqu'un qui écrit sans être écrivain*. Every moment, from line to line, from word to word, it is the virtue of one's being which distinguishes or fails to distinguish. Nevertheless, ambition comes in here, because there is the desire for *recognition*, and recognition is a matter of degrees, minor or major, standards : and these put one in competition with the others, some of them intensively competitive; and one submits in art to contemporary value judgements which are a parody of the stock exchange. Yet art is also outside the world, and what one is really and ultimately submitting to are the values of supreme judgement of existence. The poem that is born, instantly dies and sends the poet to his circle of the Divine Comedy. Luckily the poet has as many lives as he has poems. He may get to Purgatory on the next barque.

And putting all other reasons aside, work is its own

reason. Better after all to explore one's own truth, even if to discover it is a lie. So I decided to stay in for two days. To work at several things, methodically.

31 October
Worked yesterday, but did not altogether keep my resolution to stay in all day, as in the afternoon I went to the National Gallery, and from there to the Phillips. In the evening at the Library of Congress there was a concert of the New York Pro Musica Ensemble, playing fifteenth-century Florentine music on old instruments. After a bit I get bored by this kind of performance, beautiful though it is. One can't believe that these immaculately evening-dressed, black-tied beefy young men, these ladies in velvet gowns and with hair hanging loopwise over their impeccable foreheads, with their instruments perfect replicas of the original, have the passion, energy, vulgarity, aristocracy of the ladies and gentlemen who told one another stories in Boccaccio in a villa at Fiesole.

1 November
1.15 a.m. worked, but restlessly. Wrote letters. Telephoned London. Read A. J. P. Taylor's *English History 1914-1945*. Went last evening to the concert commemorating Dumbarton Oaks's twenty-fifth year. Concert of Bach, Mozart, Scarlatti, Stravinsky (the *Dumbarton Oaks Concerto*).

The concert in the marvellous hall, in which there is the El Greco of two draped figures meeting like waves, was excellent. Afterwards another party at Jack Thatcher's. Ralph Kirkpatrick – who had played five Scarlatti sonatas at the concert – started talking about the harpsichordist Raymond Russell who died recently. He described him as an eccentric Englishman who had a great flair for collecting : towards the end of his life he made, in two years, what is undoubtedly the world's finest collection of keyboard instruments. Ralph said R.R. took no interest in the world of literature. Once, when he was in London, Kirkpatrick and R.R. were walking along the Thames

Embankment when R.R. stopped to have a long conversation with a cripple who was in a wheel chair. 'In your English manner,' said Ralph, 'Raymond did not introduce me.' As they resumed their walk, Raymond explained that the cripple was John Hayward, and added as an afterthought that the tall gaunt stooping man pushing the wheel chair was an American poet called Eliot.

Two young blacks, very elegantly dressed, she with a high coiffure with jewels stuck into it, he in tails, walked through the audience of the already crowded hall, and took their places in the second row. They were so sensationally handsome as a couple that, quite literally, people stopped talking when they came in, and Mrs Purvis who was sitting next to me said, 'Tut! I wish people wouldn't react like that,' meaning that the silence perhaps conveyed to the black couple consciousness of their colour. I thought the young man had a resemblance to M—— whom I had seen in the workshop making plastic mounts a week previously, but I dismissed this thought from my mind, and I decided that they were Africans, the attaché at the Nigerian Embassy and his wife, perhaps. The couple seemed self-engrossed, looking at one another and smiling from time to time, with a turning of the two heads which made one see their profiles. The young man's was like an ebony carving or a cut black ivory silhouette. I started to think how Africans still, without irony being demanded from the artist, can look like works of a timeless kind of art, and how there was no white person in this distinguished gathering whose features were immediately transferable to canvas without their appearing either banal, or having to be interpreted by a process of subtle caricature.

As I discovered later, the young Negro was in fact M——, the maker of the beautiful plastic settings for the Byzantine objects.

9 *November*
Dinner with the youngish poet K—— before his reading. Talk about Randall Jarrell. K—— said 'the younger

generation' took no interest in his poetry or in him. He
had been a force, earlier on, whose unsparing criticisms
destroyed reputations. Perhaps he had lost too many friends
by writing such attacks. I asked who he meant by the
younger generation. 'Oh, I suppose my generation –
not that that's young – I'm forty-two. Louis Simpson,
Robert Bly, Jim Wright . . .' James Wright seems to be
the poet this intermediary generation pays most atten-
tion to. 'Why don't they put down Robert Lowell, if they
do his friend Jarrell?' asked our host. 'Uh . . . aw . . . I
don't know,' said K——. The conversation was all about
up-putting and down-putting poets. I felt rather out of it,
not down-put, or up-put, just nowhere with my consola-
tion prize of being 'an Ambassador of Letters'. Then
K—— said nice things about my long poem in the maga-
zine *Shenandoah*. 'I'm glad you liked it,' I said, 'particu-
larly so since you're the first person, apart from friends I
sent it to, who's said a word about it.' 'Well, I'm assistant
editor of *Shenandoah*.' He went on talking, he was really
flattering, adding compliments about *World Within World*.
His reading was odd, fascinating to me as someone who
also gives readings. He had a stylized anecdote or cluster
of anecdotes attached to each poem, often more absorbing
to the audience than the poem itself. They reacted to the
anecdotes, they merely listened politely to the poems. All
the anecdotes were autobiographical and the poems seemed
to be straight autobiography (as with several American
poets) like pages of a journal. One of them was a poem
called 'Adultery'. It was also attached to some anecdote
identifying the poet reading the poem with the subject of
the poem. I felt embarrassed a bit for the poet's wife who
was sitting next to me. But she did not seem in the least
concerned. American poets reading their poems let it be
taken for granted that their lives are the *matière* of their
poetry, and if one says 'I wrote this after a three-day
binge,' or 'I was needing a shot when this came to me,' or
'this is about when I was sent to Bellevue,' or (as one I
shall call Waxwrath did in his reading) 'the girl I fuck in
this poem must now be about forty-five. I look her up

Journal

sometimes,' none is any more surprised than he would be if a scientist referred to his caged rat or guinea-pig.

10 November

Read Louis MacNeice's *The Strings are False* – memories of Ireland, school, Oxford, etc. Clear and lively, sharply remembered, written with the speaking voice. Very decent and warm and courageous his attitude to politics in the 1930s: his going at the last moment, the moment of defeat, after the honeymoon of the left, to Barcelona in the autumn of 1938. His limitation (also his virtue) is the result of his excessively well trained mind and manneristic imagination which makes him rarely write the unexpected. There are no weeds, no ragged borders: flower beds planted from bright, gay, intelligent seeds out of labelled packets. If by free-associating words from time to time he allows himself some freedoms, the effect is of someone who has gone into the woods, uprooted some primroses and ferns and planted them in his own back yard. It is really like a canter by a superbly trained colt, whose whims still display his high breeding, not moving an inch beyond the curve described by the whip of the light lash. To judge from his recollections he always seems to have been fully conscious at the time of any one of his relationship of his own attitude towards it. E.g., in the account of his first marriage, it seems that he had from the moment of falling in love with her, the same dispassionate awareness of Mariette's true character. He certainly did seem to 'cast a cold eye' on the world around him. With him one was aware of his leaning back, regarding one with amused detachment through half-closed eyes. In fact his memoir shows he did regard me in this way. But I can't believe – from remembering them together at Oxford – that he judged his first wife quite as objectively, at the time of their engagement even, as here appears.

Louis's almost cold-blooded air of supercilious disdain made a great and not altogether favourable impression sometimes. During the war at the time when he was Ambassador to Moscow, Archibald Clark Kerr (later Lord

Inverchapel) on a visit to London gave a party for those English intellectuals who might be considered sympathetic to the Russian writers. Among those present was Louis MacNeice who, leaning back against the chimney piece, and holding a glass in one hand, surveyed the party through half-closed eyes, without addressing a word to anyone. As he was leaving the party, Clark Kerr went up to him, and asked: 'Are you Irish?' 'You might call it that,' said MacNeice. 'From the North?' 'Yes.' 'From the East coast?' 'Yes.' 'Well,' said Clark Kerr, 'that confirms the story I have heard that a school of seals went on shore and interbred with the people living on that part of the coast of Ireland.' He then made his ambassadorial exit from the party.

11 November
At my Poetry Consultant's office this morning, I had a call from a man who wanted me, straight away, to provide a metaphor, by telephone, for . . . I've forgotten what. He gave me examples of metaphors he had thought up. One was for a bank, which he likened to 'a dam that collects the driblets which might otherwise flow away, and banks them up, thus fitting them into the whole social spectrum.'

14 November
Dinner at Henry Brandon's. The James Restons, the Joseph Crafts and the New Zealand Ambassador and his wife were there.

Reston talked about President Johnson and the United States in a somewhat idealistic but deeply interesting way. He said the great aim of America after 1945 was not to repeat the mistake which she was reproached with after the first war of dissociating herself from the rest of the world. At Yalta Churchill and Stalin had asked Roosevelt how long he intended to stay in Europe and he had answered 'two years'. Already now they had stayed twenty. Reston said that even in Vietnam America was observing the principle that wherever there was aggression she would step in and stop it. The rest of us demurred at this point and suggested that America's aim in Vietnam was simply to stop China. I argued that America was filling the vacuum left by the European Empires in Asia. Also America was becoming obsessed by the Balance of Power (on a world scale rather than a continental one), just as Britain had been. Reston said there might be truth in this, but nonetheless America had aims far more reaching than those of Wilson, Heath, Shastri and others : and if she was not supported in these aims she would probably withdraw into some new form of isolation. He said that what Johnson now wanted from India was some sign of readiness to carry out in her own country action corresponding to Johnson's promotion in America of the idea of the Great Society. He thought the time had come when America expected some greater conception of the future from her allies than any of them had shown to date. He insisted on the idea of 'greatness', and he quoted Walt Whitman's 'O Pioneers!' Whereas in the past Americans had thought that perhaps Europeans were tired and that America must turn away and discover her own goals, since the war she had been turning to the rest of the world for an affirmation of the 'American dream' of fulfilling aims which lay beyond Empire and the use of power. 'When we expected some response from the English', one of the others said, 'all that happened was that Macmillan came to Washington to beg for some Polaris submarines.'

The conversation – as nearly always at Washington – turned to a discussion of the President, and all three said from their experience how different L.B.J. was when he talked in private from when he used his public voice. In private he was full of ideas, pithy. He employed brilliant metaphors and many anecdotes. In public he failed to communicate. 'Compared with Kennedy, he is like a man who has the words but can supply no melody,' said Reston. Reston recalled how at the White House once when he had seen Johnson being followed round by his photographer who was trying to record an image which would supersede other inferior ones, he had said to the President : 'You are using the wrong instruments. What you should have is a tape recorder to take down the things you say when you are grappling with your ideas among a few friends.'

Went to the enormous party given by Mrs Philip Graham to Truman Capote, the Alwin Deweys and Mrs Roland Tate – these people being involved in catching and sentencing Dick and Perry, the killers about whom Truman Capote has written his very interesting book of studied reportage. After the Snowdons last week, this week Washington is entertaining this extraordinary troupe. Perhaps what is really being celebrated is Truman's generosity in wanting to give the people who were both heroes and collaborators in his work, a gigantic treat. One of them at least has never been east of Kansas City. Towards the end of the evening, had some conversation with Truman Capote. He said that within a few weeks of arriving at the small mid-western town which was the scene of the murder, he had got fonder of some people in the town than of any people he had ever met. I asked him if it was true – as someone had told me – that after studying Dick and Perry he was in favour of capital punishment. He said this wasn't what he thought at all – he was against capital punishment – but he did think that real killers went on killing. People like Dick and Perry had to be put away and put away for good. They were dangerous not only to society but even to their fellow prisoners. In one prison twenty-four prisoners had – over a period of years – been killed, in the prison yard, by fellow prisoners. On the other hand, he thought that everything possible should be done behind walls to make the lives of the indefinitely detained as useful and interesting as possible. Talking about his book, he said he had a theory that a new type of literature could be based on reportage. He had arrived at this before writing this particular case history. In fact he had spent weeks scanning the newspapers before discovering the brief report which sent him to Kansas. He had spent six weeks writing his book, two and a half of them on the scene of the crime. He had cut his book down from 4000 pages to its present length of approximately 300.

[In 1966 I sent proofs of this journal to Mrs Robert Lowell (Elizabeth Hardwick). She commented :
1 'My husband has not been a Catholic for twenty years since he separated from his first wife in 1947. He has re-married and in no way keeps the obligations of the Church. He did not consider it appropriate to make a public announcement of this, but these are the facts, the existential facts.'
2 'Jarrell was not in a mental hospital at the time of his death, but being treated for a physical ailment. At the time my husband saw you he thought Jarrell had "thrown himself against a passing car". Mrs Jarrell now says it isn't true, and has gotten an official verdict of "accident" to replace the one of suicide.'
3 'My husband actually feels he has been able to write "in spite of the breakdowns". He does not consider them an aid to writing poetry, in any sense! Of course, everything is part of one's persona, as he said, like a broken leg.']

Remembering Eliot

Sewanee Review 74 (Winter 1966)

In *World Within World* I wrote that I first met Eliot in 1930 when he invited me to lunch at a London restaurant. I had forgotten that the first meeting must have been at University College, Oxford, when he addressed an undergraduate club, the Martlets, on Wednesday, 16 May 1928. There was a dinner, at the end of which the menu was passed round and signed by all present. I still have this menu, with Eliot's autograph; that I should have kept it bears witness to the aura Eliot's name already had for undergraduate poets. Eliot attended the meeting of the Martlets, on the condition that he should not give an address, but would answer questions only. Inevitably, the club being half literary, half philosophical, the discussion turned to the problem, 'How can we *prove* that a work of art is beautiful? . . .'

'. . . One generation's taste is another generation's vomit. How, then, can a work of art stand outside the changing value which it has in the mind of human generations? . . . How can we be sure that there is a consciousness in which *Hamlet* and the Acropolis forever remain the same and constant in their truth and beauty? . . .'

T——, an undergraduate who was reading philosophy and who grew tenser and tenser in his cups, and more and more voluble about Santayana, said that he did not believe there could be any absolute aesthetic criterion unless there was God. Eliot bowed his head in that almost praying attitude which I came to know well, and murmured something to the effect of : 'That is what I have come to believe.'

Already, in 1928, T. S. Eliot was a legend to the young poets. Now, when his poems seem almost inseparable from the explanations of them, may be a good time to recall the attitude of young writers to him a few years after the publication of *The Waste Land*.

The notices that appeared after his death show that there is a danger of two opposing attitudes towards him becoming crystallized. The one, that he was the Grand Master of the academy of allusiveness and strategy in deploying influences in modern poetry, and that his attitudes and beliefs did little more than provide occasion for him to push forward the 'frontiers of language'. The other view is that he was a once-revolutionary poet turned reactionary in politics, narrow-minded (and anti-Semitic) in his culture, and obscurantist in religion. In case this second view seems overstated, the reader can consult the correspondence columns of the *New Statesman* a week after Eliot's death. And I may add that when I said recently to a well-known Oxbridge don that I thought it strange that no member of the cultural branch of the British Labour Government – neither Miss Jennie Lee nor Lord Snow – had attended the Westminster Abbey memorial service to Eliot, he replied that it was entirely appropriate that a man with the liberal views of C. P. Snow should have abstained from paying homage to the author of the unfortunate 'Burbank with a Baedeker : Bleistein with a Cigar'.

I think there is a danger of people interpreting the whole of Eliot's development as the unfolding of a predetermined pattern. Philip Toynbee (in the *Observer*) seemed to suggests that Eliot conformed to the pattern of Wordsworth : the revolutionary who becomes a reactionary, disappointing his followers. Most recent critics seem to read Eliot's conversion of 1927 into *The Waste Land* which was published in 1922. They do not seem to reflect that if Joyce had late in life written novels of wry Catholic orthodoxy, instead of *Finnegans Wake*, they would have been reading his reversion into *Ulysses* (which has already been interpreted by an American critic as a hymn to the sacrament of marriage, as perhaps it may be).

With all its virtues, the danger of critical analysis is

The Thirties and After

that in tracing the graph of a writer's development it arrives at a pattern which looks like a rigid plan. Eliot lends himself particularly to this kind of treatment on account of declarations like the famous one about his being royalist and Catholic, and the still more famous one about the 'progress of an artist' being 'a continual self-sacrifice, a continual extinction of personality'. Yet the position of an artist is decided not just by himself but by an interaction between his work and his readers at various times. Part of the effect which a poem or a painting has is not what people think about it forty years later, but what they thought and felt about it when it was painted or written. In deciding, for example, whether *The Waste Land* adumbrates a Christian orthodoxy which became clarified in the *Four Quartets*, I. A. Richards's view (put forward in 1926) that it exemplified poetry 'severed from all beliefs' should be taken into account just as much as the view of someone today who using hindsight sees *The Waste Land* almost as a Christian poem. A different evolution of Eliot's ideas was possible, and if it had happened, would have made Richards right. Incidentally, if Eliot's own views are to be considered, I once heard him say to the Chilean poet Gabriela Mistral that at the time when he was writing *The Waste Land*, he seriously considered becoming a Buddhist. A Buddhist is as immanent as a Christian in *The Waste Land*.

In 1927 and 1928 writers like Eliot and D. H. Lawrence had not undergone any rigorous process of critical evaluation. They had their supporters and detractors, that was about all – except that the supporters seemed on the side of 'the future' and the detractors against it. One effect of the comparative lack of analytic discussion of contemporary writers was that we tended to relate poetry and fiction by living writers directly to the world around us, and to our own behaviour. We did not ask ourselves whether a work belonged to the Great Tradition. We felt drawn to it if it was about the world we knew we lived in, the things that deeply concerned us, and – if we wanted

240

to write – written in a way that seemed to help us to do so.

For example, it never occurred to us that Lawrence was a novelist in the Great Tradition, in direct line with the Organic Community by way of a Puritan chapel-going culture, which was a hotter line connecting with the past than T. S. Eliot's one of the Anglican communion.

This lack of critical evaluation prevented us perhaps from understanding the wealth of reference, the allusiveness of modern literature. But the fact that, if a poem or novel seemed living, we felt the presence of a force challenging us, made discussion lively. We were divided in our views about Lawrence, because although we were agreed that he was one of those very rare writers who can make the reader feel alive beyond the surroundings of his room and his armchair – we were also agreed that Lawrence's main purpose in writing was to recommend behaving in a Lawrentian way. While I, for one, felt romantically drawn by this, most of my friends felt differently. Alec Grant – one of those whose autograph is on the menu of that Martlets meeting – said, after reading *The Plumed Serpent*, that after all what Lawrence stood for was 'a dervish dance'.

Lawrence, indeed, did seem to be addressing us forthrightly, sometimes too much so. He wrote poems sneering at our 'superior Oxford' voices. And in 'Sea-Bathers' he slammed the whole younger generation:

Oh, the handsome bluey-brown bodies, they might
   just as well be gutta percha,
and the reddened limbs red india rubber tubing,
   inflated,
and the half-hidden private parts just a little
   brass tap, robinetto
turned on for different purposes.

This would seem hitting below the belt anyone determined on cool detached critical appraisal. Perhaps this is why –

apart from the frenetic trial of *Lady Chatterley* – there has been no sustained attempt to fit the later Lawrence into the approved Lawrence canon.

Even Eliot could be less than helpful if one tried to 'explicate' him. In 1929, there was a meeting of the Oxford Poetry Club at which he was the guest of honour. Before it, some of us arranged a separate meeting with Father M. C. D'Arcy, with whom we studied the text of *Ash-Wednesday*, just published. Some points were not cleared up, and at the later meeting an undergraduate asked Eliot : 'Please, sir, what do you mean by the line : "Lady, three white leopards sat under a juniper-tree"?' Eliot looked at him and said : 'I mean, "Lady, three white leopards sat under a juniper-tree" . . .'

This was not altogether a fair reply, indeed it was evasive, considering that Eliot had surely opened himself to this kind of question about his poetry with the notes to *The Waste Land*. Yet later he gave as his reason for adding those notes that Leonard and Virginia Woolf considered the poem rather short for the volume they were printing, so he added them; much as he explained to me once that some of the poems in his volume were only there because the book seemed so short. In the notes to *The Waste Land*, there is a good example of the kind of interpretation leading away from the poetic image to the literary reference which Eliot seemed to be taking exception to when he mildly snubbed the undergraduate at the Poetry Club. One note tells us : '. . . the one-eyed merchant, seller of currants, melts into the Phoenician Sailor, and the latter is not wholly distinct from Ferdinand Prince of Naples . . .'

Now this all too easily might cause the student who reads the explanation first (and the trouble now is that nearly everyone reads about the poem before he reads the poem) to write in his notebook : 'One-eyed merchant = Phoenician Sailor = Ferdinand Prince of Naples." But it is far more important to see the Phoenician Sailor as a white, new-drowned corpse, devoured by fishes, than see him as a symbol equated with other symbols. The fact that this section of the poem is a translation of an earlier poem by Eliot, written in French, confirms the suspicion that the linking-up is an arbitrary cinematic effect like a 'fade-in'. We saw the Phoenician Sailor as the Phoenician Sailor.

Thirty-five years ago, sensitive undergraduates worried a lot about what was 'real'. It would take too long to analyse all we meant by this. But looking back I can see that the concern with being 'real' or 'unreal' arose because we felt ourselves to be living in a contemporary reality from which we were somehow shut out by circumstances. One aspect of this reality was the events which had produced the war and the general strike, and were later to produce the slump and fascism, leading into yet another world war. The sense of *entre deux guerres* was pervasive, though not fully conscious, and this contributed to the sense of unreality. The other aspect was the feeling that we were prevented in some way from becoming, intellectually and physically, ourselves. We were encouraged by the writings of D. H. Lawrence and vague intimations of psychoanalysis, to think that we might discover our real instinctual selves through sex.

When we looked at what was being written, we instantly felt that some writers were concerned with the problem of 'reality' and that others were not. From our undergraduate viewpoint, writers fell roughly into three groups.

(1) The generally approved Book-Society-Chosen novelists and political poets who were names to us, mostly respected, not thought about critically, but who, though we thought of their work as literature, did not seem to touch our lives at any point.

(2) Writers who were experimental, concerned with being new at all costs, and whom we connected in our minds with new painting, new sculpture, new music, new art movements in Paris and Berlin.

(3) Writers who were directly or indirectly concerned with our own problem of living in a history which though real was extremely difficult to apprehend, and with the problems of living real lives.

The Thirties and After

The first group included Georgian poets and the novelists praised week after week by Gerald Gould, J. C. Squire, Frank Swinnerton, *et al.*, in the *Observer* and *Sunday Times*. The second group included Gertrude Stein, Edith Sitwell, E. E. Cummings, and experimental writers in the little, mostly Paris-published, magazines. Also, the occasionally published fragments of James Joyce's Work in Progress, and puzzling *Cantos* of Ezra Pound which were beginning to appear in rare editions. The third group included the James Joyce of *Ulysses*, D. H. Lawrence, E. M. Forster, W. B. Yeats (when *The Tower* appeared), and T. S. Eliot.

So *The Waste Land* was exciting in the first place because it was concerned with the modern world which we felt to be real. It excited us as poetry and yet it evoked a landscape across which armies and refugees moved. To us, in 1928, it very definitely made a pronouncement. It pronounced doom. The poet also had the sense of our problems. For him sex seemed to be rather sordid, involving 'Stockings, slippers, camisoles, and stays.' 'The young man carbuncular' who assaulted 'The typist home at teatime' had a great deal in common with any undergraduate who went down to London and had a whore in a bed-sitting room, returning, in time to climb into college, by the train called 'the fornicator'.

We connected *The Waste Land* in our minds with other great modern works of destruction and evil : Proust's volume *Sodome et Gomorrhe*; various German novels appearing about this time, notably Hermann Broch's *The Sleepwalkers*; and current philosophies of doom – the most famous of which was Spengler's now rather discredited *Decline of the West*.

Read together with *The Sacred Wood*, Eliot's poetry combined plunging into a world of chaos and absurdity with a *'rappel à l'ordre'*.

Apart from the concern with 'reality', various catchwords of the time are revealing : for instance, 'symptomatic', by which was meant that writing must not only be technically interesting but also be significant in relation to the time; and, a bit later, catching on, I think, from Leavis's *New Bearings in English Poetry*, 'contemporary sensibility'.* There was a great deal of discussion about the concept of a 'new synthesis'. In the Auden-Day Lewis Preface to *Oxford Poetry 1927*, the editors allot to poets a role in achieving a new synthesis.

> Emotion is no longer necessarily to be analysed by 'recollection in tranquillity': it is to be prehended emotionally and intellectually at once. And this is of most importance to the poet: for it is his mind that must bear the brunt of the conflict and may be the first to realise the new harmony . . .

In 1927 Eliot was the poet who seemed, in *The Waste Land*, to be fulfilling this role.

The charge of 'intellectualization' was at the centre of the subsequent battle round Eliot. That he was an intellectual was precisely the complaint of his opponents, who felt that poetry should not be intellectual.

In June 1935, *New Verse* cited some opinions of contemporaries about poets, collected by a New Zealand journalist, Ian Donnelly, and published in a book called *The Joyous Pilgrimage*. A foremost novelist is quoted as saying: 'The trouble is that all these people [i.e., Day Lewis, Auden, Spender and the rest] have been influenced by T. S. Eliot, and Eliot is definitely a bad influence. He is donnish, pedantic, cold. He is an example of the over-educated American, and Henry James was another. It would have been better for contemporary English literature if Eliot had stayed in Louisville, or wherever he came from.' Humbert Wolfe: 'Eliot is a poet who cannot write poetry. He has a great mind, but spiritually and intellectually he is muscle-bound.' Blunden: 'I don't

---

* Incidentally, I reject absolutely the legend that out generation had not discovered Eliot, Lawrence, or Gerard Manley Hopkins until the publication of this book. Already in 1928 the work of many young writers showed the influence of all three.

know why Eliot should feel so badly about things. There is no reason why he should have to write in that "I-cannot-be-gay" manner. He did not have to go through the war.'

These quotations sum up pretty well the literary establishment's dislike for Eliot even as late as 1935.

Today one can feel envious of a poet who is attacked by adversaries whose function seems to be to define only their own incomprehension, making themselves the foil to his intelligence.

Their mistake was to think that the intellect is necessarily cold. If Eliot had been cold we would not have been drawn to him. The fact is, of course, that his intellect burned white-hot. What attracted the young poets to *The Waste Land* was that rhythmically the language was so exciting. To say this is to say a great deal, for rhythmic excitement of the order of *The Waste Land* is rare in poetry. What is necessary is that rhythm should be interesting, unique to the poet, the handwriting of his sensibility, even of something beyond sensibility, the indefinable quality of his being. All Eliot's poetry has uniqueness and interest, but *The Waste Land* does more than hold the reader's interest and admiration, it makes the poetry become a passion to the reader. When this happens with a poet, his readers take up an entirely new attitude to him. Of modern poets, one could see it happen to Yeats when he published *The Tower*, which has rhythmic excitement. Although what is now perhaps Yeats's most famous poem, 'The Second Coming', was written as early as 1922, it was not until *The Tower* that readers really woke up to the fact that Yeats had emerged completely from the Celtic Twilight, and from being a minor had become a major poet of the present century.

One learned from *The Sacred Wood* of Eliot's views about tradition. But I myself enjoyed reading *The Sacred Wood* as I might any excellent critical essays, relishing particularly the quotations from the Elizabethans. It was not *The Sacred Wood* so much as the rhythmic excitement of *The Waste Land* and *The Tower* which really gave me an appetite to look for the same excitement in past poetry. It is a quality so present in the Elizabethans that when one is young one can be deluded for a time into thinking Webster and Tourneur almost as great as Shakespeare. I found it in Donne's epistles, in *Samson Agonistes*, and in passages of *The Prelude*. It occurs in one poem of Dylan Thomas ('In memory of Anne Jones'). It is the lack of it in Pound that caused Yeats to say to me once that he considered his poetry 'static'.

Apart from *The Waste Land*, Eliot's only poem which has this quality is 'Gerontion', which after *The Waste Land* is his poem the most Elizabethan in feeling. One might say that intellect in Eliot is Dantesque, but up to *Ash-Wednesday*, the passion is Elizabethan.

We formed a mental picture of Eliot. He was the poet/anti-poet – if long hair, long country walks, shaggy tweeds, beer, and bread and cheese made a poet, as one gathered they did from the Georgians. For us, his private life was summed up in the line 'The awful daring of a moment's surrender'; and apart from his pin-stripe suits, rolled umbrella, short hair, and ordinary man's job in a bank, his poetry had a good many stage properties, of a slightly music-hall kind : the boarding house, Doris padding with bare feet down the corridor, the seaside, and the beach.

The bank-clerk image was superseded by that of the editor of the *Criterion*. The loss of romantic appeal was compensated for by the possibility of being published by Eliot, of meeting him.

The secret of Eliot's influence over the young lay in a paradox of his personality. With a gesture of reversing current theories about the self-expressing poet, he dramatized a necessary shift in sensibility, from a subjective concern with the poet's self to an objective one with the values of a civilization endlessly created in men's minds. He wrote a new, a really new poetry, which set up connections with the old, the really old. He was more inimitable than any other modern poet (as would-be imitators find to their cost) yet more could be learned from his theory and practice than from those of any other writer. This man who seemed so unapproachable was the most approached by younger poets – and the most helpful to them – of any writer of his generation. Whoever had the will and intelligence to do so could grasp the principles by which he worked and lived, could read what he had read, could understand what he believed. All this was far more important than whether one agreed with all his opinions. One could see the relevance of his relation to the time in which he lived, and to the past. Religiously, poetically, and intellectually, this very private man kept open house. And all the rooms, and the garden, made clear sense. Yet in spite of all this, he was sly, ironic, a bit cagey, a bit calculating perhaps, the Eliot whom Pound called 'Old Possum'.

At the Martlets we glimpsed the Eliot of whom it was rumoured that he was being converted to Christianity. But at this time the unredeemed Eliot whom we got from the early poetry seemed more real to us. And there was some evidence in his lesser works for the existence of a street-haunting dandified night-bird Eliot. Undergraduates who went to Paris came back with copies of Charles-Louis Philippe's *Bubu of Montparnasse*, with an Introduction by T. S. Eliot. Then, later, there was the Eliot who advocated Djuna Barnes's *Nightwood*, and who admired the *Tropic of Cancer* by Henry Miller. Of course, these were literary judgements, but they also contained an obscure element of empathy.

Our meeting was the one I have described in the restaurant, which took place in 1930. Eliot inquired rather searchingly about my attitude towards my work. I said I wanted to be a poet, adding also that I wanted to write stories and novels. He said that if one wanted to write poetry one could not write anything else creative. I said : 'What about Hardy?' He said he thought that Hardy provided confirmation of his idea – his poems were amateur. 'Then what about Goethe?' 'I have always considered Goethe rather an extreme case of Hardy.' This was not meant altogether seriously, for later (in March 1932) he wrote to me that he liked Goethe's poetry but he was bored by most of his prose, with the exception of one magnificent book, 'the invaluable *Conversations with Eckermann*'. This was the year of Goethe's centenary. And he went on : 'What I chiefly dislike about Goethe is the fact that he is having a centenary. I always dislike everybody at the centenary moment . . .'

Eliot talked about poetry as being the one wholly serious activity to which a poet should devote his life. He didn't speak of it as though it were a kind of by-product of being born with a poetic gift. The phrase so often heard from the mouths of Georgian poets, 'in these lines there is a true poet', would have meant nothing to him. The question would be – 'are the lines poetry?' Poetry required concentration, dedication, and work. There was also a place for magic and inspiration, but I think one of the things that marked the difference of Eliot from the Georgian poets was that they thought that inspiration and magic preceded work, he thought that work preceded magic and inspiration. He once mentioned in a letter that he found he began a poem 'with a rhythm'. This being so, it is evident that a part of writing poetry is a kind of perpetual listening, waiting for the rhythm. One of the things that may prevent one's writing poetry or that may coarsen one's writing is filling one's mind with the rhythms of prose fiction.

The other thing I remember from that first luncheon is his answer when I asked him what future he foresaw for our civilization. 'Internecine fighting . . . People killing one another in the streets . . .'

At this point I should emphasize that although I knew him for a long time, I did not know Eliot intimately. A few times, when he was sharing a flat with his devoted friend and adviser John Hayward, my wife and I dined with him and Hayward, and after his very happy second marriage we dined two or three times with him and his wife. But between 1930 and the outbreak of war I never went to see him at any rooms where he was living. He was rather hierarchical by temperament, and in the hierarchy of his friends I was certainly in an outer circle. On the other hand, he was consistently kind and even affectionate with me. And – and I expect that others who knew him as much or as little as I did, will understand what I mean – although at the time when one spoke with him or even received a letter from him he never seemed to reveal anything of his feelings and personality, when one added up a sum of impressions got from being with him, they were very revealing of his attitudes, if never of his personal life.

His conversation could be dry and factual, and if early on one got on to some unpropitious subject – the weather or the sales of poetry – he might pursue it remorselessly, like a tram going through a slum. Rather drab yet not unmusical dialogue which occasionally breaks into shrewd observation of characterization, or irony – a bit sententious in tone – characterizes some passages of the plays. And his conversation was often like this. Some people were disappointed or bored, but to me his conversation always seemed music. His talk had a subdued metric quality which held my attention, as in the line once made at tea I have quoted elsewhere : 'I daren't take cake, and jam's too much trouble.' This has the rhythm of lines in *The Cocktail Party*. He made shrewd observations in his manner of gravely considering the problem : 'I've often noticed that it isn't what's said in a review that matters, but the length of the review.' When he laughed he bent his head forward and looked down at the table or floor and seemed to chuckle inwardly. He had a peculiar brand of sharp comment, without malice, almost affectionate, and yet to the point. Of that first conversation with me, Allen Tate has reported his saying : 'I notice that Spender spoke of wanting to be a poet, not of writing poems.' Of all my generation, he most admired Auden, but once when we were praising Auden's criticism, he said : 'All the same, he's not a scholar.' 'Why?' 'I was reading an Introduction by him to a selection of Tennyson's poems, in which he says that Tennyson is the stupidest poet in the language. Now if Auden had been a scholar

he'd have been able to think of some stupider poets . . .'
And of the anarchism of his friend Herbert Read, whom he
loved and esteemed very highly : 'Sometimes when I read
Herbert's inflammatory anarchist pamphlets I have the
impression that I am reading the pronouncements of an
old-fashioned nineteenth-century liberal.' He said that
James Joyce was the man most completely centred on his
own inner world he had ever known. We were talking
about a book which had just appeared on his *Four Quar-
tets*, and he said slyly : 'Sometimes it occurs to me that
people when they think that they are writing about my
poetry, are really writing about the kind of poetry they
would have wished to write.'

He was very deeply concerned for others. He once told
me that he always felt disturbed and unhappy that a con-
temporary of his at Harvard, Conrad Aiken, had had so
little success as a poet. 'I've always thought that he and I
were equally gifted, but I've received a large amount of
appreciation, and he has been rather neglected. I can't
understand it. It seems unjust. It always worries me.'

The very elusiveness of Eliot's poetry and character –
of which one occasionally caught glimpses like the vivid
blue flash of a kingfisher's wing – fascinated, so that younger
poets when they met him gathered up Eliotana like
crumbs that fell from the table.

Auden, who was staying with me in Hampstead in
1929, went to see Eliot about the publication of his verse
play *Paid on Both Sides* and waited an hour in a waiting
room at Faber & Faber. In 1930 Wynyard Browne when
he was an undergraduate had the temerity to call at the
Eliots' home. A lady opened the front door, asked him
what he wanted, and on hearing 'Mr Eliot' wailed, 'Why,
oh why, do they all want to see my husband !' and slammed
the door in his face.

During the war, at Eliot's request, I gave a lecture about
Yeats to something called the Tomorrow Club at which
Eliot took the chair (I have a vague impression that he
did this as the price for avoiding giving a lecture him-
self). It was terribly embarrassing to stand there talking

with Eliot sitting a yard behind me, to the side. I wrote
out the whole lecture, as though it were an essay for a
tutor. Before going to the hall where I had to speak, Eliot
took me to dinner at his club. Sherry, wine, and brandy
with the meal. I was so overcome by the liquor and my
awe that whenever in the course of my lecture I came
across the name W. B. Yeats, I said 'T. S. Eliot', and then
turned to the chairman and said, 'Sorry, I meant W. B.
Yeats.'

Among the few notes I made of Eliot's conversation,
the only ones I can find are about the first meeting of
Eliot with Igor Stravinsky, which Nicolas Nabokov asked
me to arrange. In them Stravinsky steals the show, but
that he should have done so is also characteristic of
Eliot :

I drove Eliot to the Savoy. He was in a good humour.
The conversation was carried on mostly in English,
though some of it was in French which Eliot talks
slowly and meticulously. Stravinsky started talking about
his health. He complained that all the doctors told
him to do different, sometimes quite opposite things.
He suffered from an excessive thickness of the blood.
Moving his hands as though moulding an extremely
rich substance, he said : 'They say my blood is so thick,
so rich, so very rich, it might turn into crystals, like
rubies, if I didn't drink beer, plenty of beer, and occa-
sionally whisky, all the time.' Eliot observed that a pint
of beer did him less harm in the middle of the day than
two glasses of red wine. Stravinsky returned to the
subject of the thickness of his blood.

Eliot said meditatively : 'I remember that in Heidel-
berg when I was young I went to a doctor and was
examined, and the doctor said : "Mr Eliot, you have
the thinnest blood I've ever tested." '

Stravinsky talked about Auden writing the libretto
of *The Rake's Progress*. He said it went marvellously.
Auden arrived at the Stravinskys' house in Hollywood,
ate an enormous dinner and drank much wine, went to

bed at exactly half past ten, and then was up at 8 the next morning ready to listen to Stravinsky's ideas. No sooner were these divulged than he started writing the libretto. He would think of something, write it, then ask himself where it could be fitted in, pulling out lines and phrases, and finding places in which to insert them, as though he were fitting the pieces into a puzzle. After consulting with Chester Kallman, within a few days Auden returned the libretto, neatly typed out. Only minor alterations had to be made, and Stravinsky only had to suggest that there was some difficulty somewhere and the solution to the problem would arrive by return of post.

Stravinsky started talking about the annoyance of publicity. A reporter had rung up and suggested coming to his hotel to take down notes of his reaction to the performance of one of his works on the BBC. Vera Stravinsky chipped in here and said : 'We explained that we never listened to the radio.' Stravinsky added a terse comment on the British conductor.

Eliot asked him what he did when people wrote asking for photographs. Stravinsky said he did not send them, because postage cost money. He said that when he was in Venice, where a choral work of his was performed in St Mark's, *Time* had created a link between him and T. S. Eliot by captioning their review of it : 'Murder in the Cathedral'. He said that after this performance, he waited twenty-five minutes so that the crowds might disperse, and then, accompanied by friends, walked out into the piazza. There were very few people by this time, but as he walked across the square, a few people seated at tables saw him and started clapping. He said he was extremely touched. The performance had been broadcast through amplifiers into the square, and these people, most of them young, had waited in order to applaud.

I asked Eliot how it felt to address 14,000 people at a meeting in Minneapolis. He said : 'Not 14,000 – 13,523. As I walked on to the platform, which was in the largest sports stadium there, I felt like a very small bull walking into an enormous arena. As soon as I had started talking, I found it much easier to address several thousand people than a very small audience. One has not the slightest idea what they are thinking, one sees no features of any face, and one feels exactly as if one were speaking to an anonymous unseen audience through a broadcast system. They all seemed very quiet, but I could not tell how they reacted . . .'

After our first two or three meetings in the early thirties, I was abroad in Germany and Austria for a good deal and we corresponded by mail. When one received a letter from Eliot, often it seemed flat and impersonal (and indeed most of these letters are purely about business) but on re-reading them, a good deal stands out that is revealing both of his own work and of his wish to help and advise a young man. 'I confess that personally I take so little interest in novels that I am inclined to deplore your devoting so much time to prose, instead of poetry' – this is a theme he returns to several times. His criticism of my writing is thoughtful, sympathetic, encouraging. There are flashes of self-revelation. He writes that he is very glad I am listening to the posthumous quartets of Beethoven. 'I have the A Minor Quartet on the gramophone, and find it quite inexhaustible to study. There is a sort of heavenly or at least more than human gaiety about some of his later things which one imagines might come to oneself as the fruit of reconciliation and relief after immense suffering; I should like to get something of that into verse before I die' (28 March 1931).

I have written above that I could never seriously disapprove of Eliot as a 'reactionary'. But in the spring of 1932 I seem to have written him a letter attacking the Church, calling religion an 'escape' from social struggle. He quoted this letter in a broadcast (which I did not hear) and writes excusing himself for doing so without my permission. In his letter he answers some of the points I had raised. He points out that religion is a less effective escape than that used by thousands who 'escape by reading novels, by looking at films, or best of all, by driving very fast on land or in air, which makes even dreams unnecessary.' He asks me whether I mean what I say when I write associating 'chastity, humility, austerity, discipline' with school chapels. 'If people really knew what the words mean, they would lock up or deport anyone who pronounced them.' Events of coming years in Germany (and those today in South Africa) prove that there was truth in this.

In 1933 I published a review attacking some of his views in *The Use of Poetry and the Use of Criticism.* I felt miserable in doing so, and wrote to him apologizing. He replied : 'Your criticisms are much milder than my own; in fact you give me the impression of having gone as far as possible to be generous; perhaps too far.' He then goes on to point out that some of my attack is based on my not understanding when he is being ironic. 'In short, your only weakness consists in taking the lectures too seriously.'

In a letter (9 May 1935) about my critical volume *The Destructive Element,* he is severe with me whilst also being severe with his own *After Strange Gods* (though he also writes that he thinks his criticism in that volume is more interesting than his early work; later he came to dislike it more than any other book he had published). He says the danger of this kind of criticism is that one reads in order to prove one's point. 'I was not guiltless of that,' and he insists that it is necessary to 'know one's authors from cover to cover – and I didn't,' adding with courteous irony, 'I am not quite sure that you did either.' 'You ought to have read every scrap of James before trying to fit him into any social theory . . . you don't really criticize any author to whom you have never surrendered yourself.' And : 'Even just the bewildering minute counts; you have to give yourself up, and then recover yourself, and the third moment is having something to say, before you have wholly forgotten both surrender and recovery. Of course the self recovered is never the same as the self before it was given.'

Applying these principles to his own work, he thinks his essays on Johnson, Tourneur, and Bradley good, that on Machiavelli 'rubbish'. He thinks that a study of Henry James's story 'The Friends of the Friends' would make 'otiose and irrelevant your questions about James's virility'. Rather astonishingly, he pronounces that 'James wasn't an American' because, although he had an acute sense of contemporary America, he had 'no American Sense of the Past'. Eliot adds about his own America that '*our* America came to an end in 1829, when Andrew Jackson was elected President,' and he qualifies what he has said about James by adding that James had unconsciously '*acquired*, though not inherited, something of the American tradition. He was not a descendant of the witch-hangers.'

Looking back, I see that in my twenties I was too much in awe of Eliot to realize how much trouble he was taking in seeing me and writing to me. Being over-impressed by others makes one fail to take seriously what they have to give, because one cannot really believe they take one seriously. It is almost a form of ingratitude.

Eliot was a man with the highest standards, in his poetry, his criticism, and his behaviour to others. I think it is worthwhile to draw a contrast between his attitude towards young writers and that of the magazine *Scrutiny*, which also maintained and presented high standards. Eliot encouraged, talked with, wrote to young poets. He may have been too kind, too generous, he may have made mistakes, and one (I deliberately choose the impersonal pronoun) may not have deserved his charity and trust. *Scrutiny* took none of the risks involved in charitable judgement; which did not prevent them in the exceptional cases, where they went all-out to use one or two reputations as sticks with which to beat others, from making glaring mistakes. Their frequent policy with young writers was to destroy a reputation before it was made. It was bad enough that a young poet had been published at all, but at least they could prevent their readers liking him. Moreover, the publication of their literary periodical was also bound up with theories of education. Young men reviewing were given editorial instruction as to the lines on which they should attack other young writers.

In pointing out how immensely concerned Eliot was, I want to emphasize that there are ways of encouraging literature other than being intolerant to beginners. The reason why this may be a good occasion to do so is that the English Schools in the new universities are likely to play an extremely influential role in criticism of contemporary writing during the next few years. The power of English teachers will extend beyond the universities to the BBC, the British Council, and to literary periodicals. They really have to choose between the methods of the *Criterion* and those of *Scrutiny*. Not that *Scrutiny* was not admirable in criticizing and drawing attention to works which the editors liked. Going back to Eliot's letter about my early essays on James, one might say that *Scrutiny* performed the greatest services in appreciating and criticizing some dead and a very few living writers when its critics had accepted and read them in their entirety.

So to our generation, Eliot was the poet of poets, closer to us than Yeats though Yeats might be 'greater'. We looked to the poetry, and all disagreements about the opinions seemed superficial and could be shrugged off. As a man we thought of him as sophisticated, ironic, erudite, serious, but approachable and friendly, though keeping one at a distance. On account of his seriousness, his lack of emphasis on cleverness, he seemed less alarming than, for example, Lytton Strachey, who could soar far above one with his wit and then follow this up with the depth-charge of one of his famous prolonged silences. Other than Eliot the only two older writers who made themselves *present* to contemporaries twenty years younger were E. M. Forster and Virginia Woolf.

It was astonishing to discover that to his immediate contemporaries, Eliot was a subject for endless anecdotes, in which he appeared extraordinary (that was the Bloomsbury word – '*extraordinary*') for his *naïveté*. It was not at all that they did not appreciate his genius, nor feel, indeed, extremely fond of him. But they doubted whether he put 'personal relations' as high in the scale of values as they did, and they disapproved of his being religious.

Recently I questioned a lady who knew Eliot well from 1913 onwards. The first time she met him was at Bosham in Sussex. She described him as wearing white flannels, standing by the shore looking out at the waves. Her family and the Eliots went on picnics together. What struck her about the young Mr Eliot was his inability to express himself conversationally, to enter into personal relationships. She thought he knew little about other people. His first wife, who had been a dancer (she was called by someone the 'river girl'), was gay, talkative, a chatterbox. She wanted to enjoy life, found Eliot inhibiting and inhibited, yet worshipped him. (One knows tragedies of the too-light-hearted tied to the too-serious.) There was a time when the Eliots separated, and Eliot lived by himself, wore a monocle, and was known to the neighbours as 'Captain Eliot'.

I asked her whether she thought that Prufrock and the other 'I' characters of the early poems were self-portraits. 'Oh, no,' she said, 'they weren't him. They were characters in a scene which he thought represented what life was like. Prufrock and "the young man carbuncular" who seduces the typist, with "her drying combinations touched by the sun's last rays", were vignettes of what he thought real people to be. They weren't his own life, not at all.'

Aldous Huxley used to describe Eliot taking dancing lessons, rolling back the carpet of his flat and seriously fox-trotting with his wife. He went to dances at the Hammersmith Palais de Danse. 'When I visited him at his bank,' said Aldous Huxley, 'he was the most bank-clerky of all bank clerks. He was not on the ground nor even on the floor under that, but in a sub-sub-basement sitting at a desk which was in a row of desks with other bank clerks.'

Eliot and Virginia Woolf understood each other very well on the level of their poetry. (It is unfashionable to say so but I think she had a poetic gift comparable with

Eliot's.) An extremely complex game of serious/non-seriousness was being played when one day at tea in Tavistock Square, Virginia Woolf needled Eliot about his religion. Did he go to church? Yes. Did he hand round the plate for the collection? Yes. Oh, really! Then what did he experience when he prayed? Eliot leaned forward, bowing his head in that attitude which was itself one of prayer ('Why should the agèd eagle stretch his wings?'), and described the attempt to concentrate, to forget self, to attain union with God.

There are many other anecdotes, probably most of them exaggerated and some invented. My reason for referring to them is that they do lead back into the atmosphere of Eliot's poems up to and including *Sweeney Agonistes*. The anecdotes are, as it were, the masks or *personae* created in other people's minds by Eliot the bank clerk, with his bowler hat, carrying his umbrella. After 1930 or so – that is, after the break-up of his first marriage, and after his conversion – this Eliot disappears, and that is why the early legendary Eliot seemed strange to us. But hearing such reminiscences of the early Eliot we rediscover the poet of the 'awful daring of a moment's surrender' whose character we had vaguely intuited when we first read *The Waste Land*.

I did not realize when I met him in 1928 that Eliot was just traversing a point of great unhappiness, when he was separating from his first wife, who was on the verge of insanity and who later did become insane. It is true that in conversation with outsiders Eliot gave no indication of this, and with his closest friends, I am sure, he never showed any sign of pitying himself. But I do not think it is correct to say (as some writers have done) that he never spoke to anyone about his private affairs. I suppose that he confided in Geoffrey Faber, Frank Morley, Herbert Read, and, later, John Hayward, whose advice he sought in his writing. I suspect that in the late twenties and early thirties, some of the heads of the firm of Faber & Faber were a kind of committee, advising and helping Eliot. Not only was his office a home from home, but during the most agonized years of the break-up of his first marriage Geoffrey Faber and his family provided Eliot with their own home.

In the last ten years or so of his life, after his second marriage, Eliot achieved with his radiant wife the happiness which had been denied him during most of his maturity, a happiness of which one guesses he had glimpses as a child. There are indications if a great personal assuagement in his published poetry, for example in the reference in *The Elder Statesman* to the bliss of Oepidus at Colonus, and in the dedicatory lines of that volume to his wife.

These late works are not Eliot at his best and strongest. They suggest a return to the personal, as though towards the end Eliot felt that the aim of a complete objectivity and impersonality in poetry had in it an element of pride, like that of James Joyce's Stephen Dedalus.

Eliot's last poetry does not quite round off his life-work, but it suggests how it might have been rounded off, with a return to human affection, acceptance of sensual experience, and perhaps even a less catastrophic attitude towards society. In America, shortly after the war, I once brashly said to him that in his early poetry there was a feeling of despair about this world and the next, and the imprisonment of each individual in his separateness; in *Four Quartets* and the plays, he had expressed his belief in a metaphysical world, and hope for the redemption of each individual; but he still offered no hope for civilization. My thought was that at some point he would envision people as citizens in the human city (of course, in *The Idea of a Christian Society* he did this, but he had never done so in his poetry). He smiled and said : 'Now you have put that thought into my mind, I shall instantly forget about it. But perhaps one day it will bear fruit.'

Probably I was merely being foolish, and he was being ironic. What I am trying to suggest though is that if one regards Eliot's development not as a kind of logic of the mind and imagination which developed a pattern inevitable from the start, but as an architect, then it suggests a structure planned as a whole, but which has gaps, unfinished fragments, and only indications of a crowning tower. The underlying logic of the design is everywhere felt but the whole has not been realized in the concrete imagination.

Moreover, although Eliot gives hints and indications of consistency, unity, wholeness, yet when one comes to examine the separate parts of the poetry, one has a Wyndham Lewis-like picture of a man who for the purposes of making each poem has separated part of himself from the whole. Thus in *Prufrock* and the early poems, despite the elaborate self-mockery, the point of view is essentially aesthetic. The artist, too sophisticated to be a Ruskin, a Pater, or a Wilde, nevertheless has a deep nostalgia for a past – almost any past – in which men lived by their visions. In the poetry after *The Waste Land* the poet seeks to free himself of the love of creatures, particularly human ones, and to penetrate moments outside time, moments in which the temporal intersects with eternity. The rejection of ordinary values of living, and of the animal side of human nature, is absolute. But the poetry even when it is very beautiful runs the risk of simplistic generalizations, which many people might feel to belie human experience :

> Those who sharpen the tooth of the dog, meaning
> Death
> Those who glitter with the glory of the hummingbird,
>   meaning
> Death
> Those who sit in the stye of contentment, meaning
> Death
> Those who suffer the ecstasy of the animals, meaning
> Death

Reading these lines and reading in all the plays, until the very last, the poet's doctrine of renunciation of life and of attachment to other human beings, I am struck by the fact that he has renounced so much, that the poetry, beautiful as it is, is forced into very narrow channels of

vivid spiritual experience. This narrow and concentrated
poetry is intensely beautiful, intensely expressive, with a
command of language that is absolute :

It is possible that sin may strain and struggle
In its dark instinctive birth, to come to consciousness
And so find expurgation. It is possible
You are the consciousness of your unhappy family,
Its bird sent flying through the purgatorial flame.
Indeed it is possible. You may learn hereafter,
Moving alone through flames of ice, chosen
To resolve the enchantment under which we suffer.

In its expression in controlled language with a rhythm
inseparable from a translucent imagery to which it adds
force, this is great poetry. A question arises, though, of how
much experience the poet can imagine and express in
poetry of this quality. What I think one finds in Eliot is that
in different periods his imagination dwells on different
phases of experience, but in each work the view of life is
partial. In the early poetry life is seen exclusively as hell,
in the middle poetry, everything (like marriage and work)
to do with actual living is reduced to the same grey dull
average. It is rejected too easily. The temptations of Thomas
Becket in *Murder in the Cathedral* are not tempting, and
the knights who assassinate the martyr are figures out of
Bernard Shaw. In spite of this, *Murder in the Cathedral*
is a masterpiece because it is conceived of as a great pro-
cessional scene of sacrifice rather than as a tragedy in
which there are temptations which tempt and a conflict
between good and bad forces which are fairly equal.

I cannot go further here than to suggest that Eliot's
work points towards a synthesis in which opposing worlds
are reconciled – not, of course, in the sense of good coming
to terms with evil, but in the sense of the body and the
soul, the reality of time as well as of timelessness, being
imagined with equal intensity. But the synthesis is never
complete. The two great works in which he comes nearest
to a marriage of heaven and hell are *The Waste Land* and

the *Four Quartets*. And both these poems have public and social aspects : *The Waste Land* having deep roots in the First World War, and the last three of the *Four Quartets* in the Second World War. It seems that the objectivization of his poetry towards which Eliot strove came nearest to realization when the poetry was concerned with an actual crisis of civilization : the phase of disillusion and despair against a background of revolution and collapse after the first war, the air-raids and the cause of Britain during the second. At the same time, when he turned outwards in his poetry towards society, it reflected the fragmentation of his own soul. So he was driven back on to the position that in times of the breakdown of civilization the individual becomes peculiarly responsible to himself, has to remember that he lives not just in this time of collapse, these disrupted cities, but also in eternity, and in the city of God.

Possibly, then, the centre of Eliot's work is its exploration of the truth that there cannot in our time be a synthesis between the modern city of the industrial world – bound entirely to the temporal and gambling at every moment with destruction – and the eternal city with aims of civilization outside the temporal. And therefore true art has to be, for us, fragmented art. Perhaps the force of his attack against Lawrence is not that of the Puritan against the sensualist, but of this truth – that there can be no synthesis – against the false idea of Lawrence that the modern world can be saved by the sexual relation of the human pair.

This brings me back at the end to considering again Eliot's idea that the progress of an artist is 'continual self-sacrifice, a continual extinction of personality', with its rider that 'to escape from these things' one must 'have personality and emotions'. On one level all he is doing here is opposing the kind of self-expression found in the poetry of Rupert Brooke, and upon which Owen's poetry is dependent, with the truism that the artist has to draw upon techniques and traditions which are objective and greater than himself, to surrender himself to the past. But there is also a hint of something else : that the artist has to fight against attitudes in his personality which distort his vision, with hatred, with unhappiness even. These attitudes of intense personal feeling we find in writers who agreed with Eliot's kind of classicism : in Ezra Pound and Wyndham Lewis, for instance. The problem of objectivization now becomes more complex and difficult. A programme of extinguishing the personality seems inadequate. For to achieve the kind of objectivity where the writer's view is not distorted by his personal emotions of suffering, rejection, and so on, means that he must develop as it were a personality beyond even the impersonality. And here, by tracing the progression of the sensibility which calls itself 'I' in Eliot's poetry, one is able to follow the development from the projected *personae* – the mask of Prufrock and the other 'I' characters in the early poetry – to the 'Issues from the hand of God, the simple soul,' 'I' thrown back upon itself, seeking redemption, of the *Ariel Poems* and of *Ash-Wednesday*; to the impersonal representative war-time air-raid warden and church-warden 'I' of the *Four Quartets*; and finally to the Oedipus-at-Colonus 'I' in whom there is a hint of reconciliation of body and soul, of the marriage of heaven and hell in a person beyond both personality and impersonality.

In Eliot's personal life, one can rejoice that during the last ten years the synthesis was achieved, the reconciliation was complete. This fulfilment was hinted at but not realized in his poetry. Somehow, one knew all along that it could not be, that he would hymn no Yeatsian triumph of old age.

Journal

London Magazine, new series 16, 1 (April/May 1976)

December 1975
Early in December I gave a reading in Chicago for
Poetry, the most famous and oldest poetry magazine
surviving, whose European correspondent was, before
the First World War, Ezra Pound. As an English poet, I
thought I had an excuse to read work by other English
poets than myself, who had published in *Poetry*. One of
these was Louis MacNeice. Lying on my bed in my hotel
room, I studied his 'Bagpipe Music'. In the poem
there was the word 'Ceilidh' which I could not pronounce,
and of which I did not know the meaning. I saw Louis
standing at the foot of my bed, looking down at me, with
amused contempt in his gaze.

SEEING MACNEICE STAND
BEFORE ME

Like skyscrapers with high windows staring down from
    the sun,
Some faces suggest
Elevation. Their way-up eyes
Look down at you diagonally and their aloof
Hooded glance suggests
A laugh turning somersaults in some high penthouse
Of their skulls. Seeing such a person
Looking down at you, smiling, you can't help
Looking down at yourself from his point of view : at
    the top of
Your bald head, for instance

Where the one brushed-back copper-dyed hair is noted
With precise irony. Louis
MacNeice was
Like that. Leaning
Against a marble chimney piece
With one elbow forming an angle in a Picasso cubist
    portrait,
The superior head slanted back,
With dancing eyes sizing you up
And laughter only just arrested
At some joke about you known only to himself
(Perhaps the cutting phrase sharpening in his fore-
    head)
He half beckoned you up into his high mind
For a shared view of your clumsiness —
I mean, me of mine.
Now reading his poem 'Bagpipe Music', I don't know
    how to pronounce
'C-e-i-l-i-d-h' nor what it means.
He looks down from his heaven
With mocking eyes search-lighting
My ignorance again.

Cyril Connolly, November 1974

New York Review of Books (24 June 1976)

This hews you to your statue :
Flakes away the flesh
Back to bone intellect :
Lays bare the brow, pure semi-circle,
Star-striking dome –
Sidera sublime vertice –
Proves finally the head was Roman.

This seals your eyelids : sharpens
The nose, so sensual once,
To a pure triangle; this drills
Into the base, the nostrils.

     Hid in the creviced mouth
Only the palate still
Savours the must of dying.

     She who leans over
Your shoulder, from which the sheet
Stretches in outline to the feet,
Tugs it to make you
Recognize me : 'Don't ! I pray, don't !
Don't let him see me seeing
His onyx eyeballs shout at me from marble !'

W. H. Auden

This Memorial Address was delivered in
Christ Church Cathedral, Oxford, on
27 October 1973

This gathering of friends to honour and remember Wystan
Auden is not an occasion on which I should attempt to
discuss either Wystan's personality or his place in the
history of English literature. It is, rather, one on which
to recall his presence, and express our praise and gratitude
for his life and work, in these surroundings where, intel-
lectually and as a poet, his life may be said to have come
full circle.

He was a citizen of the world, a New Yorker with a
home in Austria, in the little village of Kirchstetten, where
he is buried; and for whom Christ Church, 'The House',
had come to mean his return to his English origins. For
making this possible, the Dean and Canon and Students
are to be thanked.

I knew Wystan since the time when we were both
undergraduates, and saw him at intervals until a few
weeks before his death. It is impossible for me, in these
surroundings, not to juxtapose two images of him, one
of forty years back, and one of a year ago only.

The first is of the tow-haired undergraduate poet with
the abruptly turning head, and eyes that could quickly take
the measure of people or ideas. At that time, he was not
altogether quite un-chic, wearing a bow-tie and on occa-
sion wishing one to admire the suit he had on. He recited
poetry by heart in an almost toneless unemotional quite
unpoetical voice which submerged the intellectual meaning
under the level horizontal line of the words. He could
hold up a word or phrase like an isolated fragment or speci-
men chipped off the great granite cliff of language,
where a tragic emotion could be compressed into a coldly
joking word, as in certain phrases I recall him saying. For

268

instance : 'The icy precepts of respect', or 'Pain has an element of blank' or perhaps lines of his own just written :

> Tonight when a full storm surrounds the house
> And the fire creaks, the many come to mind
> Sent forward in the thaw with anxious marrow;
> For such might now return with a bleak face,
> An image pause half-lighted at the door . . .

A voice, really, in which he could insulate any two words so that they seemed separate from the rest of the created universe, and sent a freezing, joking thrill down one's spine. For instance, the voice in which, one summer when he was staying with me at my home in London during a heat wave and luncheon was served and the dish cover lifted, he exclaimed in tones of utter condemnation like those of a judge passing a terrible sentence : 'Boiled ham !'

The second image of Wystan is of course one with which you are all familiar : the famous poet with the face like a map of physical geography, criss-crossed and river-run and creased with lines. This was a face upon which experiences and thoughts had hammered; a face of isolated self-communing which reminded me of a phrase of Montherlant's about the artist's task of 'noble self-cultivation'; a face though that was still somehow entertaining and which could break down into a smile of benevolence or light up with gratified recognition at some anecdote recounted or thought received. It was a face at once armoured and receptive.

It is difficult to bring these two images – spaced forty years apart – together. But to do so is to find reason for our being here to praise and thank him.

His fellow undergraduates who were poets when he was also an undergraduate (John Betjeman, Day Lewis, Mac-Neice, Rex Warner and myself) saw in him a man who instead of being, like us, romantically confused, diagnosed the condition of contemporary poetry, and of civilization, and of us – with our neuroses. He found symptoms everywhere. 'Symptomatic' was his key word. But in his very strange poetry he transmogrified these symptoms into figures in a landscape of mountains, passes, streams, heroes, horses, eagles, feuds and runes of Norse sagas. He was a poet of an unanticipated kind – a different race from ourselves – and also a diagnostician of literary, social and individual psychosomatic situations, who mixed this Iceland imagery with Freudian dream symbolism. Not in the least a leader, but, rather, a clinical-minded oracle with a voice that could sound as depersonalized as a Norn's in a Norse saga. Extremely funny, and extremely hard-working : always, as Louis MacNeice put it, 'getting on with the job'. He could indulge in self-caricature, and he could decidedly shock, but he did no imitations of other people's speech or mannerisms, though he could do an excellent performance of a High Mass, including the bell tinkling. His only performance was himself.

He was in no sense public and he never wanted to start any kind of literary movement, issue any manifestoes. He was private even in public.

> Private faces in public places
> Are wiser and nicer
> Than public faces in private places.

We were grateful for a person who was so different from ourselves, not quite a person in the way that other people were. His poetry was unlike anything we had expected poetry to be, from our public-school-classical-Platonic-Romantic-Eng. Lit. education at that time.

He seemed the incarnation of a serious joke. Wystan wrote somewhere that a friend is simply someone of whom, in his absence, one thinks with pleasure. When Wystan was not there, we spoke of him not only with pleasure and a certain awe, but also, laughing. People sometimes divide others into those you laugh at and those you laugh with. The young Auden was someone you could laugh-at-with.

I should say that for most of his friends who were his immediate contemporaries, the pattern of his relationship with them was that of colleague; with his pupils, that of a teacher whom they called 'Uncle Wiz'. During the years when he was teaching at prep. school, he wrote his happiest poetry. But in those days of exuberance, merging into the vociferous and partisan 1930s, he almost became that figurehead concerning whose pronouncements he grew to be so self-critical later on : the voice of his generation. Or, rather, its several voices, under which his own voice sometimes seemed muted. For it was not true to his own voice to make public political noises. His own voice said :

> O love, the interest itself in thoughtless Heaven,
> Make simpler daily the beating of man's heart.

Nevertheless he did speak for the liveliest of the young at that time : those who wanted to throw off the private inhibitions and the public acquiescences of a decade of censorship and dictatorship and connivance with dictatorship, those who were impassioned by freedom, and some who fought for it. He gave to them their wishes which they might not have listened to otherwise. They were grateful for that. He enabled impulses to flower in individuals. All that was life-enhancing.

Thinking now of the other face, of the later Auden, a great many things about him, quite apart from his appearance, had changed. He now mistrusted his past impulsiveness and rejected in his *oeuvre* many lines and stanzas which had been the results of it. His buffoonery was now sharpened and objectified into wit. His eccentricities had rigidified into habits imposed according to a built-in time-table regulating nearly every hour of his day. This was serious but at the same time savingly comic. He never became respectable, could always be outrageous, and occasionally undermined his own interests by giving indiscreet interviews about his life. These tended to disqualify him in the eyes of members of committees dedicated to maintaining respectability.

He had also perhaps acquired some tragic quality of isolation. But with him the line of tragedy coincided almost with that of comedy. That was grace. One reason for this was his total lack of self-pity. He was grateful that he was who he was, namely W. H. Auden, received on earth as an honoured guest. His wonderfully positive gratitude for his own good luck prevented him from ever feeling in the least sorry for himself. Audiences were baffled and enchanted by this publicly appearing very private performer, serious and subtle and self-parodying, all at the same time. They could take him personally and seriously, laughing at-with-him.

He had become a Christian. There was a side to this conversion which contributed to his personal isolation. Going to Spain, because he sympathized with the Republic during the Spanish Civil War, he was nevertheless – and much to his own surprise – shocked at the gutted desolation of burned-out churches. Later, he had some signal visionary experiences. These he did not discuss. He was altered in his relations with people, withdrawn into his own world which included our world, became one of those whom others stare at, from the outside.

In his poetry Christianity appears as a literally believed-in mythical interpretation of life which reveals more truth about human nature than that provided by 'the healers at the end of city drives' – Freud, Groddeck, Homer Lane, Schweitzer, Nansen, Lawrence, Proust, Kafka – whom Auden had celebrated in his early work as those who had unlearned hatred,

> and towards the really better
> World had turned their face.

For throughout the whole development of his poetry (if one makes exception of the undergraduate work) his theme had been love : not Romantic love but love as interpreter of the world, love as individual need, and love as redeeming power in the life of society and of the individual. At first there was the Lawrentian idea of unrepressed sexual fulfilment through love, then that of the social revolution which would accomplish the change of heart that would change society; then, finally, Christianity, which looked more deeply into the heart than any of these, offered man the chance of redeeming himself and society but also without illusions showed him to himself as he really was with all the limitations of his nature. Christianity changed not only Auden's ideas but also in some respects his personality. Good qualities which he had always had, of kindness and magnanimity, now became principles of living; not principles carried out on principle, but as realizations of his deepest nature, just as prayer corresponded to his deepest need.

Of all my friends, Wystan was the best at saying 'No.' But if asked for bread, he never produced a stone. Young poets who brought him their poems were told what he thought about them. (Though, in their case, if he gave them a discourse on prosody, they may have thought that, instead of bread, he was giving them a currant bun.) He no longer believed in the efficacy of any political action a poet might undertake : but that did not mean he had no social conscience. A few years ago I told him that some writers in Budapest had said to me that if he would attend a conference of their local PEN Club which was soon to take place, the name AUDEN would impress the authorities, and their lives perhaps become a bit easier. Wystan left Vienna almost immediately and attended their meeting in Budapest.

Still, he no longer believed that anything a poet writes can influence or change the public world. All a poet can do perhaps is create verbal models of the private life : a garden where people can cultivate an imagined order like that which exists irresistibly in the music of Mozart, and perhaps really, within eternity.

Much of his later poetry was a long retreat from his earlier belief in the feasibility of healing literature, into the impregnable earthworks and fortresses of language itself, the fourteen-volume Oxford dictionary, the enchanted plots of poetic forms in George Saintsbury's book on English prosody, the liquid architecture of Mozart, and the solitaire of *The Times* crossword puzzles.

Wystan died a month ago now. How long it seems. In the course of these few weeks much has happened which makes me feel he may be glad to be rid of this world. One of his most persistent ideas was that one's physical disorders are reflections of the state of one's psyche, expressing itself in a psychosomatic language of spots and coughs and cancers, and unconsciously able to choose, I suppose, when to live and when to die. So I am hardly being superstitious in joking with him beyond the grave with the idea that his wise unconscious self chose a good day for dying, just before the most recent cacophonies of political jargon blaring destruction, which destroy the delicate, reduced and human scale of language in which individuals are able to communicate in a civilized and affectionate way with one another.

We can be grateful for the intricate, complex, handmade engines of language he produced, like the small-scale machinery he so loved, of Yorkshire mines, or like the limestone landscapes of that Northern countryside of hills and caves and freshets where he spent his childhood. He made a world of his imagination and had absorbed into his inner life our outer world which he made accessible to us in his poetry as forms and emblems to play with. His own inner world included his friends whom he thought about constantly.

He also had a relationship, which one can only describe as one of affection, with an audience, wherever that happened to be. He could project the private reality of his extraordinary presence and voice on to a public platform when he gave a public reading. He provoked some uniquely

personal reaction from each member of his audience, as
though his presence had dissolved it into all its individual
human components. The last time we met in America, I
asked him how a reading which he had given in Milwaukee
had gone. His face lit up with a smile that altered its
lines, and he said : 'They loved me !' At first I was sur-
prised at this expression of unabashed pleasure in a public
occasion. Then I thought, how right of him. For he had
turned the public occasion into everyone's private triumph.
One reason why he liked writing – and reciting – his
poetry was that a poem is written by one person writing
for one person reading or listening – however many readers
or listeners there may be. So as a public, an audience, a
meeting of his friends as separate individuals here gathered
together, may each of us think separately our gratitude for
his fulfilled life and our praise for his completed work.

Postscript

With a few exceptions the writers associated with the thirties tried after 1939 to break with their political connections. This was particularly true of Auden who edited out of his work what might be termed the Thirties Connection.

His departure with Isherwood for America in late 1939 dramatized the end of a decade. And yet the identification of this generation of writers with that decade continued and continues even today. The Thirties label stuck to certain writers just as in the last century, certain poets and novelists always seem identified with the 1890s. A few went on working their thirties preoccupations. Edward Upward in his trilogy *The Spiral Ascent* describes in fiction which is thinly disguised autobiography his hero's acceptance and then rejection of communist ideology emanating from the Soviet Union in the thirties, and then, after a period of disillusionment with Stalinism, his return to some Maoist version of communism. The two themes of ideology and autobiography here provide that continuity which in Auden's life and work is deliberately broken.

Auden was, nevertheless, very ideological. However in his poetic journey from psychoanalytic symbolism to Christian theology, Marxist materialism was the most transitory of his ideological ports of call. One might say that his Marxism dissolves into the theological, psychoanalytical and mythical idea systems of his whole work. In his self-editing, scarcely a trace of it remains. The Marxist behaviourist interpretation of life was too local, too narrowly political, too exclusively supporting one section of humanity and rejecting another, to fit into the pattern of his thinking. *Spain* (suppressed in his *Collected Poems*) explores the limits of such bearing as Marxist ideology appeared to have on events for him at a particular period of his life when, to oppose fascism seemed imperative. Thus whatever we may think about his much-criticized self-editing, it did correct the facile conclusion of some readers that Marxism was a goal in his poetry rather than a temporary stop at a position which seemed expedient, at a time when belief in expediency was itself very much in doubt.

Having colleagues like Isherwood, MacNeice and myself, whose work was very autobiographical, Auden perhaps felt it necessary to suppress clues to his own autobiography in his poetry. They would have led to misunderstanding. His poetry was far from being the autobiography of a young man who had been in Berlin, become an antifascist, and then gone to live in America. His real development was not on that level of biographical continuity. I have come to think that Auden wrote his poetry out of a personality of which his friends knew much less than they supposed. Perhaps it is this impersonality which is his deepest voice.

I myself am, it is only too clear, an autobiographer. Autobiography provides the line of continuity in my-work. I am not someone who can shed or disclaim his past. This is not merely an admission. It is something I have here tried to emphasize in presenting these records as a case history of the thirties and after. I see pretty clearly that in this particular case – my own – of the self-discoverer, the ideological has been a trap into which I have too often fallen, and from which I have only saved myself by going back to my personal as distinct from my public life. Nevertheless, coming from a political family, for me interest in politics has always been just round the corner. Perhaps it was his realization that with me the personal and the public risk being interchangeable that caused Auden to address to me the lines in the dedication to *The Orators* :

Private faces in public places
Are wiser and nicer
Than public faces in private places.

Politics without ideology and with a strong tendency towards autobiography, equals Liberalism.

All this is different from Isherwood in whom everything leads back to interest in the personal and all persons back to a self-portrait under perpetual re-examination – one way of retaining continuity while at the same time asserting the distancing of the constantly altering present from the past.

The thirties do really seem to have receded now. With the deaths of Eliot, Auden, Connolly and MacNeice with which I conclude this volume, I feel myself to have entered into the area of the posthumous. Perhaps, after all, what really maintained continuity from 1928 onwards was a dialogue between generations which had a certain mutual respect for one another : between that of Yeats and Eliot, Lawrence and Virginia Woolf, with ours. If this book shows anything I hope it will be that we looked through the eyes of an earlier generation as well as through those of our own.

Acknowledgements

The original source of each piece that is reprinted in this book is acknowledged in the text.

European Witness was first published by Hamish Hamilton. The original title of 'Notes on Revolutionaries and Reactionaries' was 'Writers and Politics'. The W. H. Auden Memorial Address, printed privately by Faber & Faber in 1973, was first published by Weidenfeld & Nicolson in *W. H. Auden: a Tribute* (edited by Stephen Spender) in 1975.

The passage on pages 32–3 from Louis MacNeice's *The Strings are False* (Faber & Faber) is reprinted by permission of David Higham Associates Ltd.

All the quotations from the published writings of W. H. Auden – from *Spain* (1937) on page 30; from 'Remember' (originally in *Paid on Both Sides*, 1930) on page 269; dedication to *The Orators* (1932) on pages 270 and 278; from the 'Prologue' (on page 271) and the 'Epilogue' (on page 272) to *Look, Stranger!* (1936) – are copyright © the Estate of W. H. Auden and Faber & Faber Ltd.

The lines from Wyndham Lewis's *One-Way Song* (Faber & Faber, 1933) are copyright © Mrs G. A. Wyndham Lewis and reprinted by permission.

E. E. Cummings's translation of *The Red Front* by Louis Aragon was first published in 1933 by Contemporary Publishers, North Carolina.

The quotations from T. S. Eliot's poems 'Burbank with a Baedeker: Bleistein with a Cigar' (on page 200) and 'Marina' (on page 261) – both in *Collected Poems 1909–62* – and (on page 262) from his play *The Family Reunion* are reprinted by permission of Faber & Faber Ltd.

The lines from John Cornford's 'Sad Poem' (on pages

Acknowledgements

191–2) and 'Full Moon at Tierz' (on page 194) and from his essay 'Art and the Class Struggle' (on pages 204–5) are in *John Cornford: a Memoir*, edited by Pat Sloan and published by Jonathan Cape in 1938.

The quotations on pages 207 and 207–8 are from Julian Bell's essay 'The Proletariat and Poetry' and from his letter of 29 November 1936 to Vanessa Bell, both in *Julian Bell: Essays, Poems and Letters*, edited by Quentin Bell and published by The Hogarth Press in 1938.

The quotations from essays by D. H. Lawrence and from his poem 'Sea-Bathers' are reprinted by permission of Lawrence Pollinger Ltd and the Estate of the late Mrs Frieda Lawrence Ravagli, and of William Heinemann Ltd, publishers of *Phoenix* and *The Complete Poems of D. H. Lawrence*.

The lines on page 201, from 'E. P. Ode Pour L'Election de Son Sepulcre' (*Hugh Selwyn Mauberley*, 1920), are in *The Collected Shorter Poems of Ezra Pound* and are reprinted by permission of Faber & Faber Ltd.

The Year of the Young Rebels, from which passages are quoted on pages 214–16, was published by Weidenfeld & Nicolson. 'The Express', quoted on pages 224–6, is in *Collected Poems* (Faber & Faber).

✳

I wish to thank my friend Keith Walker for reading the proofs and making suggestions.

Index of Names

281

Index

Index

Index

Index